YOU CAN'T MANAGE WHAT YOU DON'T MEASURE

You Can't Manage What You Don't Measure

Control and evaluation in organizations

ARYE GLOBERSON
Department of Labor Studies
Tel-Aviv University

SHLOMO GLOBERSON
School of Business Administration
Tel-Aviv University
and
College of Business Administration
Northeastern University, Boston (Visiting)

JUDITH FRAMPTON
Clinical Manager
Harvard Community Health Plan
Cambridge, Massachusetts

Avebury

Aldershot · Brookfield USA · Hong Kong · Singapore · Sydney

First published 1991

Published by
Avebury
Gower Publishing Company Limited
Gower House, Croft Road
Aldershot, Hants GU11 3HR
England

Gower Publishing Company
Old Post Road
Brookfield, Vermont 05036
USA

ISBN 1 85628 163 9

Printed and Bound in Great Britain by
Athenaeum Press Ltd., Newcastle upon Tyne.

Contents

Preface

You can't manage what you don't measure! This statement ought to be fundamental to the philosophy of all organizations. At a time when streamlining the structure of western business has made middle managers an 'endangered species' (*Business Week*, September 12, 1988), successful managers must be able to focus their attention on areas that are critical to establishing their companies' competitive edge. These managers should be able to evaluate performance by using specific performance criteria, measuring actual results, and comparing the results to expectations. Successful managers are able to *identify problem areas* and *take action to correct the situation.* This is what organizational control is all about.

The term 'control' may create a negative image for some readers, synonymous with an authoritarian or domineering leadership. In reality, however, a successful organizational control system is not a one way street. To the contrary, success must include the involvement of both management and employees in the development of measurement techniques and standards, as well as in the analysis of results and in the plans for future improvement.

You Can't Manage What You Don't Measure covers the five areas where control should be established in practically all organizations: operations, finance, marketing, human resources, and information. Although control, in each of these areas, has its own unique features and effects, there is considerable overlap among them. The book begins with the fundamental concepts of organizational control systems and moves on to dealing in detail with specific organizational functions.

Most control characteristics are common to the vast majority of organizations, and relatively few need to be tailored to any specific organization. As a result, the approach presented here is broad in nature and not limited to organizations of a particular size, structure, nor industry, and are applicable to both service and manufacturing.

A perfect management system would have completely accurate measures of all aspects of an organization's operations and would always be able to accurately identify the needed improvements and the required changes. While we are far from achieving the 'perfect system,' the field of organizational control has done much to improve our ability to recognize and respond to changes in both internal and external environments. As the competitive market becomes increasingly global and other countries and cultures show significant management skill, this field has never been more significant.

You Can't Manage What You Don't Measure covers methodological and practical issues that are relevant to all organizations wishing to design, implement and maintain a meaningful and useful control system. Our goal is two-fold. First, we want readers to gain an understanding of current theoretical concepts in organizational control. Second, we want to assist readers in applying these concepts to improve their effectiveness as managers. The many examples given throughout the book are intended to facilitate this process. In addition, each chapter ends with suggested readings for those interested in gaining further insight into selected issues. Although some reference to the subject matter appears in other business texts, this book is the first to deal thoroughly and exclusively with field of organizational control.

Boston and Tel-Aviv A.G., S.G., J.F.

1 The nature and purpose of organizational control

> Some management experts estimate that more than a million U.S. managers and staff professionals have lost their jobs in the past decade. One executive headhunter surmises that over a third of U.S. middle management jobs have been eliminated. Since 1982, Mobil has slashed its white-collar payroll by 17%, Du Pont by 15%. Ford has trimmed its worldwide salaried ranks in 35 of the past 36 quarters. In the past 18 months alone, General Electric Co.'s Medical Systems Group has cut its management ranks by 35%.
>
> *Business Week, September 12, 1988.*

In an increasingly competitive world economy, U.S. companies have been forced to cut expenses in order to remain in contention for limited markets. However, efforts to date have hardly been sufficient to ensure success. The survival of organizations, and indeed of the managers that run them, will depend on an ability to evaluate performance by measuring results, comparing them to expectations, and taking action. These are the fundamentals of organizational control. Indeed, you can't manage what you don't measure!

The organizational control system is a link between all parts of an organization. It connects major strategic decisions to policy, implementation, and detailed operations. The essence of management control is to have feedback compare achievements to organizational goals, considering environmental demands and constraints. This assists decision makers in controlling events rather than being ruled by them.

Organizational control is an ongoing process for *evaluating organizational achievement by comparing occurrences with standards or expectations*, based on relevant criteria. This general definition is acceptable to most professionals and managers who deal with the subject. However, the more detailed and specific the discussion of control, the greater become the differences in approach and application. This diversity is the result of differences in perspective brought to the subject by a variety of disciplines, such as behaviorl science, accounting and engineering.

This chapter presents control as an autonomous function and deals with structural variables that are common to all control systems. The various disciplinary approaches and the most common orientations to control are illustrated, and the goals of control are reviewed. Our emphasis is on a *dynamic* approach to control, and on its major by-products.

Separation of powers and control

A unique perspective on control arises from considering the principle of the separation of powers. This concept originated in the field of political science, the study of government and law, dating back to Montesquieu (1689-1753), and is the model on which the government of the United States is based. This perspective divides power into three authorities: the legislative, executive, and judicial. According to this principle, each of the three authorities is allotted autonomous powers which are not granted to the others.

The legislative authority establishes laws and determines the norms according to which the executive authority (that is, the government and its ministries) must function. The executive authority is thus given a normative system, which also serves as the basis for its evaluation. The central role of the judicial authority is to rule on deviations from the norms set by the legislative authority. The fundamental reason for creating the three authorities, is to establish a checks-and-balances situation in a democratic society, so that corruption can be minimized.

Operationally, 'separation of powers' means that individuals will not set their own rules, nor will they be the judges of their own deviations from the rules. The democratization of public administration, the achievements of private organizations, and the need to evaluate events as they occur, has led to the recognition of the need for *internal* controls as well as the external ones which are part of the 'checks-and-balances' model. This two-dimensional model allows for both internal control as a function of the organization, and external control, carried out on behalf of stockholders, customers, or voters. Contrary to the judiciary, whose central role is punishment of undesirable deviations, control is an ongoing process targeted at correction of deviations and improvement of organizational functioning.

The two control systems, internal and external, can be found in most large organizations. The internal system is activated by the organization's leaders; its findings serve as information used to improve performance. The external control system is handled by a party independent of the organization in order to obtain a more objective picture of the organization's performance.

Control may be internal to one body and external to another. Large concerns such as General Electric have a central control unit, which may be considered internal to the concern but external to its individual companies. In the control of a bank branch, the headquarters is 'external' to the branches, but internal for the bank as a whole.

It would be difficult to imagine a modern state, local government, or a private business, functioning without internal and external control systems. It has become increasingly common for management to recognize the need for 'control' as a fourth authority, which, like the traditional three, functions in every organization, private or public, service or manufacturing.

It is often thought that the function of control is more firmly established, at least legally, in the public sector than in the private one. Although this might be true, a private organization's obligation to itself and to its owners dictates that it, too, must define both its goals and its plans for achieving them. Management must confirm that activities which occur, are a reflection of optimal decision making. These issues are relevant to control, whether in the private or public sector.

At the organizational level, there are usually two, and sometimes three, strongly interrelated bodies which deal with control:

a. the Board of Directors, which often includes top management, and which could be compared to the 'legislative legislative» branch', setting policies and norms for the organization;

b. the operational management, which could be considered as the 'executive branch'; and,

c. those who control and evaluate the functioning and activity of the organization, who can be thought of as the 'judiciary branch'.

Control and evaluation are usually considered to be in the realm of those who set the policies and goals of the organization.

The degree of separation of powers in an organization depends, to a large extent, on the nature of the socio-political system and, management philosophy. Naturally, the role of control is not the same in a centralized government and a small local council, nor in a multi-national company and a small family business. Nevertheless, the principle of autonomy of authorities, and especially the independence of the control system, is essential to every organization that is interested in effective evaluation and control.

Structural components of control

Every control system is based on at least three basic components: information, feedback, and the organization as a system. Each of these three is relevant to all organizations, regardless of their approach to control, although the relative importance of each is influenced by the perspective of the individuals involved.

1. *The information* available to control authorities keeps them up-to-date about what is going on in the organization. By nature, control should become a reservoir of information concerning, not only the overall functioning of the organization, but highlighting its weaknesses as well. The more dynamic and integrated the control approach, the greater is its potential contribution to the organization.

The more relevant data available to an organization, the greater the potential for the control system to provide sensible evaluation, and the greater the chance of reaching reliable decisions. This is expressed in the increasingly strong relationship between planning, operation, information, and control systems. This relationship is the key to practical application.

Recent technological advances in data collection and processing have opened new channels for sophisticated analysis but, at the same time, have created new problems and difficulties. The quick and inexpensive accessibility of information sometimes leads to information flooding beyond the system's capacity. The technical ease and convenience with which data can be obtained, invites an information explosion. This is liable to be an obstacle to control because of the time and attention which is devoted to unnecessary information and trivial details.

2. *Feedback* is a response to performance and is a basic concept in control. The effective utilization of feedback requires clear definitions of norms and standards. The more detailed and precise these definitions and the more reliable the measurements, the more reliable the feedback. It is most frequently found that deviations of performance from standards result from one of three situations: an unrealistic standard which is difficult to realize; poor performance or outdated methods of operation requiring improvement; or, the need for intervention and change in both standards and performance.

Feedback is used at two levels: the comparative and the analytical level. The first is mainly technical, comparing performance to standards. The skills required at this level of control are relatively basic. The second level -- the analysis of control findings -- requires an analytical approach leading to decisions about changes in standards, performance, or both. It should be stressed that both management and control need ongoing and reliable feedback in order to carry out their tasks. Simultaneously, the existence and quality of the feedback itself is an important component examined by the control system.

3. *The organization as a system* refers to an orientation that integrates the parts of the organization with its environment. The system approach is dynamic in nature and is contingency-oriented. This means that the relative importance of each part (subsystem) is not static, and the goals of the system change according to changes in internal and external conditions.

According to this approach, the system's orientation to control is characterized by two aspects:

a. The control system aims to assist the organization by examining the achievements of the subsystems and their interactions, in order to maximize the achievement of the organization as a whole.

b. The control system examines the relationship between the organization and external systems, in order to enhance the awareness of the nature and quality of the developments in other systems, and to evaluate the readiness of the organization for external changes.

Control must consider the environment as a system that influences the organization and is influenced by it. Recognition of this is expressed by organizational standards set on the basis of the environment, as well as the internal climate.

Common disciplinary orientations

Despite the similarity in the various general definitions of control, there is considerable diversity in its disciplinary perception. This variation originates from the academic background, practical experience and preferences of the definer. These are also evidenced in the impact on the institutionalization of control in the organization. Control is relevant to all areas of activity and to all disciplines; it is therefore natural that many view this area as 'theirs'. This provides a partial explanation for the variety of approaches to control, and the variation in training of those involved in it.

Although the study of control benefits from this multidisciplinary attention, it also suffers from it, because the subject is divided into a number of areas. It is therefore not surprising to find a wide variety of attitudes toward control, ranging from a relatively narrow view of technical comparisons, all the way to a general analysis and evaluation of decision making.

Considerable attention has been devoted to finding a balance in control, fulfilling functional and social needs on one hand, and avoiding excessive control on the other. Although attempts have been made to design an optimal structure for control, no universal formula has been accepted. The design of an optimal model for control, that responds to all the needs of the system, is an impossible task. However, a pragmatic choice of a preferable control system is essential.

Observing control systems in various organizations reveals the influence of the professional background of the controller on his or her perception of its content. It is easy to find organizations similar in size, product line, and technology, yet very different in terms of the type and methods of control. This is usually the combined result of management philosophy and the disciplinary background of the controller.

The several groups of professionals involved in control represent five different orientations.

1. The *legalistic orientation* is mainly seen in controllers who have been trained in law. This category may also be extended to include most *formalistic* approaches, which resemble legalistic ones in both nature and methods of control. Professionals with this orientation have usually been educated in political science, public administration, accounting or law. These approaches are particularly well accepted in public administration, which strongly emphasizes the comparison of actual occurrences with formal rules and standards by which the organization is meant to function.

Control that stresses legal principles and formal procedures has less emphasis on ways to improve the transformation process, that is, the conversion of inputs to outputs. In these organizations, control is expected to contribute to the maximum adherence to rules and formal standards.

In principle, the emphasis on legalistic control in public administration is understandable: its clientele includes most of the population, and it enjoys monopolistic power. In order to maintain equal treatment to all, the control system must have clear and formal standards, applied as uniformly as possible.

Private organizations are also required to abide by norms such as national, state, and municipal laws. However, public institutions utilize these norms more than do private firms. There can, however, be an over-emphasis on legalistic aspects leading to inadequate attention to other essential aspects.

2. The *economic orientation* to control emphasizes input-output ratios, the major test is typically maximization on return of investments. The key macro-economic question is: Under the given conditions, could the available capital be used to yield greater returns? The demand is that control should regard profitability as a key indicator in private organizations.

This is not the case in public organizations. Although control in this sector should take economic considerations into account, this orientation is often given minimal attention. In a 9/4/88, article in the *New York Times*, J. Ronald Fox, of the Harvard Business School, stated: "Too few Government managers...are knowledgeable about industrial cost estimating, cost accounting, financial incentives, cost control, scheduling and technical performance. They also lack knowledge about the implications of contract changes on large industrial companies. As a result, they are often unable to resist pressure to expand and complicate programs and they fail to reward lean industrial contractors."

The explanation is two-fold: first, the emphasis is on formal aspects; second, public institutions generally handle other people's money.

Nevertheless, economic control is gradually penetrating into the public sector, where there are many opportunities for savings. Questions are being raised regarding the economic justification of an expensive public service as compared to lower cost provision of the same service by a privately owned organization. It has been the practice that public service is exempt from examination of cost-benefit and input-output ratios. This approach is fundamentally mistaken. A public organization with an economic orientation to control will be capable of serving the public better within the constraints of a given budget.

The economic orientation to control requires controllers who have been trained in this area. Such approaches are generally more dynamic than the traditional, formalistic, accounting approach. Among those involved in control focussing on economics, we find individuals trained in business administration and economics, accountants, tax experts, and people with extensive business experience.

3. The *accounting orientation* to control is often considered 'static', as it relies heavily on formal accounting systems comprised of reports generated by rigid rules. However, today's accounting approaches have become more sophisticated and are also used as support for decision making. A distinction should be made between two types of accounting approaches to control. One approach concentrates on verification of records, so that the internal and external controllers are satisfied that these reflect reality. The analytical approach, on the other hand, enables not only study of the past, but recommendations and preparations for future trends as well.

The focal point of management accounting has moved from the static presentation of the organization's financial situation to a dynamic and analytic interpretation. It would be difficult to imagine advanced management and control without budgeting and costing, which are essential feedback for correcting deviations. The wide variety in accounting orientations to control corresponds largely to the training and approach of the individuals involved. There is some common ground between the economic and accounting approach, as both focus on profit, although the mathematical models applied to each are different.

4. The *engineering orientation* concentrates mainly on the operations of the organization. The emphasis is on the physical conversion of inputs to outputs. Thus, the control system will focus on the examination of throughput efficiency, product quality, and scheduling. The objective is: to minimize obstacles in the production process; to identify and correct operational deviations; to assure the quality of in process and finished products; and, to maintain an adequate supply of products to customers. The engineering orientation to control is seen in individuals with technical, operations, or engineering background.

5. The *behavioral orientation* to control relates mainly to the functioning and behavior of the people in the organization. The underlying assumption is that organizational achievements depend primarily on the functioning and behavior of its personnel. Without minimizing the significance of this position, it should be noted that this approach has not yet been well integrated with the previous approaches.

Control that focuses on workers' behavior is directed mainly toward personnel policy, recruitment procedures, selection and induction, employee training, and incentive systems. It is interesting to note that those who adopt this approach come from two ends of the spectrum: those who believe that the human factor has a unique, dominant role in the organization's achievements and therefore warrants encouragement and cultivation; and those who see the employees as a production factor, with no special interest in organizational achievement, which must therefore be subject to constant control. Both claims are based on well-known behaviorist theories (McGregor, Herzberg). Most of those who adopt a behavioral orientation to control come from the behavioral sciences or have had wide experience in personnel management.

In the behavioral sciences, control has long played an important role in the study of the relationship between performance and employee behavior (Tennebaum, 1986). Behavior-oriented control deals with employee activities in order to influence their activities in accordance with standards and expectations set by the organization. From this point of view, the effectiveness of control is an expression of the degree to which it has an impact on the functioning and behavior of the members of the organization.

Another behavioral aspect of control is the degree to which it *motivates and rewards* improvement, or *provides sanctions* for poor performance. From a behavioral point of view, control can be seen as two-dimensional: it serves as a personal compass for each employee and, at the same time, as a basis for the controller and the manager to compare and evaluate employee's behavior and performance.

These five orientations to control are used by professionals of varying backgrounds and experience. Control strategies which are well formed and clear, lead to the appointment of controllers with appropriate experience. It should be emphasized that 'controller', in the context of this book, does not have the traditional meaning of a person dealing only with the financial side of the company, but with all control aspects. If management believes that control should focus on performance, it will hire an industrial engineer. Management will hire someone trained in law if a legalistic orientation is needed. If the organization's management fails to define a clear orientation to control, it is liable to be 'surprised' by the nature of the control designed by the person hired for the job.

A dynamic approach to control

A dynamic approach to control, common to the various disciplinary orientations, is evolving. This trend can be seen in four main areas:

1. A move from 'physical' control to 'abstract' control. As described above, control has traditionally concentrated on resources such as money, material, equipment, in-process inventory, completed products, and employees. Clearly, an evaluation of these elements is crucial to a full understanding of the organization's achievements. There is, however, a growing awareness of the need to examine 'non-real' items as well. These include issues such as managers' decisions, employee attitudes, customer satisfaction, -- vital factors impacting organizational performance.

2. Pre-performance control is another expression of a dynamic approach. It requires creative thinking, and involves simulation of the results of occurrences *before* they take place. This aspect of control usually accompanies policy design and planning. It encourages the examination of alternatives and preferences, prior to performance. Pre-performance control is inseparable from the decision making process in the organization; it focuses particularly on management and senior staff.

3. The growing understanding of the significance that outputs result from inputs and throughput, has shown the need for strengthening control of the *process* rather than concentrating only on output control. Process control is an approach which attempts to correct deviations *at the time of occurrence*, thus reducing defective output. This approach is particularly vital when dealing with large-scale projects.

4. The dynamic approach to control concentrates on ongoing improvement of the system rather than focusing on the identification of deviations from a static standard. Over-emphasis on a set, formal standard is often an obstacle to progress. In the same way that workers can organize job

actions by 'working by the book', (i.e. working according to standards), over-emphasis on a formal standard can lead to organizational bankruptcy. Occurrences in the organization should be compared to the *potential level*, therefore calling for a continuous revision of standards.

The dynamic nature of control introduces ongoing change in its content. According to this perspective, the basis for comparison of occurrences is in a constant state of change. Standards should be altered continuously, based on organizational and environmental developments. The organization undergoes changes in goals, work methods, skills and motives; outside the organization there are changes in market, in legislation, in technology, and so forth.

The ability to detect organizational and environmental changes depends, too, upon the skill of the controllers. The strength of dynamic control is in detecting trends that are yet unrealized; this requires a sophistication among controllers and managers. It is an innovative orientation, essentially different from traditional control. It requires a high degree of mutual trust among members of the organization, as it depends upon a process of adjusting the entire system to unknown future developments. A dynamic control system is based on the concept that a healthy organization faces constant change in aims and goals, in keeping up with changing needs and possibilities. The control system not only needs information about present occurrences and their comparison to past standards, but also predictions of future needs.

Goals and by-products

The above discussion illustrates the wide variety of control definitions and objectives influenced by the orientation and experience of the individual. A number of by-products of control also arise. These too contribute greatly to management and to organizational culture. Ten goals and by-products are presented in Exhibit 1.1; of these, three are major objectives of control, three are positive by-products, and four are negative by-products.

The *goals* are results which the control system, by definition, must attain. The *positive by-products* may often have such a strong impact that they are no less important than the goals themselves. On the other hand, control is also accompanied by a number of *negative by-products*, which warrant attention.

Goals

Correction of deviations is the most common goal in all definitions and approaches to control. This goal compares performance with planning, and initiates corrective actions. According to many orientations, this represents the central purpose of control; the initiation of change, so that occurrences meet or exceed standards and expectations.

Exhibit 1.1
Major goals and by-products of control

Major Goals:
1. correction of deviations
2. growth and development
3. protection of legitimate interests

Positive by-products:
4. definition of acceptable levels of achievement and behavior
5. reward for achievement
6. basis for communication among employees at various levels

Negative by-products
7. excess of information
8. concealment of deviations
9. work 'by the book'
10. tension between superiors and subordinates

In this context, control must ensure that the organization develops effective mechanisms for identifying and correcting deviations as early as possible.

Growth and development emphasizes the dynamic aspect of control. This goal implies that it is not sufficient for performance to conform to standards; there must be an ongoing examination of the degree to which the organization is utilizing its potential. Although the fulfillment of standards may be formally acceptable, it will be rejected by the dynamic orientation, since this approach calls for the continuous changing of standards. Accordingly, control aims to examine the system's responses to changing possibilities and changing needs in the organization and its environment. An organization that does not investigate possibilities, and does not prepare for the future, puts itself in danger of stagnation.

Protection of legitimate interests of the parties involved in the organization is an explicit goal of control, although it can also be seen as a by-product. Typical interest groups within the organization itself are managers and employees. These parties are represented either by committees or informal representatives. At the same time, control deals with interested parties outside of the organization, including customers, citizens, local and central government, stockholders, and suppliers.

In the last few decades, international control -- both permanent and ad hoc -- has been part of the scene of the Western world. Such bodies have been established to treat both 'abstract' subjects (such as civil rights) and specific issues (such as control of drugs, or child labor).

Positive by-products

Definition of acceptable achievement level and behavior is considered an essential point of departure for a number of goals: performance management, organizational climate, and the control system itself. The need for operational goals requires translating a conceptual level of achievement to performance standards. This serves as the basis for what is considered 'acceptable' and what is not. This process is twofold: it serves parties both within and outside the organization.

Reward for achievement is generally expressed by the remuneration and compensation given to those who respond to expectations, and particularly to those who exceed the standards. Similarly, it establishes an objective basis for sanctions for those who permanently fail to fulfill organizational standards.

Although a reward system serves to guide organizational members, it can be extended to outside parties, such as customers, suppliers, and taxpayers, depending on the nature and products of the organization. rewards serve the very essence of control, even when not especially intended for this purpose. In this context we should note:

a. Rewards can be set only on the basis of a standardized, clear, and accepted system, with well defined methods for measurement of performance and its comparison to standards.

b. The greater the reaction aroused by control, the higher its status and prestige, be it reward for achievement or sanctions for poor performance.

Improving communication between managers and employees occurs as a result of clarifying the definition of satisfactory level of performance. A common source of tension and misunderstanding between these parties not only comes from their real differences in interests, but also from differences in expectations and aspirations. By defining a mutual level of expectations, people are provided with a basis for reducing tension and conflict. Poor communication is a result of -- and also a cause for -- misunderstandings which usually lead to improper functioning.

Negative by-products

Excess of information is sometimes a by-product of the control process, as a result of the desire not to lose data that might seem relevant at some other stage of control. This tendency is liable to unnecessarily burden the information and communication system of the organization.

Concealing deviations from control is sometimes a consequence of the fear of sanctions that may be taken against those responsible. This tendency may be an obstacle to the control process and at the same time it reduces the ability of the organization to function properly due to lack of information.

Working 'by the book' is often a reaction of those being evaluated. These individuals may desire to 'punish' the organization by adhering strictly to standards which should really be surpassed. It can be assumed that slowdowns of this sort might also occur in the absence of control, but its formal establishment and the existence of mandatory standards emphasizes it.

Tension between managers and employees can increase because of pressure from management to attain expected levels of achievement. This 'pressurizing' factor becomes particularly troublesome when the required level of achievement is difficult to attain.

The negative by-products of control arise not only from the control process itself, but are very much the result of the organizational climate and management-employee relations. By avoiding a punitive approach to the use of control, and by including relevant parties in the establishment and ongoing evaluation of standards, these negative by-products can be brought to a minimum.

2 The control loop

As in all feedback mechanisms, the control model is a 'loop' which ensures its dynamic nature and its continuous process. Just as an increase in the level of sugar in the bloodstream sends a message to the pancreas to secrete more insulnin, the evaluation of information in the control system sends messages to management to initiate corrective actions when needed. The graphic illustration of the control loop in Exhibit 2.1, represents the process of information flow and decision making, aimed at ensuring that the organization will function according to its objectives. The following items describe and explain the content of each component in the control loop.

Aspirations, policy and planning

The aspirations of an organization; its board of directors, management, supervisors and employees, is one of the central factors which determine organizational quality. A high level of aspirations is essential to a high level of achievement. When the level of aspirations is low, regression and failure follow. High aspirations dictate high standards and a well functioning control system. Low aspirations are generally accompanied by low standards and the virtual absence of control.

The level of organizational aspirations is determined by senior management and transmitted to all employees. The clearest expression is found in policy and planning. General policy is set by upper management, where major goals and directions are defined. A clear definition of *policy* is essential in order create concrete *planning*. The organization's aspirations are expressed in the two elements of policy and planning.

Exhibit 2.1
The control loop

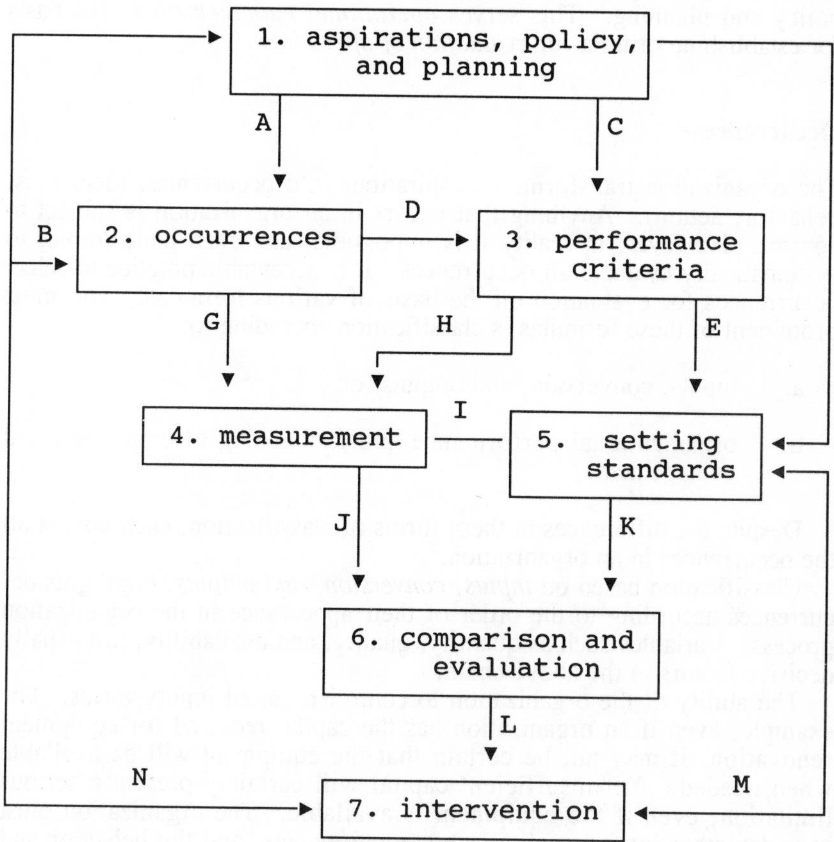

To demonstrate the relationship between levels of aspiration, policy and planning, consider the approach of two furniture factories. The management of ComfyCo intends to expand and grow by means of mass production, while the management at Excel wants to target a relatively narrow market sector by providing quality products. ComfyCo strives for maximum profits within a short period, while Excel is aiming for high quality and prestige, which in the long run should lead to high profit.

These differences in aspirations dictate the definition of different policies. The management at ComfyCo is likely to choose modular production of popular, inexpensive furniture, to be sold in low-priced chain stores with large turnover and low profit per unit. Excel's management may opt for a selective group of customers who can afford to pay high prices in return for tailor-made designs. These two policies express different objectives and directions and, therefore, require very different plans. The methods for achieving these ends, will of course, be in keeping with the spirit and level of aspirations set by management.

The 'beginning' of the control process starts with the definition of policy and planning. This serves *operational management* as the basis for establishing criteria for *evaluation of operations*.

Occurrences

The organization transforms its aspirations into occurrences (decisions, behavior, action). Anything that occurs in an organization is subject to control. However, in reality it is impossible, and even undesirable, to systematically evaluate all occurrences. It is acceptable practice to select occurrences for evaluation on the basis of various formulas. The most prominent of these formulas is classification according to:

a. inputs, conversion, and outputs; or,

b. organizational performance and functioning of employees and management.

Despite the differences in these forms of classification, each covers all the occurrences in an organization.

Classification based on *inputs, conversion, and outputs*, highlights occurrences according to the order of their appearance in the organization process. Variables such as quantity, quality, and availability, are usually decisive factors in the above chain.

The ability of the organization to control required inputs varies. For example, even if an organization has the capital required for equipment renovation, it may not be certain that the equipment will be available when needed. Yet insufficient capital will certainly present a serious limitation, even if the equipment is available. The organization must consider other inputs, such as labor requirements, and the behavior and functioning of its employees. In other words, management must verify that a proper balance exists among *all* utilized inputs.

In the course of conversion, control focuses mainly upon two areas: organizational units, and processes. In principle, each unit and subunit in the organization has a specific role. The control of occurrences in these units encompasses those activities that are part of the continuum of an activity which began in one unit and will be completed in other units. Therefore, it is necessary that the control system examine not only organizational units but processes as well, because these naturally extend across several units.

Output control relates both to the intermediate output of each subsystem in the organization, and to the end-products of the system, those designed for outside consumers.

Organizational performance and functioning of employees and management also serves as a frame of reference for the control system. It covers most of the occurrences in an organization, with emphasis on both performance and behavior. The behavior of employees in the organization is a result of several variables, including policy and procedures of human resources, management style, and motivation for achievements.

A survey of management literature gives the impression that organizational control systems deal mainly with employee operations and behavior (Burack, 1976; Brown and Moberg, 1980). The control of management activities is not treated in the systematic manner warranted by its essential nature. For the most part, the emphasis is on the control that management executes, or the results that it may get. Very little is reported regarding control of management activities, particularly that of senior management (Allcorn, 1979).

Results of occurrences in the areas noted above, are dependent upon the unique nature of each area, the quality of decisions made by management, and events outside the organization. The decisions made result from a combination of policy and planning (arrow A), and the feedback received (arrow B). The performance of the entire system is a result of the interaction of occurrences in all areas, regardless of the method used for categorizing occurrences. Therefore, managerial ability to control the quality of the occurrences and the interaction among them is a central aspect of administrative control.

Performance criteria

A key issue in control is the determination of criteria for measuring achievement. These are used to determine in which areas the organization is functioning in an acceptable manner and meeting expectations. The criteria with which achievement levels are evaluated are determined based on two characteristics.

Relative importance attributed by management to various occurrences

Specific goals and attitudes are not permanent. Changes over time require changes in organizational objectives. For instance, in one period the focus may be on human resources because of a shortage of skilled workers and high turnover; in another period the focus may shift to the purchasing department because of shortages and delays in delivery times of raw materials.

The possibility of quantifying occurrences

It is important to recognize the existence of huge differences in one's ability to quantify various areas of activity. For instance, it is easy to quantify production costs for a given product, but very difficult to quantify the correctness of the decision to produce that product.

The identification and definition of criteria for the evaluation of organizational performance is an expression of control policy and a basis for setting standards. (This subject is discussed in detail in Chapter 4.)

The effectiveness of control is unequivocally dependent on the *ability to use the specific criteria* developed for evaluating organizational performance. It is expected that the criteria will be derived from policies, planning and strategy (arrow C in the control loop). This is the basic input for criteria identification and definition. Yet, criteria are also meant to express operational needs and potential. Therefore, it is essential to develop criteria based on input and information from the field of occurrences (arrow D).

Measurement

It is not possible to compare an occurrence to a standard or to the desired situation until the occurrence has been measured. That is, the measurement of an occurrence (arrow G) must be performed for each criterion included in the control system (arrow H). If measurement of an occurrence is not reliable, the comparison of its results with the standards is meaningless. Therefore, it is of utmost importance to ensure that the process of measurement is carried out systematically and reliably. It is relatively easy to measure those areas where performance can be quantified. Measurement is more difficult in value-related criteria which are relatively abstract. For instance, it is difficult to estimate the effectiveness of communication, but easy to measure time spent waiting in line. This is the major source of difference and variety in measurement methods. (Measurement of performance is discussed in detail in Chapter 6.)

Setting standards

A standard describes that value of performance or behavior which is determined to be 'acceptable', or 'reasonable'. It is therefore necessary to define standards for every criterion (arrow E), and to determine both management's level of expectations (arrow F) and concrete measures of achievement (arrow I).

Despite the desire to define standards in operational and quantitative terms, this is not always possible. Clearly, the more quantitative the standards, the simpler the task of comparing occurrences and expectations. Often in dealing with criteria difficult to quantify, managers have relied upon subjective impressions. In such circumstances, efforts should be made to analyze the components which the subjective impression is based upon. This will help to verify the relevance of the components to the occurrence, as well as reduce the chance of a biased evaluation.

The determination of standards of different types, will require a variety of methods. The common denominator here is the recognition of the need for a standard on the basis of which the organization can function, measure, and evaluate occurrences -- whether they are technical processes or human behavior. (A detailed discussion of setting standards can be found in Chapter 5.)

Comparison and evaluation

Most experts consider the comparison of occurrences to standards, and the evaluation of results, as the heart of control. Almost every supervisor or manager conducts such activity. As noted, the more defined and clear the criterion, the easier is the comparison of occurrences to standards.

The evaluation of findings derived from the comparison of occurrences to standards is the creative aspect of control. Reaching conclusions about the fit between measurement findings (arrow J) and standards (arrow K) is the most complex part of the control process. At this stage, attention is focused to determine whether the activity achieved the objectives set by the organization. The more significant the evaluated subject, the higher the management level needed to carry out this evaluation and initiate change.

The evaluation of deviations from standards entails the examination of both the nature of the deviation and its cause. Deviations are desirable if performance exceeds the standard, but undesirable when performance falls below expectations. The causes of deviations lie in internal and external, objective and subjective, technical and human variables. Random deviations indicate an uncontrolled system, since a fully controlled one can usually lead to desired outcomes without undesired or unpredicted fluctuations. The control system strives to locate these factors in order to eliminate them and help to ensure proper functioning of the organization.

While the significance of evaluation in specific areas can not be underestimated, the overall evaluation of an organization requires an integrated criterion. (Special attention to this issue is given in Chapter 4.)

Intervention

There is no justification for the existence of a control system without the ability to introduce change. This may be done in order to reduce undesirable deviations or to adopt and generate 'positive deviations'.

The very existence of a criteria system implies the ability and the authority to make corrections designed to improve the organization.

There are two main possible reactions to evaluation: one requires intervention (arrow L), while the other does not. According to the common approach to control, there is no need for intervention if the system is functioning according to expectations. On the other hand, there are at least two types of situations in which evaluation by the control system leads to intervention.

Lack of fit between standards and performance

Comparison between the two may indicate that the standards are unrealistic; that the standards are too low and that occurrences have surpassed expectations; that occurrences do not fulfill expectations because they are carried out poorly; or, that both expectations and performance are at fault. In light of this imbalance, action is taken to create a better fit between occurrences and standards (arrows M and N).

A vision of potential, rather than actual, deviation in existing activities

In this case as well, changes in performance standards are called for, but this type of intervention involves future expectations rather than immediate corrections based on past performance.

The concept of the control loop is meant to emphasize the dynamic nature of a system in which all organizational levels are involved, with senior management holding central responsibility. One of the most important tasks of the control function itself is to ensure the dynamic process of the control system as a permanent tool for organizational improvement and growth.

3 Control items and timing trichotomy

We have discussed the purpose of control and the process of the control loop. But as a manager, you must ask yourself what items need to be controlled, how extensive the control should be, and when and how often will an evaluation be needed. What, how, and when, are the three issues of control planning.

What items to control

If you think that 'everything' should be subject to control, you are liable to end up with a system that ignores important items and exerts too much effort examining others. Clearly then, it is important to define which items should be evaluated. Determining the list of control items is an ongoing process; on-the-spot decisions are not sufficient. When determining if an item should be subjected to control, a cost-benefit analysis applies. You must ask yourself two questions:

1. What is the cost if an error is not detected and corrected? The cost may be felt immediately and have an obvious monetary value, or, it may have consequences that are not felt for a long time. For example, the cost of a mistake in assembling an item may be easy to detect and quantify, if it is impossible to properly finalize the assembly with the error. But errors which damage the reputation of your organization, have a long term impact, and are difficult to quantify.

2. What is the cost of control? To be worthwhile, the benefit derived from controlling an item must exceed the cost of its control. This is discussed further in Chapter 15.

There are various types of control systems. One of these is presented below, and consists of four categories; organizational units, processes, resources, and outputs.

Four major control categories

Organizational units. With this orientation, the control system examines each organizational unit separately. This is referred to as *vertical control.* The more autonomous the unit, the greater the significance of this type of control. If a unit is highly integrated in a continuous process, this control structure is less useful.

A good guideline is that the decision to concentrate on organizational units should be influenced by the relative autonomy of the units, as well as by the ability to clearly define each unit's outputs. In unit-oriented control, strong emphasis is placed on comparison either to other units, or to the unit itself at different points in time.

A unit can be classified by: the impact it has on the survival of the organization; the ability of the organization to handle malfunctioning in the unit before it is detected by customers; and, the degree of standardization in the processes of the unit. Organizational units can also be classified functionally, such as R&D, production, marketing, and finance. These distinctions are useful in planning the control system. The structure that is appropriate for the control of a research and development unit will be different from that of a production department, since time frames, outputs, and standards will be very different.

Products or processes. A completely different orientation to control defines an item as a 'product' or a 'process'. In order to complete a product or service, a series of activities should be performed. These generally involve a number of organizational units. It is the series of occurrences in the process that concerns control, and the boundaries between subunits are disregarded. This is what is known as *horizontal control.*

Examples of processes are varied. The process of absorbing a new employee involves his department, personnel, payroll, and other units. Ordering materials involves the department needing the materials, the warehouse, and the purchasing department. Obtaining a building permit typically entails the involvement of more than ten organizational units. Those who apply for the permit are not at all interested in the performance of any single unit.

Most frequently, comparisons in process control are made between the same occurrences, performed either by different organizational units at the same time, or by a single one at different times. The dynamic orientation to control invests in the examination of products and processes, which change more frequently than organizational units.

Resources. Control of resources focuses on the characteristics and utilization of resources in a specific unit or in the organization as a whole. This occurs prior to, during, and following the use of the resources.

Organizational resources can be divided into six groups, referred to as the 6 m's: members, money, machines, materials, methods, and management. This diversity in content, as well as in the feasibility of control, necessitates a discussion of each group separately.

Members, or more precisely, human resources, is probably the most common element in control. It is easy to identify, and quantitative data on the relevant attributes is generally available. This resource is undoubtedly one of the most important to the success of the organization, but its success depends upon other resources. Control of the performance and behavior of employees is sometimes overemphasized in management control, and this at the expense of attention to other areas. Human resources control is so central and complex, that Chapter 13 has been devoted entirely to it.

Money is generally considered to be the primary indicator of the activity and success of an organization. However, not everything in an organization can be measured in monetary terms, and therefore we deal with this as just one of the six resources, albeit a very important one.

If the control of an organization was expressed only in monetary terms, it would be very limited. Consider, for instance, company A, a poor performer whose profits are high because its major competitor was wiped out by the San Francisco earthquake. The complexity of this situation is not captured by an exclusively monetary approach.

Utilization of financial resources, however, is part of almost every aspect of organizational activity, and is integral to determining the quality of all other resources. It is a major component for control itself, and is an essential element for all other components. This resource is also dealt with separately, in Chapter 11.

Machinery and equipment, in a broad sense, refers to the technological resources of the organization. Investment, utilization, renewal, and maintenance of this resource are basic issues for control. Equipment may be evaluated for the entire organization, or for particular subunits. Control often examines whether equipment reaches a satisfactory level of utilization, whether it is properly maintained, and to what extent it is renewed. Subunits in the same organization, or similar units in different ones, can be compared with regard to the performance of their equipment.

Materials control involves the examination of policy, planning, purchasing, inventory, storage, allocation, waste, and the flow of materials in the production process.

A large part of a company's assets is invested in raw materials, products in process, or final products. A poor materials policy can result in problems such as overstocking financed by high-interest loans. Effective inventory policy and proper flow of materials is crucial to the survival of any organization, particularly in companies that maintain large stocks.

Methods used by organizations are instituted and reviewed by departments such as systems analysis, industrial engineering and organizational development. The role of such functions includes ongoing evaluation and control of work methods aimed at performance improvement.

Methods evaluation and control provides the dynamic potential for ongoing improvement. Methods, once considered optimal, do become outdated. Control should assure that the organization is geared toward adapting to new developments and work methods.

Management is a resource critical to the success of an organization, but particularly difficult to control and evaluate. Control of management should start with management philosophy and end with applied managerial tools. Management control involves a paradox: the more senior the level, the less intensive the control. An item that is concrete and clear and easily standardized, lends itself to a simple control procedure. Yet the quality of executive decision making, critical to organizational survival, is in fact, less controlled.

Management is both a complex resource and a basic input, requiring intensive control despite the practical difficulty. It is essential that the processes of recruitment, selection, and development of managers; management style; and the process and quality of decision making be systematically examined and evaluated. Because of the importance of this resource, it is discussed in detail in Chapter 7.

Outputs. Outputs are tangible in manufacturing and intangible in service organizations. In purchasing tangible items, such as refrigerators and textile goods, customers are interested in the final product and do not care about the production process. This is not the case when dealing with many service companies, since the process is part of the product itself. For example, when dining in a restaurant, the customer considers not only the quality of the food, but also the way in which it is served.

An organization developing output control must first concentrate on a clear definition of its products. It should examine the characteristic of the outputs from two different perspectives: that of the organization, and that of the customer. An organization is interested in evaluating the profit it makes from every single product, while its customer is interested in the price and quality. In establishing a control and evaluation system for an organization's outputs, customers' interests must be represented.

Extent of control

Once control items are determined, it is imperative to define the extent of control for each item. Three control levels are commonly used: strategic, tactical, and operational (Devenna, et al, 1981).

Three control levels

The strategic level. Strategic control focuses on policies and planning. This can be for the entire organization or specific subjects and resources. Is an optimal strategy being applied? At this level, control is expected to examine the leadership of the organization, usually directed at the quality of top management's decisions.

The tactical level. Tactical decisions are those that determine the way in which the organization will carry out what it has decided to do. For instance, a decision was made to manufacture and market a new product. It is at the tactical level that it will be decided which operations to carry out in which departments. Tactical-level control is intended to ensure the optimal utilization of resources in the conversion process.

Tactical decisions are implemented by senior and middle-level management. They have a significant impact on both the utilization of inputs and the operation of the system. Control at this level must devote special attention to the ability of managers to motivate their subordinates in the most effective manner, since the quality of the human resource is a crucial factor in success at this level.

The operational level. This is the most detailed level of control. The operational level deals with scheduling orders and available resources in order to match deliveries in the most effective manner.

The three levels of control discussed above can be seen in the following example. Senior management of an airline company has decided to expand its services (a decision at the strategic level). This decision may be implemented in several ways. New lines could be added, or changes in the existing lines with the addition of stopovers could be employed instead (a decision at the tactical level).

Once the tactical decisions are made, the flight schedule must be developed, including which planes will fly the new route, when they will fly, and which crew members will be involved (the operational level).

When to evaluate -- the timing trichotomy

In designing the control system, you must determine when and how often to initiate control. The continuum is longer than it may seem. The operation begins with its conceptualization and ends with its completion.

The appropriate timing for control depends on the specific organization and the occurrence in question. However, in principle, it is correct to view each occurrence in three significant stages: pre-occurrence; during-occurrence; and post-occurrence.

We prefer the terms pre-, during-, and post-occurrence, although the literature commonly uses, 'precontrol', 'currentcontrol', and 'postcontrol' (Gerloff, 1985). This terminology is misleading, since we want to refer not to a period prior to control, but rather to control prior to the occurrence.

Pre-occurrence control

Before an activity begins, its possible outcomes should be assessed. Although it may seem difficult to evaluate an outcome before the occurrence actually begins, it is commonly done. In fact, techniques such as simulation to aid in this assessment are becoming increasingly popular.

Pre-occurrence control is particularly suitable to certain conditions. These include situations of high risk, technological uncertainty, or the irreversibility of errors.

Risk. The greater the risk entailed in an operation, the more rigid the pre-occurrence control should be. Consider the decision to develop a complicated product such as a pilotless-airplane. The most reliable instruments available must be applied in order to predict the possible results of the occurrence and their probabilities. The importance of this kind of control explains the development of methods and tools which attempt to simulate potential occurrences, in order to predict the eventual outcome.

Technological uncertainty. Uncertainty is the reason to construct experimental models and pilot studies before initiating a full-scale operation. It is usually better to invest in an experimental model than to discover in the course of the occurrence that the approach is fundamentally wrong.

Irreversibility of errors. Errors which could lead to plant shutdowns, injury to employees or customers, or damage to the environment, are alone reason for pre-occurrence control. Perhaps less dramatic, but potentially as irreversible, are errors which result in damaged reputation.

Every test, examination, analysis, experiment, simulation, or brainstorming, carried out prior to operation, can be considered pre-occurrence control. Although pre-occurrence control is often useful, and in some cases absolutely necessary, it is not an alternative to during-occurrence control.

During-occurrence control

This type of control, often referred to as in-process control, is aimed at identifying, correcting, and preventing deviations and defects in the course of operation. Such control is based on the assumption that even if great investment is made in the pre-occurrence period, there remain many opportunities for errors during the occurrence itself. If these are not discovered and corrected, it is likely that their cumulative effect will be damaging.

In practice, during-occurrence control strives to oversee the occurrence and to correct any deviation as soon as it is detected. The need arises because pre-occurrence control is not capable of predicting the outcome of the operation in detail and post-occurrence control may identify problems too late to prevent extensive damage.

Although it is neither practically nor financially feasible to check every item and step at every point in time, we strive for a system with built-in control to evaluate and correct deviations throughout the course of the occurrence. Built-in controls are typically characterized by a fast response time. The smaller the time lapse between the start of a malfunction and its correction, the smaller the cumulative error, and the more likely that outputs will meet expectations.

The need for built-in controls can be evaluated by examining these areas:

a. *The need for speed of correction* is the most obvious indication for built-in control. For example, it would be difficult to imagine the operation of planes and missiles, without built-in control systems that receive and correct deviations from course.

b. *The need for change in plans* is an important reason for built-in control. Comparing performance to plans almost always reveals that they do not match completely. Control is responsible for this comparison, for analyzing its causes, and for suggesting possible ways to correct it. Whether the deviation is the result of defective operation or of poor planning, its correction requires a change in plans.

c. *Automation* necessitates the existence of a built-in control system that will identify and respond to problems in real-time. For example, in work centers such as FMS (flexible manufacturing systems), machines automatically move from one item to a different item. The dimensions of tools are measured automatically and continuously, and adjustments are automatically made to correct undesired deviations. If a cutting tool breaks, the machine stops immediately. Control is integrated into the occurrence process and prevents errors.

d. *Critical points in a process* indicate the need for during occurrence control. A critical point is identified by its impact on the final output.

Post-occurrence control

Post-occurrence control concentrates on the evaluation of outputs. It is the most conventional form of control. With post-occurrence evaluation, the damage has already been done and, in some cases, may not be repairable. This cannot replace pre- or during-occurrence control, but focuses on ensuring that the outputs meet specifications. There are some situations in which post-occurrence control is very significant. This is particularly true if the output can be evaluated only on the basis of the finished product. There are three variations in which post-occurrence control is essential.

As a conclusive basis for comparison of organizational performance. Criteria for output evaluation are relatively easily traced and measured. Post-occurrence evaluation can be within an organization, comparing performance between periods, or between various organizations. The more effective and efficient an organization, the more successful its functioning. An overall evaluation of this type is feasible only through post-occurrence control.

Where there are legal requirements for post-occurrence control. This most often takes the form of balance sheets and performance reports. Control here is performed after the occurrence.

Public opinion is a very powerful form of post-occurrence control. For example, criticism of a play may determine the fate of the production. Similarly, a consumers' picket line is likely to reduce business. In such cases, the control refers to the product or service, which signifies post-occurrence timing.

Although post-occurrence control relates to the 'bottom line' of the organization's performance, it is important to note that the emphasis should be placed on pre- or during-occurrence control. In this way the organization hopes to avoid undesirable outputs at the time of post-occurrence evaluation.

When to evaluate -- timing and frequency

A number of considerations go into determining the timing and frequency of control.

Cost-benefit of control time. A cost-benefit analysis will be needed to determine optimal timing in order minimize damage. If pre-occurrence control cannot prevent errors, it is not worthwhile to make a large investment in this area. Economic considerations regarding control and its location on the continuum of the occurrence is vital, and in some cases, the decisive factor.

The relative importance of timing and frequency of control varies from one occurrence to another. For instance, in a car assembly plant, current performance control is not sufficient, and strict post-performance control of the completed vehicle is essential. The determining factors here are feasibility of control and the nature of the item.

Reliability of data is a vital factor in control. Erroneous data leads to erroneous analysis and decisions. Control must be timed, and data collected, so that the sources of defects can be accurately identified.

The law often determines the timing and frequency of control. Almost all organizations, particularly those in the public sector, are periodically required to examine the consequences of their operations. Public organizations, and most businesses, are subject to extensive post-occurrence controls, including the obligation to present balance sheets and performance reports to the public and shareholders. The emphasis in competitive companies must be on pre-occurrence and duringcontrol; since the more a company relies on output control, the greater is the risk of producing defective items.

There exists a strong logical connection between two variables discussed here, control items and the timing of control. This is demonstrated in Exhibit 3.1, which shows the relationship between timing and the continuum of occurrences, from policy to the finished product. There is, of course, some degree of overlap in the levels of occurrence and timing.

Exhibit 3.1
Relationship between timing trichotomy and the occurrence continuum

Timing	Pre-occurrence	During-occurence	Post-occurrence
Occurrence	Policy and Planning	Operations and Performance	Performance and Output

In general, investment in pre-occurrence control will mean fewer problems during operations, and, effort put into during-occurrence control, will pay off in fewer post-occurrence problems. This approach, also known as the 'life cycle cost' concept, states that the impact of each activity should be evaluated based on its overall impact on the project life cycle.

4 Evaluation criteria

As presented in Chapter 2 on The Control Loop, the evaluation process of information flow and decision making, is comprised of four consecutive activities. These activities include:

a. the identification and definition of control criteria

b. the measurement of each criterion

c. the determination of a standard for each criterion

d. the comparison of actual performance to these standards.

In order to evaluate occurrences (decisions, actions, etc.) in an organization, performance criteria must be established as a basis for comparison. A relevant performance criterion is a *measurable* indicator that can be used to discern improvement or deterioration in organizational performance. Examples of criteria include indicators such as product cost, customer satisfaction, percentage of defective products, rate of employee turnover, or overall organizational profitability.

Relevant criteria are developed through an analysis of the organization's objectives. Very often, these objectives are expressed only in general terms and the relevant performance criteria are not explicitly stated. However, specific performance criteria must be developed on the basis of these more general goals.

For example, a university wishes to improve the quality of registration processing. In order to achieve this general goal, the university has to establish quality criteria and a satisfactory level of performance, also referred to as standards. Even after establishing a standard, say an error rate of 4%, the goal is not specific enough to enable operational control nor the proper response when the goal is not achieved. Therefore, specific goals should be established for each department involved in the process. For example, the percentage of errors allowed in the data entry department might be 2% while in accounts receivable, a 1% error rate might be appropriate.

Types of criteria

In developing performance criteria, both vertical and horizontal criteria should be established.

Vertical criteria are those used in evaluating the performance of an *organizational unit*, such as a production, marketing, purchasing, personnel, or finance department.

Horizontal criteria are those used for the evaluation of *processes*. A process may begin and end in one department (e.g. changing a large bill to coins), or it may involve several organizational units (e.g. applying for a loan). Since horizontal analysis crosses departmental boundaries, it is the appropriate approach for evaluating the *utilization of organizational resources* such as the labor force.

The characteristics of both vertical and horizontal criteria are discussed below in greater detail.

Vertical criteria

Vertical criteria can be developed in each of the following areas: outputs, inputs, productivity, and quality. The significance of each of these areas and the circumstances in which each is likely to be essential are as follows.

Outputs. Output criteria are those criteria that relate to final products or services and are expressed as quantities of output per unit of time. Examples of such criteria are the number of ovens produced in a month, the number of university graduates in a year, the number of insurance policies sold per month, or the annual revenue of a company.

These criteria are often applied to stimulate the growth of an organization by evaluating the level of growth in particular outputs. Such evaluations should include consideration of both *absolute criteria*, such as the increase in the number of items sold in a year, or of *relative criteria*, such as the rate of increase in the number of items sold in a year. This type of criterion is even used to evaluate the performance of the nation. Many readers are familiar with 'production indicators'. These output criteria, such as tons of steel produced per week or units of automobiles produced per week, are used to evaluate national growth.

Inputs. Input criteria deal with the resources required in the process of production, or delivery of service. These resources usually include materials, equipment, the labor force and capital. Input criteria are generally expressed in terms of units of input per unit of time, for instance: three tons of fuel per year, 240 machine hours in a month, 400 labor hours (400 people working for one hour or 40 people for 10 hours), $1,000 for advertising per month.

Certain circumstances demand control of a specific resource even if it is not included in the routine control system of the organization. For instance, a company manufacturing small appliances routinely monitors the criterion of labor hours per week. At a certain point, management realized that workers were idle as they waited for available machines. It then became critical to investigate equipment utilization in order to determine whether there was a real need for additional equipment. Perhaps the problem of idle time was simply the result of poor scheduling. Each scenario would lead to very different solutions with very different costs!

Another way in which input criteria are particularly useful is in examining the ratio of one input to another. For example, the ratio of machine hours utilized to labor hours paid, expresses the number of hours of machine work per employee hours paid. The use of this ratio helps management to better understand situations such as the idle time problem in the above example.

Productivity. Productivity criteria are based on the ratio of outputs to inputs, or the number of output units produced per input unit. *Overall productivity* is the ratio of *all the outputs* of the organization to *all its inputs*. Naturally, in order to create this ratio, the outputs and inputs must be reduced to a common denominator, such as money.

Consider an organization that produces merchandise valued at $100,000 at the factory. For the production of this merchandise, the organization purchases materials and services valued at $30,000. The value of the other inputs (labor, equipment, energy, etc.) is $40,000. The overall productivity of the organization is:

$$\text{overall productivity} = \frac{100{,}000}{40{,}000 + 30{,}000} = 1.43$$

In other words, the organization generated production at the value of $1.43 from each dollar invested in input. It is important to note that if the value of this ratio is equal to 1, the organization is at break even. If the value is less than 1, the organization is losing money.

In addition to overall productivity, organizations are often interested in *partial productivity* criteria. These criteria represent the ratio of production, or *output*, to *specific inputs* used by the organization. For instance, a partial productivity criterion might be the number of finished units per employee hour, the number of units per machine hour, the number of patients per hospital bed, or the number of units per square foot of space.

Generally, an organization's overall objective is to increase productivity. This can be accomplished by working faster, but even more importantly, by working smarter. Improving productivity usually means increasing the organization's output while using the same resources, or attaining the same output using fewer resources. Organizational productivity can be measured employing a number of different criteria. The relative importance of each of these will vary according to specific circumstances.

For example, a furniture manufacturer is interested in increasing its output. Analysis of the production process identifies that the utilization of resources is unbalanced, and that work is piling up at one of the gluing stations. It is realized, that in order to increase the organization's output, productivity at that station must improve. This can be achieved by increasing the number of units produced per labor labor hour, which is a *partial productivity criterion*. As you can see, the focus on productivity criteria does not stem only from the desire to reduce the cost of production, but also from a desire to increase output.

Quality. Quality criteria refer to characteristics of the product or service, regardless of the quantity of resources utilized in the production process. A container manufacturer specifies that certain aluminum cans will withstand 30 pounds of pressure per square inch. This is a quality criterion, and as such, does not concern itself with inputs or productivity measures. Very often, the quality features of a product are expressed in labeling, commercial advertising, and usually in the consumer's expectations as well.

Frequently, productivity and quality criteria complement one another, as each emphasizes a different aspect of performance. The slogan "fast and courteous service" is a familiar example of such a balance. The company will provide fast service, a productivity criterion, without sacrificing courtesy, a quality criterion.

Horizontal criteria

There are two types of horizontal criteria, process criteria and resources criteria.

Process criteria. Many issues that a company deals with involve of a number of different departments. This involvement may take place simultaneously or consecutively, as illustrated by the process chart shown in Exhibit 4.1.

These visual aids are generally used for planning and control in process analysis. Process performance is generally measured on the basis of criteria from three areas: *quality*, *cost* and *time*.

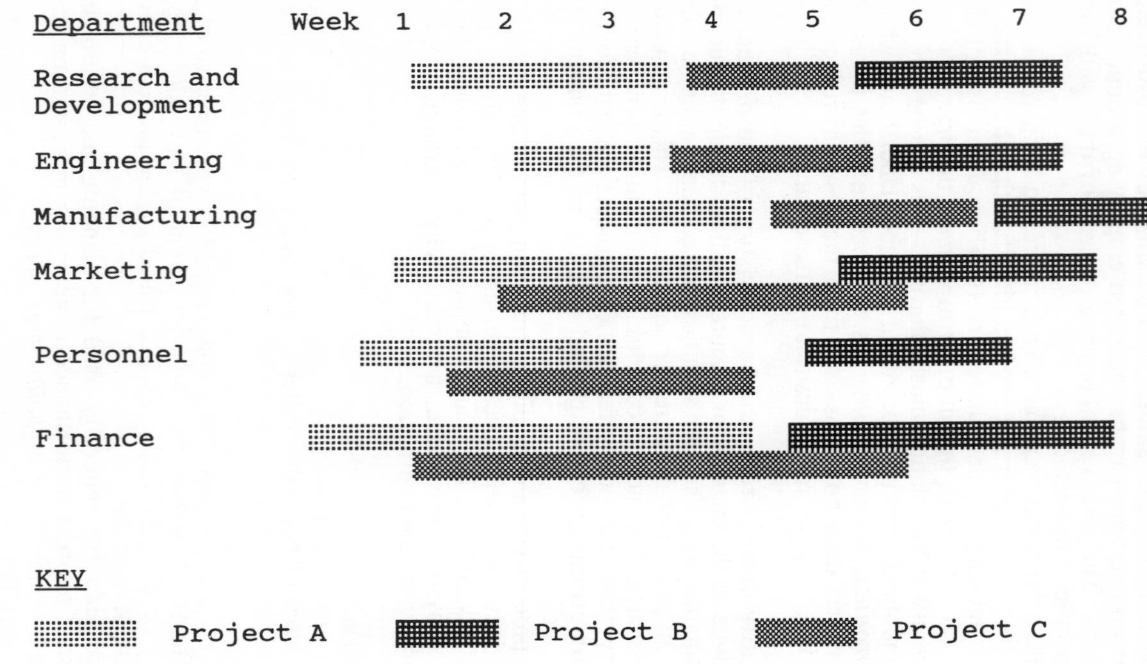

Exhibit 4.1 Process flow chart

Quality. When a city issues a building permit, its *quality* can be expressed in terms of accuracy and politeness. That is, if the building permit is not in keeping with necessary regulations, or the contact with the staff was not helpful, then there may be a defect in the quality of the product. On this basis, the percentage of cases in which the treatment was of the desired quality can be used as a process criterion.

Cost. The processing *cost* in this case refers to the expenditures required of the municipality for complete handling of a request for a building permit. The cost of all resources required includes labor, energy, building, equipment, and the like.

Time. With respect to *time*, we are interested in the period required for completing the process. In the case above, time criteria could include a number of measures, such as the average time it takes to handle a request or the percentage of permits issued within a given period.

Resource criteria. The primary resource used in the operation of the entire organizational network is *capital*. This resource may be exchanged for other resources such as labor, material, equipment, energy, and know-how. After most of the capital has been exchanged for the resources needed to run the organization, there is still a certain level of operating capital maintained; cash, liquid assets, etc. This operating capital is also considered to be a resource. Control criteria must be developed for both capital and the other resources.

In the following discussion, we present performance criteria for the *major resources* most commonly found in organizations: *equipment*, *labor*, *material*, and *operating capital*.

There is considerable difference between the criteria methodology applied in the analysis of processes, and that appropriate for resources. In process analysis, the general criteria of cost, quality, and time can be applied to each process. In contrast, while some resource criteria are of a general nature and can be applied to each resource, others are specific and can only be applied to a single resource.

We will examine two important *general criteria* -- *efficiency* and the *ratio between resources and outputs*. Later we will demonstrate some *special criteria.*

Efficiency

Equipment. One of the most important general criteria for the control of resources is the efficiency in *resource utilization*. This criterion examines the level of use in relation to potential use. With reference to equipment, the term 'utilization' is more commonly used than 'efficiency'. For instance, utilization of equipment signifies the percentage of output produced by the equipment, as compared to the maximum, or output capacity specified by the manufacturer. For example, a manufacturer indicates the output capacity of a laser printer to be 600 pages per hour. If, in actual operation, your company is realizing an output of 540 pages per hour, then utilization is 90% (540/600). Frequently, there is greater interest in the inverse of utilization, that is, the criterion of 'idle time'. The reason this is useful in practice becomes clear in Exhibit 4.2.

Exhibit 4.2
Reasons for equipment idle time

Reason	Likelihood
equipment awaiting repair	13%
equipment presently being repaired	2%
lack of work	3%
no operator for equipment	11%
Total percentage of lack of utilization	29%

Labor. Labor efficiency can be similarly evaluated and analyzed. The output produced by the employees in an organization is compared to *standard output*, that is, the output produced by a trained employee working at a normal pace. Standard output is determined by the use of work measurement methods, such as time study or work sampling. In the case of labor, efficiency can often exceed 100%. This is true because performance often improves over time, as employees gain experience, and therefore, can produce more output than that considered to be 'standard'. Labor efficiency is calculated using the following formula:

$$\text{Labor Efficiency} = \frac{\text{actual output}}{\text{standard output}} \tag{1}$$

Separate calculations for each resource may be carried out with relative ease. However, an integrated criterion, or overall measure, is a difficult one to establish. In measuring performance in producing fliers for an advertising campaign, for instance, the efficiency in the use of a copying machine and a computer can each be established without great difficulty. However, it is more complicated to determine a common efficiency coefficient for the two together.

Material. The common criterion of efficiency in material utilization is *inventory turnover*, calculated using the following formula:

$$\text{Inventory Turnover} = \frac{\text{annual value of all material used by company}}{\text{current value of material presently in company}} \tag{2}$$

In order to evaluate the efficiency in use of materials in an organization, a comparison must be made between the turnover in that company and the accepted turnover in the industry. This is done using the following formula:

$$\text{Efficiency in Use of Materials} = \frac{\text{turnover in organization}}{\text{accepted turnover in industry}} \qquad (3)$$

Let us look at a specific example. A manufacturer of aluminum products has an annual value of materials of $3,000,000 and a current inventory valued at $300,000. The manufacturer's inventory turnover then, is 10 times, or 3,000,000/300,000. The average turnover for the industry is 9 times. This manufacturer's material utilization, therefore, compares favorably with the industry average. The more the organization 'turns over' its inventory of materials, the higher its efficiency in the use of materials.

Operating capital. The measurement of efficiency in the use of operating capital differs completely from that of the three resources mentioned previously. The criterion most commonly used to measure this type of efficiency involves evaluating the interest gained from it. This criterion is determined by comparing the actual interest received, with the interest that would have been gained from an optimal financial policy. That is, the efficiency coefficient for operating capital can be defined as follows:

$$\text{Efficiency of Operating Capital Gain} = \frac{\text{interest paid}}{\text{maximum possible interest}} \qquad (4)$$

Exhibit 4.3 summarizes the significance of the concept of resource efficiency, as reviewed here.

Exhibit 4.3
Efficiency coefficients for four major organizational resources

Resource	Method of Calculation
equipment	$\frac{\text{equipment output}}{\text{maximum output capacity}}$
manpower	$\frac{\text{manpower output}}{\text{normal output}}$
materials	$\frac{\text{turnover in organization}}{\text{common turnover in same industry}}$
capital	$\frac{\text{interest from operating capital}}{\text{maximum possible interest}}$

Ratio of resources to output. This ratio has been used for the evaluation of resource performance for several decades. One classic example was formulated for the development of an organizational incentive system, the Scanlon Plan, (Globerson, 1985). According to this method, *labor* cost (a resource) is divided by the total value of production to obtain 'required labor cost per dollar of production value', as a criterion for performance evaluation.

For example, labor costs for a book publisher in 1987 were $6,500,000 when production value was $21,000,000. This yields a labor cost to production value ratio of .31 (6.5/21); for every $1 of production, $.31 must be spent on labor. The following year, the same company's production was valued at $22,500,00 with labor costs of $7,500,00. The new ratio is .33, meaning that performance has deteriorated since it now costs $.33 to produce $1 of output.

It has been found that these relationships are significantly dependent on the industry to which the organization belongs. Therefore, ratios within organizations in a given industry, are similar.

Another ratio of resource to output can be developed for *materials*. The cost of materials is divided by the value of production during a given period of time, such as annual expenditure on materials divided by the value of annual output.

It is not as straight forward to calculate this ratio for equipment and for operating capital. The major problem in calculating the ratio of the value of *equipment* to the value of production is the difficulty in estimating the value of equipment. This is an accounting problem, which may be resolved in a number of ways. Each way leads to a different result, and the method chosen affects the result in different ways. One simple approach is to calculate the value of the equipment according to its cost of purchase, discounting the inflation factor only. A more accurate, and complicated, approach takes into account the salvage value of the equipment.

Calculation of the ratio of *operating capital* to the value of production is also problematic. This is due to constant changes in the level of operating capital in most organizations. The average monthly operating capital can be used as the basis for the calculation.

Special criteria for resources. For each major resource there are also special criteria which cannot be used for the other resources. The following are examples:

> *Labor*: employee turnover, absenteeism, labor grievances, improvement proposals, training pace of new employees, percentage of employees capable of fulfilling more than one position.
>
> *Materials*: percentage of materials at different stages of production process (raw materials, works in process, final products), percentage of time during which material is worked on out of total time material is in organization, level of standardization of materials, percentage of material rejected, waste of material.

Equipment: cost of maintenance per given period of time, setup time, down time, interchangeability to other products.

Operating capital: percentage of various components of operating capital, e.g. cash, liquid assets, etc.

Choice of effective criteria

The list of feasible performance criteria for evaluating an organization is quite long. However, for practical purposes, a few dozen relevant criteria are usually sufficient. Below we describe ten factors that are most useful in developing relevant criteria.

Factors used in developing performance criteria

Organizational objectives. A significant performance criterion is one which is derived with organizational objectives as a starting point. Developing criteria with this principle in mind, forces management to express its objectives in clear-cut terms. For instance, an organization may state that one of its objectives is to improve quality. In order to implement this policy, the general goal must be translated into operational criteria. Examples of such concrete criteria include; the number of defects per 1,000 pieces, the time it takes to respond to a request for service, or the score of client responses to a customer service survey. Because the criteria are derived from objectives, it is usually necessary to change criteria when the organization alters its objectives or its priorities.

Making comparisons. By establishing relevant performance criteria, management is able to contrast performance in areas that are similar. This includes the comparison of *similar organizational units* such as branches of a bank, supermarket or insurance company, or departments within a plant, such as production units. Such comparisons can be used to explore the possible range of performance, identify the more successful units, and adopt their methods in the less successful ones.

Like the comparison of similar organizational units, the comparison of *similar subjects* can also be carried out with certain performance criteria. A subject might be a product (tire) or a service (house cleaning). Organizations that belong to the same industry can also compare their use of *similar resources*, using generally accepted industry-wide standards. This concept was discussed in the previous section on resource criteria.

Process of criteria selection. The criteria chosen are determined not only by the organizational objectives but also by the process of criteria selection. In order for the criteria to represent the needs of the entire organization, it is important that the selection process include all interested parties; customers, employees, and management. The process of choosing criteria is discussed in greater detail later in this chapter.

Clarity of purpose. The purpose of a criterion must be clear in order to enable its proper application. For instance, 'customer satisfaction' is an important criterion, but it is too vague and cannot be quantified unless further clarified. Precise and measurable criteria, such as customer waiting time, percentage of returns of defective products and, rate of return customers, must be used.

Appropriateness for specific organizational units. For a criterion to be of value, the results of the measure must be influenced by the efforts of the department or organizational unit being evaluated. If a criterion is not affected by the performance of a particular unit, it is not appropriate for the evaluation of that unit. For instance, the number of customers handled hourly at a bank is a relevant criterion for the advertising department, however, it would not be relevant for the performance evaluation of the purchasing department of that bank.

There are situations in which a unit has an impact on only a portion of the process and therefore only a portion of a given criterion. In these cases, a special criterion must be developed for the part of the operation that is influenced by the performance of the unit under evaluation. For instance, when a customer turns to an organization for the installation of an appliance, the request goes through a number of stages, including registration of the request, preparation of the order, and the actual installation. The response time is the total time it takes to perform all of the operations. However, total response time cannot be used as a relevant criterion of performance for each stage of the process.

Ratio criteria and absolute criteria. An absolute criterion is expressed by a number, while a ratio criterion compares one numerical value to another. For instance, the *present* revenue of an organization constitutes an absolute criterion, say $3,000,000, while the *growth* in revenue is a ratio criterion, say 2.8%. A control system requires both types of criteria for organizational evaluation.

Objective and subjective criteria. Objective criteria are more reliable and therefore preferable to subjective ones. However, in some cases there is no choice but to use subjective criteria. For instance, it is difficult to make an objective assessment of the cordiality with which service is provided, or to objectively estimate whether a research and development project was completed with optimal results. In such cases, the subjective evaluation of those involved or of reliable experts is usually used.

It is even the case that objective criteria used alone may miss important aspects of performance which can only be measured using subjective criteria. Consider the customer service department in a telephone company. One significant, objective measure of performance would be the length of time it took to handle customer inquiries.

However, if this measure were used alone, it would not take into consideration subjective criteria such as attitude or courtesy, critical to the successful performance of a customer service department.

Reliability of measurement. Reliability of a measure means that the repeated measurement of a criterion at the same performance level should result in the same outcome. However, it is difficult to maintain absolute control over the measuring process and for people to perform measurements with absolute accuracy. These factors may account for some differences in results.

Another common reason for variation in the results of repeated measurements is the use of a sample, rather than the entire population. It is expected that the results obtained from each sample would be somewhat different from the others. If repeated measurement of performance at the same level results in widely different outcomes, the measure is not reliable. (See Chapter 6, Measuring Performance.)

Calculation methods. It is important to be precise about what methods will be used for data collection. It is equally important to be clear as to how each performance criterion will be calculated. Let us go back to the example of the customer service department at the telephone company. We have agreed that the length of time it takes to handle customer inquiries is a relevant performance criterion, but we can collect data on this criterion in different ways. For example, supervisors could time telephone conversations periodically, random samples of call times could be calculated by a computerized phone system, or data might be collected on all calls via the phone system.

Once the data has been collected, the method by which the criterion will be calculated must be specified. In the case above, we could use measures such as average call time, the standard deviation of the time, the coefficient of variation (the standard deviation divided by the average), or the percentage of customers that had to wait for more than a specified time.

Does the criterion measure what you want it to measure?

In developing criteria, mistakes are often made when specific criteria are chosen because they are obvious or easy to measure. This can be done while neglecting more relevant criteria because they are more difficult to measure and calculate.

To continue with the example of the customer service department, clearly, handling customers' calls quickly would be good for service. Clients would be happy to spend as little time on the phone as possible, calls would not get backed-up and callers would not be kept waiting on hold. However, if this were our only criterion for customer service, we might find that we would give high ratings to employees who were curt and did not extend themselves for fear of taking too long on a call.

Let us look at another example that causes errors such as this. This time, using an example from the insurance industry, a claims department wishes to evaluate accuracy in claims payments. One method frequently used is to track the volume of customer complaints and returned checks. The flaw in this method of calculation, is that over-payments to clients rarely result in complaints or returns. Under this system, if an employee is faced with a question about the value of a claim, one obvious solution is to pay the highest amount to avoid an inquiry. What was originally designed to reward accuracy, actually ends up motivating over-payment of claims.

Selection of preferred criteria

Two stages are necessary for criteria selection; first, the generation of a list of possible performance criteria and second, selection of significant criteria out of the more extensive list.

Generation of a list of possible criteria

Recent research has concluded that the most significant cause of the decline in productivity in the United States lies in the overemphasis and exclusive attention of management to cost savings (Judson, 1982). The inclusion of a number of significant criteria related to other critical aspects of the organization would likely prove to be a more effective instrument in the process of improving organizational performance.

Each employee, manager or shop floor worker, is capable of making a list of possible evaluation criteria for the organization. Nevertheless, in order to create a list that is as representative as possible of the needs of the organization, input from various members of the organization should be applied. The following is an example of the possible composition of a team assigned to compose a list of performance criteria.

* The head of the team, who should be knowledgeable in those areas related to the establishment of the control infrastructure, such as evaluation systems, industrial engineering, information systems, systems analysis, and administration and control systems.
* The manager of the unit for which the control system is being developed.
* The senior manager to whom the unit manager reports.
* A respected employee from the unit in question, and alternatively or additionally, an employee from an appropriate headquarter unit, such as the controller's office.
* A representative from departments directly affected by the work of the unit. In certain cases, the representative should be an end customer who is not an employee of the organization.

The team is intended to concentrate on these subjects:

* Formulation of the objectives of the unit in question.

* The structure of the control unit in the organization and in the unit.
* The significance of performance criteria in general, and in the unit in particular.
* The development of general guidelines for the choice of criteria and their application in the unit.
* Finally, the generation of a list of possible criteria for the unit.

It is important to note that *the purpose of the first stage of the team's work is to generate a representative list of performance criteria*. Below is an example of such a list. This was generated by a team assigned the responsibility of developing performance criteria for a service department dealing with repairs of home appliances. The list is presented in the same sequence that was generated by the team:

- average cost of a repair
- average price of a repair
- cost of materials for repair
- number of repairs per month per employee
- time elapsed between customer request and filling of request (response time)
- percentage of services improperly performed
- level of satisfaction with service
- employee absentee rate
- time wasted as a result of tardiness
- increase in number of requests for service
- number of customer complaints
- increase in number of customers
- efficiency of service

A careful look at the list reveals that the team has identified a number of areas of interest to the organization. These include the areas of:

- productivity - (number of repairs per month per employee, average cost of a repair);
- quality - (percentage of services improperly performed, customer satisfaction);
- time - (response time between request and provision of service);
- growth rate - (increase in number of requests, increase in number of customers)
- employee behavior - (rate of absenteeism, time wasted because of tardiness).

Selecting a representative list

Because it is possible to make a long list of criteria, it is necessary to develop a method by which a representative list can be generated. It is best to choose the preferred criteria on the basis of two considerations: e *optimal number of criteria* that should be included in the control system, and a *rational method for selecting* these criteria.

To include all relevant criteria in the control system would present a tremendous burden in terms of data collection, analysis, and cost. Therefore, it is recommended, that organizations avoid using a large number of criteria. Research on the number of criteria generally accepted for use in incentive systems found that three criteria were most commonly used (Globerson and Parsons, 1985). In a small percentage (3%) of organizations using such systems, the reward was based on seven or more criteria.

Additional evidence in the literature, indicates that there are a limited number of critical areas necessary to the successful functioning of an organization (Rockart, 1979). Focussing on performance criteria in those areas would be the basis for an effective control system. While there is no hard and fast rule as to the 'correct' number of criteria to use, it is recommended that development teams focus on not more than seven central criteria.

The optimal number of criteria is also a function of the degree of effort required for data collection and analysis. In cases in which the work process is computer-aided, and data is automatically collected and processed, more criteria can be generated and used. In cases where data collection is manual, a smaller number of criteria should be employed.

Once the development team has made an extensive list of criteria, it must develop a process for selecting preferred criteria from this list. The selection process would be simple if it were possible to compare the relative merit of each criterion. Unfortunately, this is rarely possible.

Comparison in pairs, *graphic comparison*, and *simultaneous comparison*, are three common methods used in the selection process. With comparison in pairs, relative weights are assigned to each criterion and these weights are compared, by pairs, to determine the most important ones. In graphic comparison, the relative weight of each criterion is expressed on a graphic scale. These two methods are not discussed in detail here, as they have been found to be less efficient than the *simultaneous comparison method*, which is described below in detail. In this process too, each criterion is assigned a relative weight. The difference in simultaneous comparison, is that the comparison is made of all criteria *at the same time*.

When making a list of criteria that are to be weighed against each other, you must be certain that the various criteria are exclusive of one another. That is, that there are no two criteria that measure the same factor. For example, if you look at the list of 13 criteria above, 'level of customer satisfaction', and 'number of customer complaints', are overlapping criteria. The final list should contain only one of them. If one of these criteria is included in the final selection, it should be 'number of customer complaints', since it is the more concrete, measurable and objective of the two.

A further look at the list reveals that the criterion 'efficiency of service', lacks clarity. The concept of efficiency is probably better stated by using a combination of the criteria; 'average cost of repair', 'response time', and the 'quality' measure. The vague criterion should also be rejected from the final list.

A critical aspect of the selection process, is to ensure that all criteria chosen are under the control of the unit being evaluated. Again, looking at the list of 13 criteria, we notice the criterion, 'average price per repair'. This is a value determined by management and one that is not directly affected by the service department. Therefore, it is not an appropriate criterion for evaluating the service workers. It too should be rejected.

Having eliminated three criteria, there are 10 remaining. The selection of the preferred criteria out of these 10, is the next step to be carried out by the team. Each member assigns a relative weight to each criteria, using a total possible weight of 100. A combined weighted average is then calculated in order to determine which criteria the team members have considered the most important. Exhibit 4.4 below demonstrates how this method would be used for the 10 remaining criteria for the customer service department.

Exhibit 4.4
Relative weights of criteria assigned by committee members and weighted average

	Member 1	Member 2	Member 3	Weighted Average
Average cost of repair	10	15	10	12
Cost of materials for repair	5	5	5	5
Number of repairs/ month/employee	15	10	10	12
Response time between request for service and provision	14	10	15	13
Percentage of cases in which service was performed improperly	12	15	15	12
Number of customer complaints	10	15	20	15
Percentage of employee absenteeism	5	5	8	6
Time wasted because of tardiness	4	5	4	4
Increase in number of requests for service	10	5	10	8
Increase in number of customers	15	15	10	13
	100	100	100	100

According to the method, the team members would select the criteria having the highest weighted averages. In our example, the team members preferred the following six criteria:

- average cost of repair
- number of repairs per month per employee
- response time between request for service and its provision
- percentage of services improperly performed
- number of customer complaints
- increase in number of customers

By using a group selection process, the team clarifies priorities and increases the probability of generating a set of performance criteria that properly represent the organizational objectives.

Integrated criteria

An *integrated criterion* is one that expresses the achievements of the entire system by integrating within it a number of criteria. Profit, for instance, is considered to be an integrated criterion. Profit is calculated on the basis of other criteria, such as revenue and expenditures, each of which can be divided further into secondary criteria, such as materials cost and labor cost. For a factory competing in the consumer market, profit is a significant indicator of the overall achievement of the organization.

In some cases, the value of an integrated criterion can be *calculated directly*. This is demonstrated by the Quality of Service Survey Form shown below in Exhibit 4.5. Customers of a health insurance company were asked to use this form in order to evaluate the service they received when contacting nurses reviewing their claims.

Creating an integrated criterion that is *represented by a formula* requires a different process. It is necessary to go through the following stages:

a. the determination of each of the specific criterion to be included in the integrated criteria;

b. the assignment of relative weights to each of the specific criteria;

c. the assignment of ratings to various levels of performance within each criterion; and

d. the creation of the formula for calculating the integrated criterion.

Exhibit 4.5
Quality of service survey form

Please circle the appropriate number beside each statement below. In your telephone conversation with the nurse reviewer, do you agree that the reviewer:

	strongly disagree		agree		strongly agree
1. acted politely	1	2	3	4	5
2. acted professionally	1	2	3	4	5
3. was informative	1	2	3	4	5
4. was efficient	1	2	3	4	5
5. was accurate	1	2	3	4	5

Additional comments:____

Thank you for you assistance in maintaining our high quality of service.

The following is an example of how such a formula was developed for the integrated criterion of quality of service for a bank. In the first stage of the process, it was decided to use three criteria:

1. average line length per teller (total customers divided by total tellers),
2. number of complaints per 1,000 customers,
3. number of errors per 10,000 transactions.

In the second stage, each criterion was assigned its relative weight, out of a total possible weight of 1.00. This process is detailed in Exhibit 4.6 below.

The weights given each of the criteria express their relative importance as established by the members of the team. These weights are an expression of the organization's strategy and indicate the significance of each criterion in achieving the goals of the organization. In the example above, the team at the bank determined that the number of errors, with a weight of .5, was the most important criterion in the integrated criterion of quality of service. This was followed by the average length of the line (.3), and the number of complaints (.2). As you can see, the total of the weights of each criterion is 1.0.

Exhibit 4.6
Weights of criteria and values for various levels of performance

Criterion		Average length of line (LN)	Number of complaints (CM)	Number of errors (ER)
Relative weight		0.3	0.2	0.5
	poor (2)	6+	8+	40+
	fair (4)	4-5.9	6-7.9	30-39.9
Value (points)	satisfactory (6)	2-3.9	4-5.9	20-29.9
	good (8)	1-1.9	2-3.9	10-19.9
	excellent (10)	1-	2-	10-

Once this stage is complete, ratings for performance levels can be established. Five levels of performance were chosen for each of the criteria in the example above. In Exhibit 4.6 you can see the levels go from 'poor' with a value of 2 points, to 'excellent' with a value of 10 points.

The decision on the range within each level is based on the actual performance at the time of designing the method and on the team's perceptions of the preferred levels of performance. For instance, an average line of 2.0 to 3.9 customers was considered satisfactory.

Now the team is ready for the final stage and can develop a formula for representing the integrated criterion. Simply take the weight of each specific criterion and multiply it by its performance level. Adding these products together will produce the numerical representation of the given integrated criterion. Using the example of the bank again, the formula for calculating quality of service is:

$$QUAL = (0.3 \times LN) + (0.2 \times CM) + (0.5 \times ER) \qquad (5)$$

where:

QUAL = the integrated criterion for quality of service
LN = length of line, expressed in points
CM = number of complaints, expressed in points
ER = number of errors, expressed in points

For example, during the observations, the following values were measured:

1. average length of line = 2.7 customers;
   according to Exhibit 4.6, LN = 6,

2. number of complaints per 1,000 customers = 3.1;
   according to Exhibit 4.6, CM = 8

3. number of errors per 10,000 transactions = 12;
   according to Exhibit 4.6, ER = 8

Substituting these values into formula 5, we get:

$$QUAL = (0.3 \times 6) + (0.2 \times 8) + (0.5 \times 8) = 7.4$$

Thus, the overall performance of the bank, in terms of quality of service, is slightly lower than 'good'. This is because a score of '8' represents 'good' and '6' represents 'satisfactory', and the performance rating calculated was 7.4.

Considerable effort has been invested recently in developing integrated criteria in order to evaluate *job design and job enrichment*. An analysis of job design examines the methods, tasks, inputs, responsibilities, and atmosphere in which the organization operates. One accepted view, the *socio-technical* approach, maintains that the organization is composed of two subsystems: the human, or social system, and the technological system. Organizational performance is determined on the basis of the performance of each subsystem and the interaction between them.

The technological subsystem is evaluated with the use of such criteria as level of automation, cost of equipment, and reliability of equipment. The social subsystem is evaluated using such criteria as the level of motivation, rate of employee turnover, and absenteeism. The values of these are affected strongly by the employee's perception of the richness of his or her job and the satisfaction derived from it.

'Job richness' can be considered an integrated criterion by which to evaluate an important aspect of organizational performance. As an integrated criterion, it would be comprised of various other criteria. Two commonly accepted methods for determining job richness are: requisite task analysis (RTA) and job diagnostic survey (JDS), (see Turner and Lawrence, 1965; Hackman and Oldman, 1975; and Beatty, 1980). Both of these can be used for the purpose of evaluating the effect of changes in job design on job richness.

As an example, let us review the criteria included in JDS, which are:

1. *Skill variety*: the degree of variety in the skills the employee requires for the effective performance of the job.

2. *Task identity*: the extent to which the employee performs the entire task rather than only limited parts of the task.

3. *Task significance*: the impact of the task on the lives of people.

4. *Autonomy*: the degree of freedom granted the performer of the task.

5. *Job feedback*: the extent of feedback received by the employee directly from the job itself.

6. *Feedback from other parties*: the extent of feedback received by the employee from other people, such as the manager and peers.

7. *Relationships with others*: the degree of interaction with others (employees and customers) required of the employee for the purpose of performing the job.

The evaluation of each of these criteria is conducted subjectively using a seven point rating scale. The integrated criterion is then calculated. (For a more detailed description of the calculation, see Griffin, 1982.)

Integrated criteria are also frequently used in the area of *finance and accounting*. Here, the integrated criteria typically involve the translation of all organizational operations and assets into monetary values. Some of these criteria can be described in terms of a *performance criteria hierarchy*. Initially, the basic operations of the organization are dealt with. Then other operations and assets are added, until an integrated criterion is created which can be used for the evaluation of the organization as a whole. An example of such a hierarchy of criteria is presented in Exhibit 4.7.

Each level of the hierarchy of criteria can be attached to a certain level of the organization. For instance, the production manager is evaluated on the basis of criteria derived from the cost of sales, while the factory manager is evaluated according to operational profit as a percentage of sales. The return on investment is a relevant criterion for the evaluation of the performance of the general director, as he has an impact on all organizational operations as well as on the assets structure of the organization.

In summary, the choice of criteria and the weights assigned to them, is an expression of the objectives and policies of the organization. The process is a dynamic one and, therefore, it is essential to examine the correctness of the criteria system periodically. Determining specific criteria as well as integrated criteria, should be seen as the starting point in expressing the aspirations and standards of the organization. As performance improves and conditions change, performance criteria must change as well.

Exhibit 4.7
Return on assets as an integrated criterion

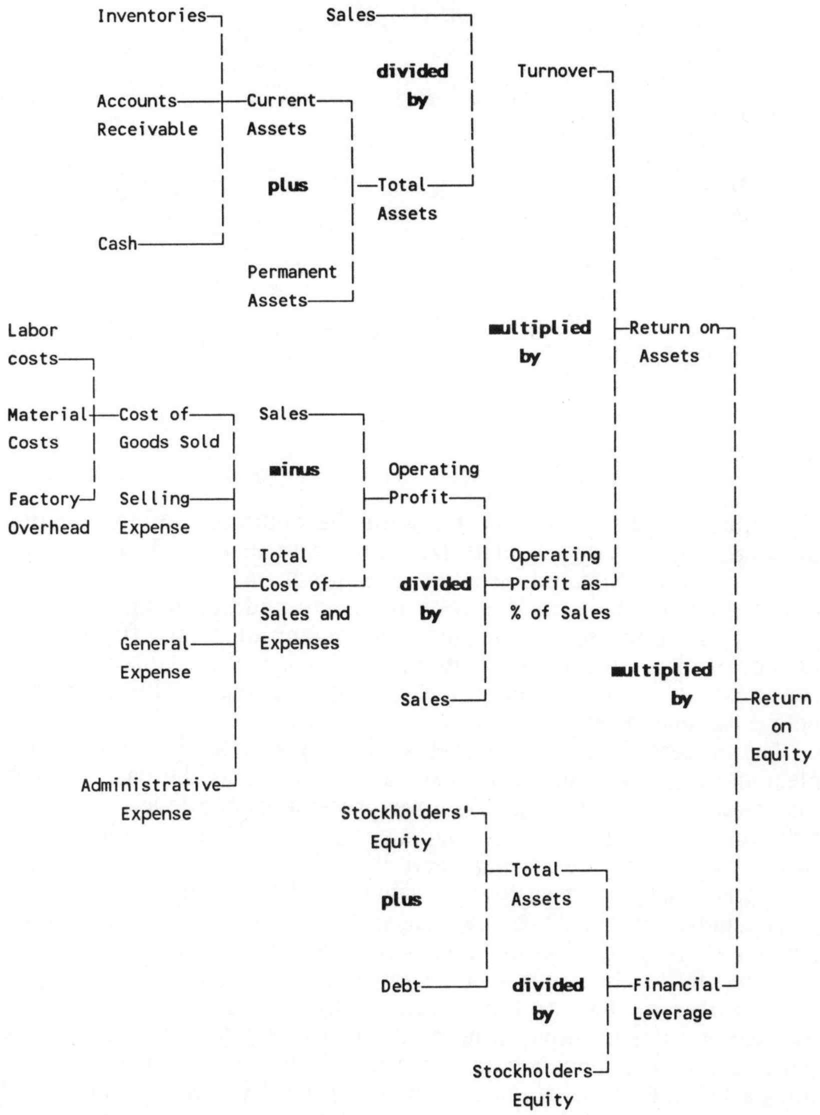

5 Standards of performance

You must certainly be familiar with the common notion that in an organization 'everyone criticizes everyone else'. It is true that individuals are compared, achievements are characterized, and activities are evaluated. This can be done regularly and systematically, or at random. As discussed in Chapter 4, no organization can afford the cost of incidental control and evaluation. It is essential to the well being of the organization and its employees, to institutionalize the comparison between actual events and objectives.

The process of comparing events with expectations is facilitated by a clear definition of the *standards* that will serve as the basis for those expectations. The standard is an expression of the level of expected achievement or behavior. Its attainment is perceived as the obligation of those involved in the relevant activity. Standards serve as a basis of comparison and as a measure for evaluation of achievements.

A standard can relate to any area, and to every level of organizational activity -- from decision making to cost-per-unit, to reporting for work on time. In the absence of clear, known, and accepted standards, serious misunderstandings and problems may emerge in the course of evaluation. For example, a hospital which permitted 12 paid, sick day per year, used attendance as one criterion for evaluating nurses. The nurses felt that good attendance was defined by using fewer than the allotted number of sick days. The managers, however, were giving poor ratings to nurses who used more than six sick days during the year. There were two standards existing at the same time, a formal one (12 days) and an informal one (6 days). The misunderstandings that resulted from having two different standards, were the source of much friction.

Although some ambiguity may occasionally arise regarding the difference between criteria and standards, in principle, criteria define the content for testing organizational achievement, while standards determine the accepted level of occurrences defined as much as possible in quantitative terms. For example, a quality related criterion would be the number of complaints per 1,000 customers per month, where the acceptable level, or standard, would be a specific number, say 15. Nevertheless, many standards, do remain at the level of concepts or values, and require some degree of judgment in the process of comparison. In the following pages: four aspects of standards are examined: setting standards, the use of standards, the qualities of standards, and the classification of standards.

Setting standards

Once an organization has determined the criteria with which it will evaluate its functioning and performance, it must set specific standards in relation to these criteria. There are various methods for setting standards; the choice of method is greatly dependent on the nature of the organization and its outputs. An electronics component assembly line, a shipbuilding company, and a university, would apply different methods for establishing standards. Regardless of which method is used, economic and legal considerations must always be taken into account.

Although economic forces play different roles depending on whether the organization is private or public, they are relevant to both types. The survival of a business enterprise is dependent on its ability to produce a product or service at a cost lower than its selling price. This limits the amount of resources the organization can invest in a product or unit.

The budgeted, non-profit organization, differs in this respect. Nevertheless, if the public organization wishes to perform its tasks, it must make sure that it does not invest too much in one activity, leaving inadequate resources for other essential activities. Although non-profit organizations are obliged to use some additional standards, as a result of their public nature and objectives, there are no substantial differences between these and for-profit organizations (Anthony and Herzlinger, 1980).

Similarly, legal considerations are relevant to all organizations, public as well as private. These relate to such factors as the permissible number of work hours per day, safety issues, human resource policies, negotiated agreements, and certain wage and benefit requirements.

The various methods for setting standards may be divided into four major groups: work measurement, past performance, management by objectives (MBO), and interorganizational comparison. These methods vary widely, and it is essential to determine the suitability of any specific method to the organization's operation, nature, products, and staff. The needs and concerns regarding standards would be different for a commercial firm, a scientific institute, a tax collecting authority, or a sports club.

Work measurement

The objective of work measurement is *to determine the standard time for performing various tasks*. Therefore, techniques of work measurement are used only to evaluate the effectiveness of the use of time by employees. A survey of the degree to which such techniques are applied, revealed that 89 percent of the organizations studied used them frequently (Rice, 1977). It has also been found that successful service organizations are characterized by the intensive use of work measurement (Kearney, 1975). In light of the popularity and usefulness of work measurement for setting standards in various types of organizations, we review the four most common techniques of this method.

Time study involves measuring the length of time actually required to perform a task. The standard time is derived from the actual time, corrected by the work pace as estimated by the time study analyst. Exhibit 5.1 illustrates the results of a time study, based on ten observations of a given task.

Exhibit 5.1
Time study results

Observation number	1	2	3	4	5	6	7	8	9	10
time in minutes	1.70	2.20	1.85	1.95	2.10	2.05	1.75	2.00	1.80	1.90

Average of 10 observations: 1.93 minutes

Since the figures in the exhibit are the observations of just one worker, to make the findings meaningful as a basis of comparison, an assessment of this worker's speed must be made by the time study analyst. It was estimated that this employee worked at a somewhat slow pace of 90 percent, where a normal pace is defined as 100 percent. Hence, the *performance time of the task at a normal work pace* is:

$$1.93 \times (90/100) = 1.737 \text{ minutes}$$

In order to calculate the standard time, *allowances for personal needs and fatigue must be added to the normal time*. For instance, an addition of 10 percent to the normal time is generally accepted for office work activities. The inclusion of this addition in the time calculation results in the following standard time:

$$1.737 \times (1 + 10/100) = 1.91$$

The general formula for calculating standard time then is:

STANDARD TIME = OBSERVED TIME x PACE ADJUSTMENT x (1 + ALLOWANCE)

Predetermined time standards is a technique that entails the use of tables noting the normal time required for the performance of the elements which make up tasks. The normal times for these elements are located on tables and added together to calculate the normal time for the task as a whole. The most well known of these are the MTM, methods time measurement tables, from the MTM Association for Standards and Research. The more tables of predetermined time standards an organization prepares, the greater is its ability to use this approach.

The table in Exhibit 5.2 is an example of the breakdown of the task 'message delivery' into its basic elements, and the calculation of the normal time required to perform that task.

Exhibit 5.2
Task division by basic elements

Element	Normal time (in seconds)
Writing down message	30
Folding message and placing in envelope	8
Writing address	20
Pasting stamp	5
Total	63 seconds

The advantage of this technique lies in its modularity; elements are easily omitted, added or changed. For example, in the case above, if a sealing machine were used instead of pasting stamps, the normal time for this element would be changed from five to two seconds.

Work sampling, as the name implies, uses samples of work activity in order to determine a time standard. The samples are used to estimate the percentage of time spent actually working, and the pace at which the work was performed.

For example: there are 45 employees in a department, all of whom perform the same assignments. A sampling was conducted, spread through the full work day, covering 8 net hours of work. The sample included 40 employees (5 were absent on that day). Thus the number of production hours included was:

$$H = 8x40 = 320$$

The estimation of the net time that the employees were working was based on a multi-observation sampling. The sampling was performed by making random observations of all employees and identifying whether work or non-work activities were being performed. A record was kept of the total number of times each activity was observed, as illustrated in Exhibit 5.3.

Exhibit 5.3
Example of work sampling results

Activity	Number of observations
Working on task	300
Not working	50
Not found at work station	150
Total	500 observations

This data is used to estimate the percentage of time directly devoted to work on the task. In this case, task work was being performed in 300 out of 500 observations. Thus, the work ratio, or percentage, is 60%:

$$P = 300/500 = .6$$

As is the case of time studies mentioned earlier, in the course of observation, the time study analyst must estimate the average work pace of the employees included in the sample. In this case, the pace, or rate, was determined to be:

$$R = 110\%$$

Next, we must establish the number of units produced during the sampling period. In the given example, the total number of units completed, the quantity, was:

$$Q = 270\%$$

Now we can calculate the normal time, NT, per item. The calculation is based on the formula:

$$NT = (P \times H \times R/100)/Q \qquad (1)$$

By substituting the values for our case, we get

$$NT = (0.6 \times 320 \times 110/100)/270 = 0.782 \text{ hours, or}$$

$$0.782 \times 60 = 46.9 \text{ minutes}$$

Again, as in time studies, personal and fatigue allowances should be added to this figure in order to determine the standard time.

The determination of standards using work sampling is quite common, and increases in effectiveness, with the number of employees performing identical assignments.

Statistical time standard, is based on the fact that, the time required to perform a task, is a function of the characteristics of that task. Using *multiple regression analysis*, makes it possible to develop an equation that relates these characteristics (independent variables) to the time required to perform the task (dependent variable). Data for the equation is often generated from information on past performance.

The following is an example of standard time estimation for building a new product based on its preliminary design. For this purpose, information was gathered about previous models of the same product. This data included the time it took to assemble the product, as well as information about relevant variables such as; weight, volume, construction material, required accuracy, and number of tools used.

Using *step wise multiple regression analysis*, independent variables are introduced to the equation one at a time, and those with the greatest impact on the dependent variable, are chosen. In the first stage, the equation includes only the most influential variable on work time, then the second most influential variable is added, and so on, for all the variables. After the addition of each variable, the degree of improvement in the predictive ability of the equation is statistically evaluated. The process of adding variables to the equation ends when the addition of variables no longer improves its predictive ability. An example of a result of such analysis is shown in the following equation:

$$T = (5.7 \times X_1) + (0.3 \times X_2) + (23 \times X_3) + (0.09 \times X_4) \qquad (2)$$

where

T = standard time for building a particular model,
X_1 = number of different parts in the model,
X_2 = volume in cubic inches,
X_3 = number of drawings,
X_4 = required accuracy.

Knowing the values of the independent variables, makes it possible to estimate expected performance time and to adopt it as a standard.

Past performance

In setting standards according to past performance, the following parameters may be used: average past performance, median performance, and the general trend. To illustrate this method of setting standards, we present an example dealing with the percentage of errors made by each of 20 employees in the claims department of an insurance company. The breakdown of the percentage of errors made in one month by the department staff is described in Exhibit 5.4.

This breakdown leads to a number of conclusions:

* 50% of employees (the median) had an error rate of 6% or less, and 50% had a rate of 7% or more.
* The average percentage of errors was 7.
* 25% of the employees had an error rate of 3% or less.

In order to use past performance in setting future standards, any of the values noted above can be adopted. For example, if the median is taken as a standard, then an error rate of 6 percent is defined as a satisfactory level; any employee with an error rate greater than 6%, works below the satisfactory level and is expected to improve.

By adopting the median as a standard, employees with performance below the median are motivated to improve. At the same time, it can be reasonably assumed that it does not lead employees with better than median performance, to lower their performance level. This can be expected to lead to a dynamic process of improvement, and achievement in the following period will be better than those of the past period.

The analysis of past trends may also be used in setting future standards. When this approach is employed, the expected changes are calculated, as in the example below. We will use sales data from the branch of a large supermarket chain as shown in Exhibit 5.5.

On the basis of the existing trend, it can be expected that sales in 1990 will be close to $2.4 million. Analysis of past data indicates that growth was due mainly to two factors: increase in local population, and an aggressive marketing policy. Unfortunately for this store, a competitor recently opened a supermarket in the same area; an event that will have a significant effect on sales. The management of the supermarket chain must evaluate the potential negative impact of the competitor.

Past experience shows that a similar store belonging to the chain lost 20 percent of its sales in such a situation. Based on this data, the expected sales for 1993 can be estimated to be:

$$2.4 - (.20 \times 2.4) = 1.92 \text{ million}$$

The standard can now be set based on the data presented in Exhibit 5.5 and adjusted according to expected future constraints.

```
FREQUENCY

                    X       X
        X           X       X                                      PERCENTAGE
        X           X       X       X                                      OF
X   X   X   X       X   X   X       X       X       X           X       X  ERRORS
_________________________________________________________________________________
0   1   2   3   4   5   6   7   8   9   10  11  12  13  14  15  16  17  18  19  20
```

Exhibit 5.4 Percentage of errors made by claims department

Exhibit 5.5
Annual sales volume

ANNUAL SALES
IN DOLLARS

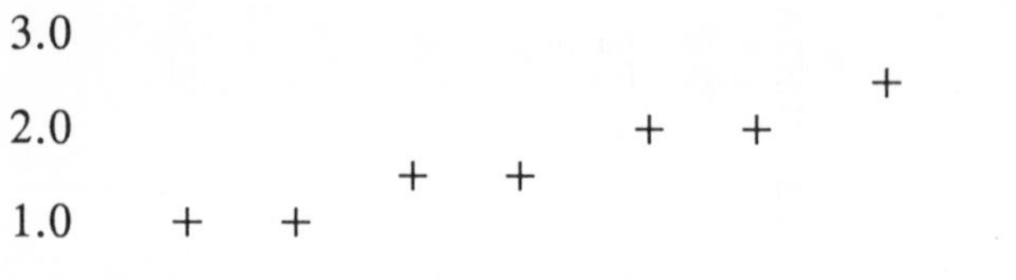

YEAR 1985 1986 1987 1988 1989 1990 1991 1992

Management by objectives (MBO)

Objectives are often based on considerations of present needs and the availability of resources. According to the MBO approach, objectives are determined on the basis of analysis and group discussion. This management method is also used in setting standards, and is based on interaction between management and employees. (For a detailed description, see: Carroll, S.J. and Tosi, H.L., 1973; French, W.L. and Hollman, R.W., 1975; Lee, S.M., 1981.)

The basic assumption of MBO, which is derived primarily from the behavioral sciences, is that people are highly motivated to achieve goals that they have been involved in determining. The emphasis then, is on the process of setting objectives by means of a dialogue between managers and subordinates, leading to an agreement on performance levels.

Let us return to the supermarket example. Using the MBO approach, the regional manager and the store manager came to the conclusion that the location of their store was much more advantageous than that of the competitor. They concluded that, if the store manager conducted advertising and promotional campaigns, the expected drop in sales would be only around 10 percent, and the gain would more than cover the marketing expenses.

Thus, you can see that, the MBO approach is not only a management style, but also a pragmatic method for dealing with necessary relations between supervisors and employees. The MBO technique can be applied in a variety of situations and is a form of management that involves employees at all organizational levels in the standard setting process.

Comparison of performance

A standard can be based on a comparison of performance in organizations that are of similar character. These can include organizations with identical products or processes, that use the same technology, or are situated in similar environments. For instance, this would apply to a comparison of the performance of branches of a bank located in a specific country. On the other hand, comparison of a branch in England and a branch in the United States would be of questionable validity, since there are substantial differences between the two countries in this area.

Using the comparison approach, an organization can develop standards by using one of two methods or a combination of both:

a. performance of other organizations; and/or,

b. past performance of the organization itself, or performance of similar units within the organization.

A typical example of a standard based on the performance of other organizations in the same industry is that of sales per employee. Average annual sales per employee in the electronics industry is $140,000. Therefore, an organization with individual employee sales exceeding this figure can consider its achievements as above average.

The use of comparisons within an organization, is relatively simple in a situation where there are similar branches, such as in a bank, a supermarket, or a retail outlet. For example, this method is frequently used to determine standards for staffing bank branches. The required size of the staff is a function of the types and quantity of transactions processed by the branch. Using data from all bank branches, a comparative equation can be developed for the relationship between the number of transactions and the personnel required. Exhibit 5.6 shows the number of transactions processed in one month by a given number of employees in various branches.

Exhibit 5.6
Transactions processed and staff size in ten bank branches

Transaction	T_1	T_2	T_3	T_4	T_5	Employee Months
Branch						
A	49.8	4.1	63.1	6.2	14.6	36
B	53.3	12.6	22.6	4.2	8.6	34
C	19.6	7.6	12.6	4.0	7.9	27
D	22.0	7.7	4.2	3.5	6.7	25
E	23.2	4.6	15.8	2.3	4.7	22
F	15.3	3.6	18.5	2.9	5.3	16
G	13.2	1.0	3.6	0.8	2.8	14
H	12.3	0.9	15.0	1.2	3.7	13
I	9.4	1.1	48.7	1.0	2.4	12
J	5.9	0.7	0.4	2.2	4.4	10

Stepwise multiple regression can be employed in order to develop an equation for the correlation between the number of each type of transaction and the required number of staff. As illustrated in the previous example (equation (2)), this method of regression analysis, includes independent variables, (here, T_1 to T_5), according to their impact on staff size. The analysis in this case yields the equation:

$$STf = 6.72 + (0.34 \text{ x } T_1) + (2.33 \text{ x } T_4) \qquad (3)$$

where the correlation is $r^2 = 0.927$. The value of r^2, the coefficient of determination, denotes the strength of the correlation between the independent variables, that is T_1 and T_4, and the dependent variable, that is, required staff. The maximum value of r^2 is ± 1.00, and values of ± 0.8 or greater, are considered high. The high value of r^2 in our example, indicates that the two types of transactions included in the comparison, (of the five presented in the exhibit), have a significant impact on the requirements for staff.

Using this equation, it is possible to calculate a staffing standard for every branch, and to compare that with the existing staffing. For example, in order to calculate the standard staff for branch A, we substitute the values from Exhibit 5.6 in the equation:

$$STf = 6.72 + (0.34 \text{ x } 49.8) + (2.33 \text{ x } 6.2) = 38.1$$

In other words, according to this equation, branch A requires 38.1 employee months. Because Branch A used only 36 employee months for the number of transactions processed, we can conclude that the branch is operating above 100% efficiency. In this case, its efficiency is (38.1/36) x 100, or 105.8%.

Use of standards

The importance of standards for the organization may be illustrated by examining five groups of essential uses.

Operational expression of policy and planning

Standards represent the translation of concepts, general objectives and goals into concrete terms of desired events and operative specifications. These specifications are binding for most definitions of input, throughput and output. They relate to material or equipment, work methods and output, management and employee behavior, work priorities or general administration. Standards are the basis for any planning process, and its translation into operational terms.

Mutual understanding between managers and subordinates

A major cause for misunderstanding is differences in expectations among various parties. The standard, as determined and recognized by all involved, serves to ensure that managers and employees know what is expected of them and what will be considered 'normal' and 'acceptable' in terms of achievements and behavior. Standards are essential to the entire system in order to facilitate effective communication in the organization. The fact that recognition of standards by managers and employees reduces misunderstandings and conflicts, has been widely treated in the relevant literature (e.g. Alewine, 1982).

The process of control and evaluation

Without standards it would be impossible to maintain a control process. There are situations in which standards are not formally and unequivocally defined, but mutual expectations are recognized and known to all those involved. In practice, control is organized and carried out on the basis of standards, whether formal or informal, explicitly written or implicit, legal or functional, specific or general. The emphasis is on the current standard, which is expected to be realistic and acceptable for all the parties that are meant to comply with it.

Incentives and rewards

It would be impossible to determine a method for encouragement of achievements without a definition of achievement criteria, and particularly, of the 'normal' level, beyond which the employee is eligible for special rewards. The standard serves as the starting point for any form of reward in an achievement-oriented system. The most well known and popular methods are wage incentives; because of their importance to control systems, they treated separately in Chapter 14.

Growth and development

Because standards express the reasonable level of expectations in an organization, it may be assumed, that in an achievement-oriented society, individuals and organizations will strive for higher standards. For example, if a certain position is defined as requiring an MBA, it can be assumed that those interested in it will consciously direct themselves toward completing graduate studies. A manufacturer interested in supplying products to customers that demand high quality, or to countries with strict quality control, will have to invest a great deal in raising its standards. This principle, however, also works in the opposite direction: low requirements by customers and a non-competitive market, tend to lower standards. This is a dynamic view of standards, as discussed in detail on various occasions in this book. In principle, the dynamics of standards should be considered as an integral part of strategic management (Tabatoni and Jarniou, 1976).

Qualities of standards

An organization that operates on the basis of binding standards, needs rules to establish them. Yet the use of standards is accompanied by the danger of rigidity and the drive to apply a standard even when it has become outmoded and obsolete. In such a case, the standard may become an oppressive, detrimental factor.

An example of this situation occurred in the patient registration department of a large hospital. Employees were required to record demographic, insurance, and other pertinent data for every patient admitted to the hospital each day. This was done by hand, and each employee was expected to complete the process within 12 minutes. Unfortunately, under this manual system, it was possible to omit vital information, causing delays in other areas.

When the hospital introduced a computerized medical records process, there was a tremendous improvement in the quality of the admissions record, because the computer did not allow certain information to be left out of the record. This saved significant amounts of time for other departments, such as billing and insurance, but added to the time it took to register a patient. This change in work method was not reflected in a change in the standard time for processing patient admissions. As a result, management thought that the work pace was deteriorating.

Setting standards is an ongoing process, requiring constant monitoring. The following section highlights eight essential characteristics of standards and their maintenance.

Knowledge of standards

Those expected to function according to the standards, must know and be informed about their existence. They must understand the meaning of each standard and be clear about the performance that is expected. Failure to do so would be like having a society governed by binding laws, about which the citizens knew nothing.

Fairness

In designing a standard, the interests of all parties involved -- even contradicting interests -- must be seen as legitimate and worthy of consideration. It is essential, therefore, that in the stage of its creation, the standard be examined from various angles; from different vantage points and interests. In particular, a standard intended for long term functioning must not ignore the needs and interests of those expected to live according to it. The use of a standard as a management tool is doomed to be short-lived if it does not consider the viewpoints and needs of various interested parties.

For example, consider the process of setting standards in the areas of nutrition and medicine. In the course of the process many varied and opposing groups are involved, such as: manufacturers; consumers;

marketing agents; health-related organizations; agricultural institutions; commercial and industrial authorities. All must become legitimate partners in the process of setting standards, even though this often lengthens and complicates the process.

Agreement of involved parties

It is preferable to have a standard that is 'less good', but acceptable to all partners, than a 'better' standard that is forced and requires frequent sanctions in order to be maintained. This entails not only consideration of the legitimate interests of the parties involved, but it requires the attainment of as high a level of agreement as possible. The use of a vague values such as 'organizational interest' as a justification for coercion, is likely to impede the achievement of this goal since it is one sided. It is not sufficient that management or the systems analyst determine work loads. Employees should feel that the standards are fair, realistically attainable, and that working according to them will be rewarded.

Benefits from working according to standards

The factors taken into account in setting standards should include an understanding of the benefits of functioning according to them. The combination of incentives and appropriate rewards for meeting standards is a significant factor in designing standards, as well as in the evaluation process. Concepts such as 'positive and negative reinforcement' have become meaningful, both in terms of management style and the evaluation process. It is appropriate to consider the standard as a realistic and achievable level of functioning, which is possible to achieve on an ongoing basis. It should be worthwhile to the individual, and the organization, to function according to standards, and to improve performance and achievement.

Ongoing performance

It is essential to set standards at an achievable level. Levels that are set too high, may be achieved some of the time but cannot be maintained. Assume for example, that with maximum effort and on one occasion only, an employee is able to produce an output of 160 units per work hour. On a continuous basis however, with reasonable effort, for which he receives incentive pay, he is able to produce an average of 125 units per hour. The production standard in this case should not be 160 units, but closer to 100.

Reliability of standards

Methods for establishing standards must be reliable, that is, identical methods must produce identical results, given the same data. This is essential for the proper functioning of any control system. For example, two experts, using the same instrument, measure the level of carbon monoxide emissions in testing for quality in an auto plant. If a discrepancy of 20% exists in their results, it arouses suspicion regarding both the measurement technique and the standard. Lack of trust in standards, in methods of setting them, and measurement procedures, represent a source of multiple behavioral problems. This issue is given special attention in Chapter 6.

Coverage

Not all the activities of an organization will be covered by standards. Standards are typically developed for those activities that occur frequently and are repetitive, or are ongoing. However, there are times when technical difficulties and restrictions, prevent setting standards for a specific area. In a situation when many of an organization's activities are not covered by standards, it is essential that the control system develop methods to promote intensive communication and dialogue among participants in order to coordinate the normative approach (see Chapter 7).

Monitoring and revision

Monitoring and revision is required for both the maintenance and control of standards. Standards become outdated because of advances in knowledge and skills, improved technology, and new work methods. The test of a standard is whether it suits a number of variables which are in the process of frequent change. Thus, standards require constant maintenance, including complete change. The more complex and dynamic the organization, the greater the tendency of its standards to become outdated. You must be cautious however, as too frequent revision of standards can lead to confusion among the people involved. Standards must be monitored and revised only when the difference justifies it.

Classification of standards

Standards may be classified in various groups. However, because standards serve a number of purposes in an organization, there is often overlap in the classification, with some standards properly falling into several groups. We suggest five models of classification of standards based on the following criteria: degree of formality; level of conceptualization; level of quantification; the function hierarchy of standards; and the dynamic approach to standards.

Model 1: Degree of formality

The degree of formality of a standard is determined by the extent to which the standard has been established and publicized by an authorized body in the organization. Standards can be set in a formal manner, or informally developed over the course of the life of the organization.

There is a strong correlation between the degree of formality in setting standards, and both management style and style of interpersonal relations (Todd, 1977). A management style that favors extensive involvement and participation by employees will more favorably view the development of informal standards. A more authoritarian style relies on the formal approach to setting standards.

There are certain generalizations which can be made regarding formal and informal standards:

a. *The absence of a formal standard* invites the development of an informal one, in order to fill the 'vacuum' created by having no standards at all.

b. *Defects in an existing standard* lead to gradual abandonment of that standard, and its replacement by an informal one, as long as the defective one still exists.

c. *Power conflicts* in the organization tend to give rise to new standards, which deviate and often even contradict the formal ones.

Control systems have generally related only to the formal standards in an organization, and have failed to adequately study the essence and creation of informal ones. Perhaps this reflects the belief that informality is inferior, or detrimental, to an organization. Yet the more dynamic and sophisticated the organization, the less likely it will be to have its functioning fully covered by standards. Those areas not covered, will be so extensive, that the organization's survival would be endangered if informal standards were to not develop in the course of its activity.

The key to the control strategy required in dealing with informal standards, begins with the recognition that they exist in the organization. An understanding of the factors leading to their generation is required. To the extent that the informal standards conform to the needs of the organization, and do not contradict its interest, a de facto adoption of these standards is indicated.

Model 2: Level of conceptualization of standards

This model is based on a hierarchical grading of standards in terms of four conceptual levels. This classification fits most organizations, from a small organization to one as large as a government. The emphasis is on the levels of concepts and generalization of the standard, and go from the abstract to the particular. The four levels in this model are: demonstrative, strategic, tactical and operational standards.

Demonstrative standards express organizational aspirations and are determined by the highest level of the organization (e.g. the board of directors). Their purpose is to let the people know what the organization is striving for and what can be expected of it in the future. These standards are usually proclamatory in nature, and are particularly common in statements of long range goals. They most often characterize large enterprises and public institutions, such as the executive board of a large concern, or the legislature of a country. Due to their proclamatory and non-operational nature, such standards are sometimes treated as policy declaration. An example of a demonstrative standard is: "To become the market leader in diet soft drinks."

Strategic standards are derived from the demonstrative standards (if those exist). They usually express long term plans and do not deal with specific implementation programs. In this respect, strategic standards are complementary to planning: planning may indicate the direction, while the standard indicates its force. Both translate the intentions and policies of the organizational leaders into long term programs. Development programs and multi-annual budgets may be included as strategic standards. Management control should be aware that, because there is a high level of uncertainty associated with strategic standards, substantial deviation from the goal should be tolerated. As example of a strategic standard is: "To win contracts with Burger King and Macdonald's."

Tactical standards cover shorter term programs and objectives, as derived from the strategic standards. The life span of tactical standards is relatively short, and therefore, they are revised more frequently than are strategic standards. These serve as the basis for operational, or performance standards. An example of a tactical standard is: "To offer introductory price promotions and service contracts to fast food chains."

Operational standards are the practical expression of the concepts set by top level management. They are intended to live in conformity with the demonstrative standards and are a direct materialization of the tactical standards. An example of an operational standard is: "Regional sales force A will reach $4,000,000 in new fast food contracts in the first quarter."

Demonstrative and strategic standards are meant to state policy and directions, while tactical and operational standards determine the specific programs and specifications for performance. The control system must examine the extent to which these standards are consistent. An organization functioning according to tactical and operational standards, without a proper set of strategic standards, resembles a ship sailing in the open seas without a compass.

Another aspect of this classification is the relatively high degree of flexibility required in the process of designing tactical and operational standards. This is in contrast to the more stable nature of demonstrative and strategic standards. Tactical and operational standards should follow the higher level standards and not be objectives by themselves; they are not intended to replace the strategic standards of the organization.

Model 3: Objective and subjective standards

Standards may be classified according to the degree of quantification, with the two dichotomous groups: (a) objective standards, and (b) subjective standards.

An objective standard is characterized by its unequivocal determination. Objective standards are usually formal and operative. Examples are: work hours are from 8-4; an item with 5-10 defects is class C; a basketball player must be over 6 feet tall; the minimum punishment for theft is one month imprisonment; the standard output for one labor hour is 24 units. Objective standards are an obvious necessity in the daily life of every organization.

Subjective standards are also essential, and may serve as the source of objective ones. However, in contrast to objective standards, subjective ones are generally value-related and less operative. The existence of objective standards is more stable and ongoing than that of subjective ones since they are more simple to evaluate.

For example, a computer service company wishes to set as a subjective standard, to respond to requests for service in a prompt manner. To quantify this standard the company must specify variables, such as customer satisfaction, on which to base the evaluation.

Other examples of subjective standards that require quantification are: 'for normal working hours, employees will receive normal pay' (both, work hours and pay must be quantified); or 'the plant will supply only products of high quality' (how will high quality be defined?) It is doubtful whether there are any objective standards that do not have subjective ones as their foundation, and the control system must periodically examine the origins of the latter standards.

Model 4: Hierarchy of standards

This model combines the three previous models and adds to them certain environmental factors that have an impact on organizational behavior. We consider the organization as an open system, and its employees, as members of a number of social subsystems. As such, they are meant to operate according to a variety of standards, some of which are determined outside of their work place, while others are specific to the organization. Furthermore, some of the inner organizational standards are based on *conventions* set outside of the organization.

While tactical and operational standards are set on the basis of organizational policy, both must be in line with *legal requirements* developed outside the organization. Operational standards that result from organizational needs must not conflict with legal standards, and at the same time, must consider conventional standards. The maintenance of legal standards in setting organizational standards is mandatory. The consideration of conventional standards may prevent pragmatic decisions on standards which would be impossible to maintain, and thereby fail to achieve the desired results.

According to this model, standards are classified into four groups, closely related to one another. The first two are primarily determined outside the organization, while the other two are based on the considerations and needs of the organization itself: (1-2) legal and conventional standards, and (3-4) value-related and operational standards.

Legal standards originate with the legislature, or, in formal agreements between two or more parties (such as nationwide industrial agreements). They are binding for the organization and restrict its freedom in setting its own internal standards. In general, organizations have little influence on legal standards, however, the more powerful the organization, the greater the impact it can have. Such attempts are permissible, if they comply with the law and the social code of ethics. Lobbying groups, and interest organizations such as agriculturists, industrialists, unions, landowners, senior citizens, and minorities, serve to pressure the designers of legal standards.

Conventional standards are created by force of habit and custom. They generally develop outside of the organization, and usually dictate the personal and group behavior of members of the organization. Even though these standards have no legal validity, they are very powerful and organizational standards should consider them. Thorough familiarity with these standards is particularly essential in a pluralistic society, whether they be ethnic, cultural, or religious. Conventional standards, which are culturally based, may be different from one region to another. For example, it may be typical to use flexible time in a certain region, where it may be treated as a conventional standard.

It is likely that implementation of both legal and operational standards will be difficult if they severely contradict conventional standards. For this reason, the control system must always investigate whether the failure of a standard is the result of a lack of conformity with conventional standards.

Value-related standards belong to the group of conceptual standards of the organization and usually include expressions of policy. Even if not formally stated, they represent the values and inclinations of the founders and leaders of the organization. There is a strong resemblance between value-related standards and the demonstrative and strategic standards mentioned in the previous classifications. While these standard are not always expressed in writing, their recognition is extremely important. This is true since organizations are not always completely covered by operational standards, yet employees are still required to function 'in the spirit of management's intentions'. Thus, value-related standards have a significant impact on the nature of operational standards.

Operational standards are derived from organizational policy and serve the routine for daily functioning of the organization, both in production and service. They should not contradict external standards, and they must conform to the behavior and customs of the people who are to comply with them.

The central features of these standards are:

a. employees must have a knowledge of the standards according to which they are expected to function;

b. there must be adequate belief in the fairness of the standards and in the organization's ability to function according to them on an ongoing bases;

c. there must be rewards for achievement according to and above the standard;

d. standards must be set using reliable tools which yield identical results in repeated measurements; and,

e. there must be reliable, ongoing maintenance and revision of standards in order to prevent obsolescence.

Model 5: Dynamic standards

Every organization is capable of improving its performance. Improvement in organizational performance is derived from such elements as improving employee's abilities, introduction of changes in technology and work processes, or logistical changes in areas such as material flow and purchasing. Analysis of past performance of organizations, using learning curves, reveals that the process of improvement is sustained as long as there is motivation to improve performance. Assuming that once the degree of expected improvement is determined, management and employees will find ways to realize these improvements.

Some organizations, such as Texas Instruments, use this approach for the purpose of continuously updating their standards. For example, if direct labor cost for the production of a certain calculator was $2.40 per unit last quarter it will be revised to a lower cost next quarter say, $2.20 per unit. The ability to introduce improvements is not infinite; its pace declines. This is illustrated in Exhibit 5.7, which provides an example of a learning curve.

As shown by the exhibit, the rate of improvement decreases as the number of repetitions of the task increases. This signifies that the potential for improvement decreases over time. Use of the learning curve enables an organization to determine improvement standards. This is possible, of course, only after an estimation of the parameters of the graph. Typical learning curve models are described by Yelle.

Exhibit 5.7
The relationship between the number of repetitions and performance of the learning curve

Unit Number	Labor Hours For Unit	Cumulative Labor Hours	Average Labor Hours
1	100	100	100.0
2	75	175	87.5
4	56	295	73.7
8	42	480	60.0
16	32	764	47.7
32	24	1192	37.3

The use of the dynamic approach for setting standards requires the creation of a suitable atmosphere in the organization. This is one in which where there is a drive for continuous improvement along with the recognition that improvement can be attained without extraordinary struggle. For instance, a senior employee is expected to perform her task in standard time or less, that is to work at 100% efficiency or better. In contrast, it is clear that the expected performance of a new employee is lower, say 50% efficiency, but it too will be adjusted over the course of time. It is possible to deal in a similar manner with performance at the division level, where the expectations are that managers initiate appropriate changes in order to achieve desired improvements.

The dynamic approach to standards is thus, both a management philosophy and a technological conviction that 'standards are a basis for change'. For this concept to become a reality, the organization must have the ability to visualize potential rather than present performance. It is a permanent process that strives towards improvement rather than being satisfied with current results.

6 Measuring performance

Imagine you are the manager of a firm which manufactures components for electronic equipment. It is your goal to improve the quality of your product, so you establish measurable quality assurance standards for the coming quarter. These include; decreasing the number of reworks to 3%, improving product conformity to no greater than ±1% of standard, and decreasing the rejection of faulty raw materials from vendors to 0.5%.

This looks like a good plan on the surface. Clearly the criteria you have chosen are important to improving the overall quality of your product. However, your plan is flawed because it does not adequately represent the content of what you intend to measure. It is possible to imagine products which pass inspection as they leave your plant, but breakdown shortly after being placed in radios manufactured by your customers. Your customer return rate is too high, and you have not included that in your measure of quality.

Any control system not only requires a solid set of performance criteria and standards, but proper measurement methods as well. Performance measurement is an integral part of proper management and control, and the starting point for any evaluation process. "Measurement is the assignment of numerals to objects or events according to rules" (Stevens, 1951). Key to this definition is the notion of rules. It is essential that employees, raters, and management understand these rules, and know how individual and organizational performance is being measured. This chapter will cover measurement scales and their use, the validity, reliability and sensitivity of measurement techniques, sampling, and control of measurement errors. But first, data collection must be considered, since this is obviously the basis of any measurement process.

Data collection

No decisions can be more accurate or reliable than the data which is used to make those decisions. Yet a major problem we face, is that data collection is often not considered to be productive work. It is frequently viewed as 'extra', not part of the necessary activity of the firm. Consequently, the task of data collection is often the first to go when busy managers are looking for ways to save time or money. This is true even though the lost information may have pointed the way to more effective operations.

Because of this, whenever possible, data collection should be an integral part of the regular activity of operations, rather than a task which is performed separately. Implementing this approach not only guarantees that the cost of data collection will be less, but also ensures that data will be collected consistently.

The use of computers facilitates this task. For example, monitoring inventory level is crucial to the proper operation of organizations. In many settings however, it is no longer necessary to actually count remaining inventory. Utilizing the bar code system as part of the checkout routine in department stores and supermarkets, cashiers enter the code number of an item, and data is processed by computer providing the basis for programmed reports on inventory level, demand rate, and so forth. Obviously, individual performance data can also be captured in this type of environment. For example, by assigning each individual an identification code which is keyed into the register, the system can process data for performance criteria such as percentage of errors and production rate per employee.

In many cases though, management must rely on a manual system for data collection. We must remember that a manual system is more sensitive to interruptions and is bound to deteriorate unless there is a very strong motivation to keep it active. For example, service organizations, such as banks and insurance companies, employ internal auditors to monitor daily work. These monitors look for errors, identify consistent sources of deviations, or measure work quality. In these circumstances however, there is a strong tendency to see the auditor's role as expendable. When short-staffing occurs, the auditor is usually moved to replace an absent employee, and data collection is placed on the back burner.

Measurement scales and uses

There are four common measurement scales: nominal, ordinal, interval and ratio, and each has a different set of rules. The following is a description of the nature of each scale, with examples taken from various organizational environments.

Nominal scale

This scale classifies objects or events into specific categories; nothing is stated concerning the relative value of one category as compared to another. For example, a nominal scale would be used when classifying organizations according to their nature, such as 1 for service and 2 for manufacturing, or for classifying employees according to sex, such as 1 for male and 2 for female. These figures cannot be used for calculations since the numbers themselves are meaningless; the class afforded the number '2' is not higher in value than that represented by '1'. The coding is used merely as an aid for grouping and identification.

The ordinal scale

With an ordinal scale, the numbers have meaning and rank objects in order of the extent to which they possess a particular attribute. For example, employees may be ranked according to a criterion such as quality of work by utilizing the following scale:

1 - very poor quality
2 - poor quality
3 - acceptable quality
4 - good quality
5 - very good quality

While an ordinal scale indicates the order of the objects being measured, it cannot be used to measure how much better one is than the other. For example, even though Joe's quality is ranked as 2 and Ruth's is ranked as 4, it would be incorrect to say that Ruth's quality is twice as good as Joe's. However, one may say correctly that Ruth's quality of work is better than Joe's.

The interval scale

This measurement utilizes equal distances on a scale to represent equal distances in the attribute being measured. Using this measure, values *can* be mathematically manipulated. For example, if the performance criterion is dollar-profit, and A has an annual profit of $500,000 and B has only $400,000 profit, then the difference between the two can be determined. The resulting figure does have meaning, A's profit is $100,000 more than B's.

The ratio scale

This measurement also uses an equal distance scale. The minimum value on a ratio scale is zero. For example, percentage of defects, cost per item, machine utilization, or response time, cannot be a negative value. Although some of the ratio criteria are obtained by the division of two variables, this does not alter the nature of the scale. For example, machine utilization can be defined as the ratio of the actual time the machine was in use to the available machine time, and has a minimum of zero. If machine A is utilized 30% and machine B is utilized 60%, then machine B is utilized twice as much as machine A.

Use of the scales

Some people say that the nominal scale is not a measurement scale at all since it does not compare the intensities of a measured criterion. It is nevertheless included for two reasons: first, to cover all possible scales reviewed in the relevant literature and currently used in practice. Second, draw your attention to the fact that numerical values assigned to categories do not necessarily indicate the superiority of one category to another and cannot be used for purposes of comparison.

It is also important to re-emphasize that the ordinal scale is subjectively defined and the values on the scale are not mathematically meaningful values. As a result, addition and subtraction cannot be performed on the ordinal scale in order to determine the difference between compared measurements. This is not the case with the interval and ratio scales. With these, equal measurement intervals are used. For this reason, in many situations, it is preferable to use the interval or the ratio scales. There are, however, some cases in which it is necessary to use several different types of scales, and where use of the ordinal scale is appropriate. The following example illustrates such a case.

Look at the data in Exhibit 6.1. This data summarizes the performance auditing in several branches of an insurance company. This was an integral part of the semi-annual control procedure used by the company. As part of its activities, each branch dealt with hundreds of customer inquiries daily. Since the branches were distributed all around the country and were managed quite independently by their local managers, each developed its own approach to responding to customer inquiries. Six alternative approaches were identified by the control manager at the corporate headquarters, and she wanted to analyze and compare them. Four performance criteria were used for the comparison: cost, visual attractiveness, response time, and percent of inquiries handled.

The analysis of the alternatives employed both ratio and ordinal scales. Ratio scales were used for cost per response, reaction time, and percent handled. The ordinal scale was used to rate attractiveness, using a five-point scale:

1 - very unattractive
2 - unattractive
3 - indifferent
4 - attractive
5 - very attractive

Exhibit 6.1
Comparison of alternative methods to respond to customer inquiries

Alternative	Reponse Cost $	Attractiveness of Response	Response time days	Percent Handled*
Use of standard forms filled out by hand	0.96	3	1.0	70
Typing of standard texts	1.88	5	3.5	90
Response on letter received	1.94	1	1.0	80
Use of computer generated letter	2.26	3	2.5	90
Hand-written response	2.26	2	1.0	100
Tape recorded response	4.42	5	5.5	100

*Estimated percentage of inquiries that could be answered using the given alternative without undue effort. For example, approximately 90% of the responses could be answered by using computer generated letters.

This example is typical of a situation in which management would use a combination of scales to appropriately evaluate alternatives and improve decision making. Once the data was available so that comparisons could be made, the next stage was to choose the preferred alternative. Each of the four criteria (cost, attractiveness, response time, and percent handled) had a different unit of measurement. It was impossible to simply add them in order to find the best option. How then can me make decisions using these ratings?

Much has been written about multi-criteria decision making providing us with quite a few approaches to use in making the decisions. A common denominator to all is the need to present the results in a table similar to Exhibit 6.1, using the relative importance of each as perceived be the decision maker.

Validity, reliability, and sensitivity

The usefulness and accuracy of a measure depends on three characteristics: validity, reliability, and sensitivity. They must all be considered when designing a control system for an organization, or when auditing an existing one. A control system is not acceptable if the performance criteria used are not valid, reliable, and sensitive.

Validity

A valid measure is one which actually measures what it is supposed to. For example, imagine that you have been asked to calculate the cost of employee turnover in your company. You decide to get this figure by adding the cost of recruitment, screening and interviewing candidates, and training new employees. Have you measured what you wanted to? What about a new employee's affect on other workers' efficiency, what is its cost? What about the cost of decreased morale among your staff when co-workers leave? Why include training costs, don't some of these cost go toward employee retention? Don't employees stay longer and do well in jobs for which they have been well trained? Is your calculation a valid measure of the cost of employee turnover?

There are three major types of validation: criterion-related, content-oriented, and construct-oriented (Cronbach and Meehl, 1981).

Criterion-related validity identifies a criterion which can be used to *predict* success in a given area. That is, an independent variable is used as a predictor of the results of a dependent variable. For example, an employer who wants to predict the potential performance of a candidate uses an aptitude test as part of the screening process. It is not only good business sense, but it is also the law, that if the test results are used as a basis for employment decisions, the test must prove to have predictive power. That is, those who score well on the test, should be the same individuals who will do well on the job.

Criterion-related validity can be proved using statistical techniques, such as correlation analysis. The independent variable (the test score), must correlate directly (doing well on one is associated with doing well on the other), with the dependent variable (job performance). This correlation is depicted graphically in Exhibit 6.2. If the correlation is sufficiently strong, the criterion (the test score) can be considered a valid measure for the prediction of potential performance.

Criterion-related validity has been the basis for SATs, GMATs, and other standardized tests. You may be aware that these exams have been strongly criticized for racial and class bias. In fact, racial minorities and students from low income families do less well, on average, than members of the white middle class, even though they do not on average possess lower intelligence. These standardized tests, however, are valid predictors of academic success. What this implies, is that racial and class bias is functioning in universities and affect success rates, but not that the tests are invalid as predictors of academic success in those environments.

Content validity is established by verifying that the content of what is measured is relevant to the subject being measured, and that the criteria used adequately represent the content of the job or subject. Very often, individual employee performance appraisals do not adequately represent the content of the job that the worker does. For example, hospital nurses are regularly reviewed for their punctuality and attendance, quality of patient care, medication and treatment accuracy, and continuing professional education. However, not usually included in these evaluations is the nurse's teaching/coaching skills, even though these nurses are regularly expected to train new employees, and their abilities in this area have a significant impact on the quality of work in the unit.

Exhibit 6.2
Criterion-related validity

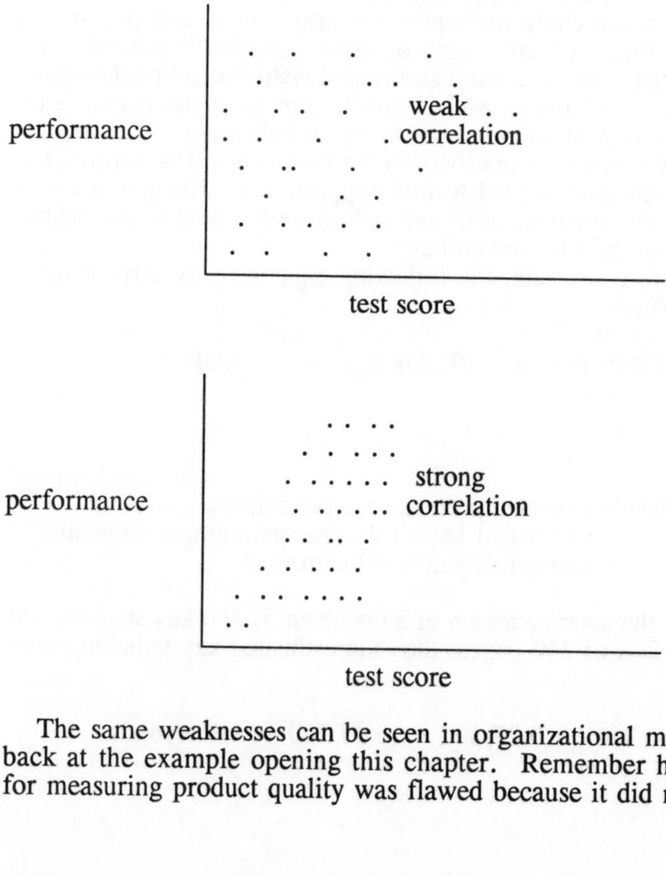

performance

weak correlation

test score

performance

strong correlation

test score

The same weaknesses can be seen in organizational measures. Look back at the example opening this chapter. Remember how the system for measuring product quality was flawed because it did not measure an important component of the content under evaluation. That measure did not have content validity.

Construct validity is required whenever a test is used to measure an attribute which it does not measure directly. The 'constructs' are elements that account for variance in performance. Once they are determined, a causal model is constructed so that each construct, and the way these variables relate to one another, is included in the model.

A very familiar measure which uses constructs is the individual performance appraisal. Often these rely on constructs such as 'maturity', 'interpersonal skills', or 'initiative', as measures of job performance. The validity of this measure is highly questionable. First, it is unclear how these variables would be accurately measured. Second, the construct validity of the system is highly questionable. We would ask, to what extent are 'interpersonal skills' related to effective performance in a particular job, for example, that of a meter maid?

Let us consider the effective use of constructs by describing a model to estimate claim processing time in an insurance company. After a work process analysis, the various activities in which the clerks were involved were identified as; copying information from the claim form into the computer, searching for supporting information, and performing other short activities. Clearly, each of these variables is related to the total time required to complete a claim, and constructs can be developed as a representative measure of each element. For example, counting the number of keystrokes in an entry would be an indication of the amount of time needed to copy information into the computer. The construct to estimate the search time needed to find supportive information could be the thickness of the documentation manual, since the thicker the manual the longer it would take to find an item.

Based on these constructs, the following equation was derived using regression analysis:

$$\text{TIME} = 230 + (0.25)\text{KS} + (0.15)\text{PAGE}$$

where:

TIME (in seconds)	= expected process time per claim
KS	= number of key strokes needed to input the claim
PAGE	= number of pages in the manual

For example, if the average length of a document is 300 key strokes, and the manual consists of 240 pages, then the estimated key punching time is:

$$\text{TIME} = 230 + (0.25)300 + (0.15)240 = 341 \text{ seconds.}$$

The correlation coefficient, r^2, or strength of the association between dependent and independent variables, varies between -1 and 1. Here $r^2=0.83$, and is used as a measure of the construct validity of the model.

Reliability

Reliability, the second characteristic essential for a meaningful measurement, refers to the extent to which repeated measurements under constant conditions generate constant results. Suppose that five industrial engineers were asked to estimate the time required to produce products A, B, and C. The engineers were required to use the same method when timing the same product, however, they were permitted to measure item A using a different method than for items B or C. Exhibit 6.3 demonstrates the results of their findings.

Exhibit 6.3
Estimation of production time for 3 products by 5 industrial engineers
(in minutes per item)

	Industrial Engineer				
Product	1	2	3	4	5
A	26.5	23.0	24.0	24.5	23.5
B	4.9	5.1	4.9	5.0	5.1
C	7.5	5.0	6.0	6.5	5.5

As can be seen from the exhibit, repeated measurements of each of the three products produces different results. However, the discrepancy in the measurements for product B is relatively small (4.9 to 5.1) compared to the results for products A and C. We can conclude from this that the measurement procedures applied to product B were more consistent, and therefore more reliable, than the procedures applied to the other two products. This demonstrates *inter-rater reliability*, that is, that measurement technique will produce results that will be stable from one rater to another.

Other forms of reliability are *test-retest reliability* and *internal consistency*. As the name implies, with test-retest reliability, a procedure for measuring will give the same results over time, all other things remaining the same. For example, the accuracy of a scale can be determined from the distribution of the reading while using the same weight.

With internal consistency, a test will be consistent within broad areas or 'dimensions'. For example, in our quality assurance test in the previous section, a reliable measure would mean that a good score on the quality of raw materials would also be reflected in a decrease in the number of defects produced.

In general, the concept of reliability implies that results are repeatable. Reliability can be viewed as a test of error: the less the result deviates from the true value, the greater the reliability. In order to quantify that statement, and to calculate an error term which may be used as an indicator of reliability, the real value of the measured condition must be known. It may not be sufficient to use the average of several measurements as an estimate of the real value because the average may be biased. Bias exists when a measurement systematically overestimates, or underestimates, the value of a variable,

For example, using the data in Exhibit 6.3, the average time to produce product B is 5.0 minutes. However, it turns out that all the engineers failed to include an activity in their calculations which would have added 1 minute to the total time. The true value, therefore, would be closer to 6.0 minutes. The measured value of B, which is around 5, is 1 unit away from the true value of 6. This is an *error* of 1/6, or 17%. What this shows is that a small error term is necessary, but not sufficient, to guarantee a reliable system of measurement.

To compensate for the fact that a measurement range does not evaluate the magnitude of the error term relative to the average, a coefficient of variation should be employed:

$$COV = \frac{STD}{AVG} \tag{1}$$

where:

COV = coefficient of variation
STD = standard deviation of the measurements
AVG = average value of the measured phenomenon

The average value is calculated by the following equation:

$$AVG = \frac{\sum_{i=1}^{n} X_i}{n} \tag{2}$$

and the STD is calculated from the variance (VAR), using the following equations:

$$VAR = \frac{\sum_{i=1}^{n} (X_i - AVG)^2}{n} \tag{3}$$

$$STD = VAR^{1/2} \tag{4}$$

where:

n = number of measurements
X_i = the value established by the ith measurer or measurement.

For example, let us calculate the COV for the three products described in the Exhibit.

$$AVG_A = \frac{25.5 + 23.0 + 24.0 + 24.5 + 23.5}{5} = 24.1$$

$$VAR_A = \frac{(1.4)^2 + (-1.1)^2 + (-.1)^2 + (.4)^2 + (-.6)^2}{5}$$

$$= \frac{1.96 + 1.21 + .01 + .16 + .36}{5}$$

$$= \frac{3.68}{5}$$

$$= .74$$

$$STD_A = (.74)^{1/2}$$

$$= .86$$

$$COV_A = \frac{0.86}{24.1} = 0.036$$

The values for the other two products were similarly calculated and found to be $COV_B = 0.018$; $COV_C = 0.141$. There does seem to be more consistency in the way that product B was measured. Measurement of product C appears to be the least consistent, and therefore the least reliable.

If the real value of the measured criterion is available, then we can substitute it for the average (AVG) and use equations (1) and (4) to calculate the COV. The results can be used as a true test of the reliability of the measurement system, since the error term is proportional to the real value rather than to the average of the measured values.

Even tests in laboratories with precision instruments do not produce exactly the same results. Reliability is a critical element in meaningful measurement, and must be carefully examined in any control system.

Sensitivity

The third characteristic of measurement deals with its ability to identify changes in the attribute which is being measured. The greater this ability, the more sensitive the measure. A highly sensitive measure is preferred to a measure with low sensitivity, because the auditor is able to identify very small differences.

The following example demonstrates this point. A manufacturing company wants to estimate the inventory level of bolts. This estimate can be reached through the use of one of the following measurement processes:

a. Weighing all the bolts and dividing by the average weight of one bolt;

b. Counting the number of containers of bolts and multiplying this by the number of bolts in one container;

c. Counting each bolt.

Alternative C is more sensitive since it can detect a difference of a single item. It is also more reliable since repetition of the same measure will lead to the same, or very similar, results. Alternatives a and b are less capable of identifying a difference of a few items; they are less sensitive. However, the company may decide to use one of the less sensitive alternatives since either one of them is cheaper to implement than c, and sensitive enough for the company's needs.

When an organization decides to establish a performance criterion, it must decide on the tolerable discrepancy between the real value and the measured one. The tolerable discrepancy can be stated either in absolute or relative values. In order to make a final choice, this consideration must be coupled with other factors, such as the time and cost of administering the measurement technique.

To return to the example of estimating the inventory of bolts, the company may find that a difference of up to ± 10 bolts between the real value and the measured one is sensitive enough for its purposes. Exhibit 6.4 provides the results of the three measurement methods.

Exhibit 6.4

Comparison of three inventory measurement alternatives

Alternative	Cost per 100 Items	Maximum Discrepancy (95% Confidence Interval)
a. Weighing	.30	3 items regardless of the number
b. Counting containers	.75	4 items per container
c. Counting bolts	1.10	1 item per 100

The conclusion we arrive at from the data is obvious: weighing the bolts is the preferred method since it is sufficiently sensitive to identify a change of more than 3 bolts, and is less expensive than counting. Using the container method is not acceptable since, even with only three containers, the cumulative discrepancy (3x4=12) would exceeded the boundary of ±10.

Measurement errors

Errors are a 'normal', albeit undesirable, phenomenon in organizational activities. The potential for error exists in all organizations whenever human beings are involved, and the design and implementation of control systems is no exception. In measurement, an error is a discrepancy between the 'real' value and the reported one. Prior knowledge of possible sources of errors can help in designing a more reliable and more accurate measurement and evaluation system.

There are three main sources of error: human, technological, and errors due to the nature of the organization. Through a better understanding of the nature of errors, a control system which minimizes the potential for error can be designed.

Human errors

A human error is one which is generated by people, which sometimes cannot be foreseen, understood, or prevented. Human errors generally stem from two major causes: physiological constraints and psychological factors. A better understanding of these subjects will help to improve the design and implementation of a control system.

Physiological constraints. These errors are usually the result of human sensory limitations -- vision, hearing, touch, taste, and smell. The constraints may be defined by determining the range over which a person can detect that the phenomenon exists, or by the minimum difference between two values that would be detectable by the person. This concept is known as the *Just Noticeable difference*, or *JND*. An example of these kinds of constraints is human hearing, with a range of 20-20,000 hertz, and a JND of around 1800 hertz.

As a general rule, you can use 10% for the JND. That is, a difference of 10% will be perceived as a significant difference by the majority of people (Sheridan and Ferrell, 1981). Whenever a measurement system is designed, such constraints must be considered.

Take for example the design of a quality system to measure the level of cleanliness of painted surfaces. The quality auditor rates the size and number of dots on the surface; the larger the size and number, the less clean the surface. In defining these indicators of quality, you must consider the visual ability of the auditor in order to ensure consistency in measurement results. It is important to emphasize that there are individual differences in people's ability to use the senses. Therefore, you can expect two individuals to arrive at different values for the same measured phenomenon.

A knowledge of the limitations of the use of the senses and the physiological constraints of the human body is of crucial importance in designing equipment and processes as well as in measurement and control. For example, in designing a car, the designer must consider the ability of the driver to detect the light which indicates that the oil level is low, as well as his ability to discriminate between this and other lights, such as the high beam signal. In any design you must evaluate whether all physiological and other constraints have been taken into account, so that the end product will function properly. This subject has developed into a distinct scientific discipline known as ergonomics.

Psychological factors. When people are involved in collecting and interpreting data, or in rating performance, psychological factors can intentionally, or unintentionally, lead to errors. Studies have shown that in individual performance appraisals, supervisors are prone to several types of errors (Hampton, et al, 1982).

- *Central tendency*, is the inclination to rate everyone as average, giving little meaning to the evaluation. This is likely to occur when raters have little training, little time, or feel uncomfortable with the role of evaluating others.
- *Halo effect*, is the tendency to rate a person in all areas as you perceive him in one area. A secretary who was a very quick and accurate typist might receive an excellent rating in all areas even if her performance on the telephone, or her attendance, was inferior.
- *Recentcy of events*, occurs when raters remember only what has just happened, even though the evaluation may cover a period of a year. An employee who calls in sick for several days before a performance appraisal, runs the risk of being rated lower than he deserves. Employees are aware of this rater error and often work at peak performance prior to an evaluation,
- *Leniency or strictness*, occurs when raters artificially score employees either too high or too low.

Many raters are unaware of the potential for these errors and have no idea that they may be making them. Despite the fact that errors can be significantly decreased through rater training, most supervisors conducting evaluations today have had no formal training as raters.

Other psychological factors contribute to measurement errors as well. These derive from sources such as:

- A strong desire to reduce the discrepancy between what is considered to be acceptable and the reported value. The larger the discrepancy between the real situation and the situation which is desired by the individual, the more likely he is to close the gap. The fear of a large discrepancy between actual and desired performance is probably one of the major sources of resistance to control systems.

- Lack of organizational concern regarding the importance of measurement accuracy. If management puts little emphasis on accuracy, there is little reason for others to work to reduce errors.
- Misunderstandings created by the participants in the measurement process. If data is collected by one individual, calculations are performed by another, and analyzed by a third, misinterpretations may result.
- Possible advantage to an organization in hiding or falsifying information. The future of an organization often depends on its reported performance. This may generate a strong motivation for an organization to manipulate data, if the reality does not conform with a positive profile.

In order to reduce the probability of these types of errors, a control mechanism on the monitoring system must be developed. The three common control mechanisms are:

a. objective monitoring;

b. double checking, where the same object is measured twice by different individuals;

c. checks and balances, where measurement is performed by someone who will not benefit from a specific result.

Checks and balances are particularly useful when the measured objects move from one unit to the other, where the output of one unit is the input of another. For example, if it is to the advantage of unit A to report a high value in order to achieve a high performance rating, then the opposite should be true for the next unit. This occurs, for instance, when unit A is a production unit and unit B is the warehouse. If such a conflict of interests exists between two units, the measurement process is more reliable, since it has a built-in system of checks and balances.

Errors due to technology

Many measurement procedures require the use of equipment. Equipment may consist of different types of gauges, watches, calculators, computers, and so on. Measurement with the aid of equipment also has its own 'built-in' level of accuracy which can not be exceeded. For example, a typical gauge is unable to identify a difference of less than 0.0004 of an inch. Quite a few calculators are unable to deal with numbers of more than 8 digits, so that numbers have to be rounded off.

Human control is crucial even if the process is considered to be fully automated. Although a fully automated system is usually equipped with its own control mechanisms, these mechanisms are not able to respond properly to all possible circumstances. This has been recognized by the

Japanese and is reflected in the approach they call 'selfmation', or automation which is managed and controlled by the employees. In selfmation human discretion plays a major role in evaluating and controlling fully automated systems and employees are empowered to override such systems. This orientation stems from the recognition that even a very sophisticated system cannot be programmed to respond properly to all exigencies. A technological error may sometimes be corrected by the appropriate human response, but keep in mind that errors may be introduced by the human as well.

Errors due to the nature of the activities

The magnitude of the potential error depends to a large extent on the nature of the organization -- its input, throughput, and output.

Input is composed of either materials, customers, or both. There is always uncertainty regarding the nature of the input. For example, material may not reach the plant at the right time, the quality of the material may be different from one batch to the next, customers may arrive randomly, what one customer wants may have nothing to do with the demands of the next. Because of this, if measurement of input is required, a statistical analysis must by performed. Such an analysis always entails an estimation of reality, and therefore, recognition of the fact that there is a possible difference between the estimated and the real value. This difference is the error term.

Throughput consists of activities performed on the inputs by equipment and employees. As such, any uncertainties regarding the inputs will have effects on the throughput. Additional uncertainties are introduced by equipment and employee variations. For example, old equipment is less reliable than new; an experienced worker is more competent than one who is inexperienced.

Output attributes are also a function of the organization's nature. For example, physical products are within the company's control for a given length of time. This is not the case with service companies where customers walk out immediately after the service has been rendered. In the first case, the company has some time to measure characteristics of the completed product, which because it is tangible, is also more easily measured.

Use of sampling

Data may be collected either by measuring the entire population of events, or on a sample basis, that is measuring only a subset of all events. The decision will depend on the cost, work flow, and complexity of measurement.

It is often impractical to measure each item. Imagine that you need to determine the percentage of items assembled correctly by your production unit. Is it essential that you examine all the items, and if not, how many items should be examined? You correctly realize that if all the items are checked, this will significantly increase your production costs. If too few items are examined your results may not be sufficiently accurate since they do not properly represent the batch from which they were sampled.

The size of the sample you chose to measure is of great concern: a sample which is too small may call measurement validity into question, while too large a sample may be unnecessarily costly. It is of major significance for any control system to be aware of the problem of sample size, and the two main sampling methods: success-failure sampling and value sampling.

Sample size

The larger the variation in measurement results, the greater will be the number of observations (the sample size) necessary to guarantee a given level of accuracy. This is valid for all cases in which there is variation between measurement readings. If no variation ever occurs, then one reading is sufficient.

Two other factors which influence the sample size are the desired *accuracy* and the *confidence level.* Accuracy is measured by specifying an 'allowable error', that is, the acceptable difference between the estimate you get measuring the sample and the true population value. For example, assume that based on a sample, it was found that the average time needed to perform an activity to be 12.5 minutes, and that ±10% is considered the required accuracy (or ±1.25 minutes). It means that the real value may lie within a range of ±10% around the calculated value. If however, it is decided that the range is too broad, then the accuracy requirements must be raised. This would necessitate increasing the sample size, thus increasing the cost of the control process.

The confidence level, refers to the extent to which we can be certain that an actual value lies within a specified range, keeping in mind that it is not possible to obtain 100% confidence. A common confidence level is 95%; that is, if the range of 11.25 to 13.75 (in the previous sample) has a confidence level of 95%, this means that there is a 5% chance that the real value is outside of this range. The desired confidence level is built into the measurement system. The larger the confidence level, the more certain we are of the accuracy of our results, and the greater the required sample size.

The proper sample size as a function of the parameters mentioned, can be determined by using certain equations, presented below. It is important to note that these equations assume that the statistical distribution of the calculated value is a normal distribution. This assumption is valid as long as the sample size is large enough (more than 10 for practical purposes). Clarifications of this, as well as other issues discussed in this section, may be found in most basic statistics books (e.g. Berenson and Levin, 1983).

There are two types of equations for determining proper sample size. The first is used when the results of each measurement are classified as success or failure (the box is properly sealed or it is not). The second is used when continuous values are assigned to each measurement (the weight of the contents of the box).

Success-failure sampling

In this type of sampling there are only two possible results for each measurement: an item is either defective or not, the customer has or has not filed a claim, the activity has been completed within the specified time or it has not. The required sample size is computed as follows:

$$N = \frac{1-P}{P}\left[\frac{K}{A}\right]^2 \qquad (4)$$

where:

N = sample size
P = probability of 'success' on each observation
A = the desired accuracy
K = the desired confidence level expressed by number of standard deviation units required

The process of computing the sample size requires two decisions:

1. The desired accuracy level. You may decide that 10% accuracy is sufficient, in which case, A would be set at A = 0.10, or if greater accuracy is required, say 5%, then A = .05, etc.

2. The desired confidence level, which determines the value of K.

Table 6.1 may be used in order to find the value of K as a function of the desired confidence level.

Table 6.1
Conversion of confidence level to the value of K
(assuming a normal distribution)

Confidence Level	80%	85%	90%	95%	99%
Value of K	1.28	1.44	1.65	1.96	2.58

If confidence levels other than those included in Table 6.1 are desired, the appropriate value for K can be generated from a normal distribution table to be found in any basic statistics book.

Once the values of A and K have been established, the following three steps are needed to compute the necessary sample size.

1. Take an initial sample of N_1 observations ($N_1 > 10$) and calculate the value of P. Let's say that the criterion under investigation is the percentage of customers that are not served within a certain time period. Out of $N_1 = 100$ customers that were examined in the initial sample, 35 exceeded the desired value. Hence, P = 35/100 = 0.35.

2. Substitute the values into equation (4), assume a 95% confidence level, and a desired accuracy of ±10%:

$$N = \frac{(1 - 0.35)}{0.35} \left[\frac{1.96}{0.10}\right]^2 = 713$$

That is, the total required sample size is 713. Since 100 observations have already been considered, then an additional 613 observations are needed. If this number is too high for practical purposes, then either the accuracy and/or confidence level must be revised. For example, if the confidence level were revised to 90% or K = 1.65, then the new total required sample size would be:

$$N = \frac{(1 - 0.35)}{0.35} \left[\frac{1.65}{0.10}\right]^2 = 506$$

That is, 207 fewer observations are needed for 90% confidence.

3. Take the additional observations, recalculate the value of P based on all the observations, and then recalculate the new required sample size. For example, if out of a total of N = 713 observations, 264 observations exceeded the desired value, then P = 264/713 = 0.37. Substituting this value together with the others in equation (4) we get:

$$N = \frac{(1 - 0.35)}{0.35} \left[\frac{1.96}{0.10}\right]^2 = 654$$

Since the new required size is 654, and 713 observations have been performed, there is no need to take additional observations. If more observations than needed are taken, the answer will simply be more reliable.

Value sampling

In this type of sampling, each measurement results in a number that can be of various values, rather than only 'yes' or 'no', for example, cost per item, time per activity, weight of a bag, value of a stock, and so on. Determining sample size is again of great importance for measurement, and therefore control, since an improper sample size would result in an incorrect estimated value. The following steps are needed to establish sample size in the case of value sampling.

The following equation is used to determine the sample size:

$$N = \left[\frac{STD}{AVG}\right]^2 \left[\frac{K}{A}\right]^2 \qquad (5)$$

where:

N, K, A are the same as in equation (4)
AVG is the average value as calculated using equation (2)
STD is the standard deviation, and is calculated by equation (3)

An iterative approach similar to the one used for the previous case is also employed here, as shown by the following example.

1. Determine the desired level of A, say A = 0.05.

2. Determine the desired value of K, say K = 1.96.

3. Take an initial sample (N ≥ 10) and calculate the average. Assume N = 10 observations were taken of the time it took to perform an activity with the following results:

   55, 53, 49, 52, 48, 47, 56, 61, 47, 58.

   The average is AVG = 52.6.

4. Calculate the value of STD. Substituting the values into equation (3) we get STD = 4.88.

5. Calculate the required sample size by using equation (5).

$$N = \left[\frac{4.88}{52.6}\right]^2 \left[\frac{1.96}{0.05}\right]^2 \qquad (5)$$

That is, according to the first 10 observations, a total of 14 observations are required in order to obtain the accuracy and desired confidence levels. However, a situation might arise where the additional four observations lead to a greater variance and a sample larger than 14 observations is needed. For example, if the four additional observations produced the values 40, 59, 63, 41, the new parameters of the sample, based on the 14 observations, would be AVG = 52.07, STD = 7.09, and the desired sample size will become 28.48.

Let us assume that the additional 15 observations taken to complete the sample of 29 produced the following result: AVG = 52.5, STD = 6.52, N = 23.7. In this case the sample of 29 observations produced an accuracy or a confidence level higher than required, since the required sample size, N, was only 24.

A control system is valueless without proper measurement routines. Yet, measurements are not without cost, and if they are redundant or exaggerated, they may be very costly and of limited value. Measurement is a function of what information is needed, and has its own cost-benefit ratio, like any other managerial activity.

Therefore we may generalize by stating that it is preferable for the control process to utilize, as far as possible, data and measurements produced by the organization in the normal course of its activities. A major objective of control is to ensure that the organization uses proper and reliable data, and that the measurements conducted are relevant and reliable.

7 Control of the decision-making process

A 'decision' is both an outcome of a process and an input for every operation. This is true at every organizational level. Therefore, the quality of a decision determines the quality of the operational outcome. By viewing an organization as a decision making system, it is easy to see that an improvement in the decision making process will result in an improvement in the organization as a whole.

Management literature treats the subject of decision making extensively from two perspectives. The first recognizes that an examination of the decision making process is an excellent approach to an analysis of the organization. The second focuses on decision making as a tool for managers in performing their jobs. The central purpose of this chapter is to examine ways to evaluate and control the decision making process, in order to achieve that best possible results.

The normative base

It is obvious that the more reliable its decisions, the greater will be the achievements of an organization. The key question then, is whether it is possible to identify a sound formula for an optimal decision making process. One of the complex dilemmas facing decision makers is how to ensure that the optimum amount of relevant information has been considered, and that reasonable alternatives have been reliably examined.

There are various approaches to decision making, and a wide variety of methods for evaluation. Some of these are very rational and sophisticated, generally analytical and quantitative. Typically, these approaches are based on establishing a *decision tree*, made up of possible events and their probabilities. Assuming that there is a payoff for every combination of events, one selects the combination which best fits the situation and personality of the decision maker. Exhibit 7.1 gives an example of such a decision tree. In this example, a developer must decide whether to build housing on an existing plot of land, or to attempt to have the parcel rezoned for use as a medical facility.

The value at Chance Node A equals:

.3 x 1 x 10	=	3
.5 x .75 x 10	=	3.75
.2 x .1 x 10	=	.2
		$6.95 million

The value at Chance Node B equals:

.5 [(5 x 10)-10]	=	20
.5 x 0	=	0
		$20 million

The following table compares the results of the two alternatives:

	Initial Investment	Expected Revenue	Net Profit
Housing	$4,000,000	6,950,000	2,950,000
Medical Facility	100,000	20,000,000	19,900,000

Using the above approach, building the medical facility is the preferred option.

Some models of decision making rely on a *pragmatic* approach, based on experience and intuition. With these methods, the decision makers base their conclusions on previous results and expert opinions.

A completely different approach is that of the *determinist method*, which in some ways 'eases' the task of decision making. According to this approach, present decisions are an outcome of past activities and decisions. As a result, the decision maker is 'compelled' to decide in a given way, with minimal freedom of choice.

The larger and more decentralized the organization, the more significant the high-level decisions are for its existence. It is only natural then, that intensive effort is currently being invested in the search for improved models for high level decision making. Yet, despite considerable research, there is serious doubt as to the existence of one best model. No matter what model you use, it is preferable that the decision be not only rational and feasible, but that it also satisfy the decision makers.

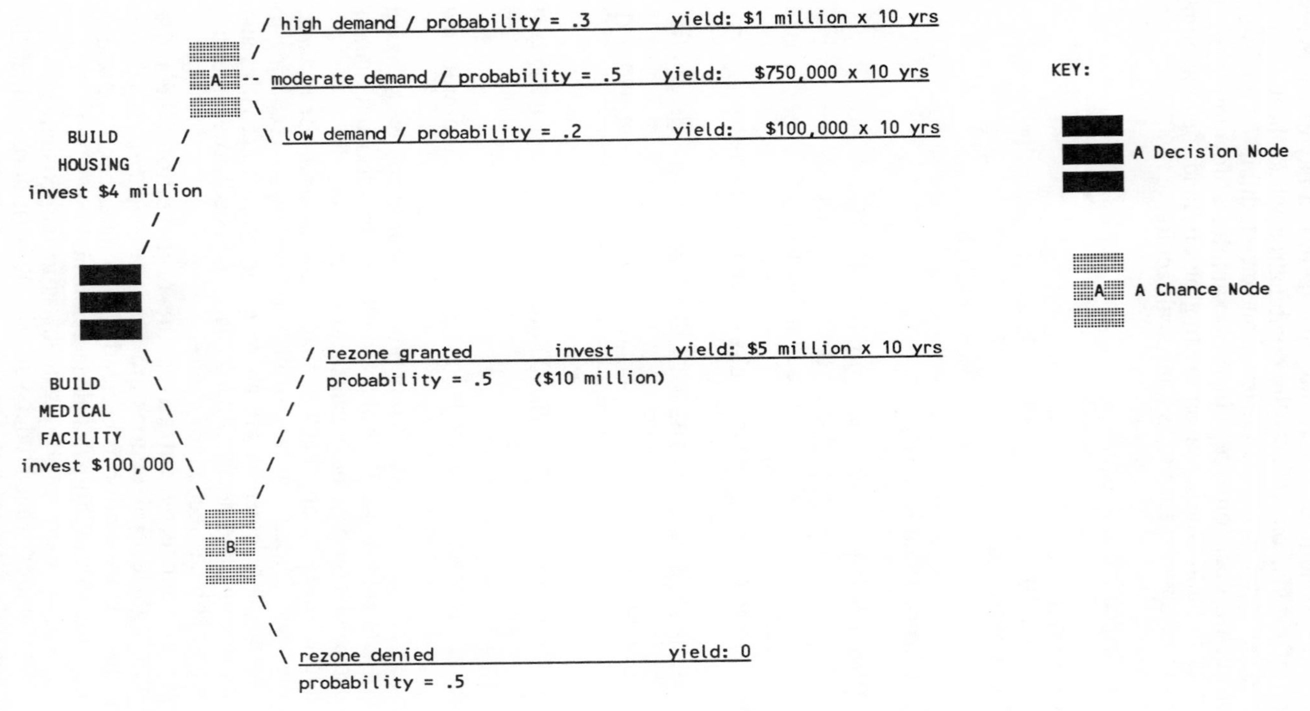

Exhibit 7.1 Using the decision tree

Due to the absence of one catch-all formula for optimal decision making, there is renewed interest in some normative, or standard, approaches. These emphasize the importance and implications of group consultation and team consensus, negotiations between partners in a decision, participatory management, and involvement of employees in the decision making process.

Surely you have complained about spending too much time in meetings, and although individual decision making appears to be a speedier process, groups tend to make more accurate choices. Individuals tend to be more innovative, yet surprisingly, groups are more willing to take risks (Hampton, et al, 1982). However, the most important reason for the popularity of the group process, is the evidence that people are more likely to accept and to help support decisions that they have been involved in making. All these are relevant not only to the improvement of decision making; they become important elements of the control loop, as well.

Attempts have also been made to learn about the process of decision making which is based on experience and intuition. This is of particular interest given the absence of any clear distinction between the rational and the pragmatic models.

"How did you make that decision?"

The high level of interest in understanding the decision making process, is a reflection of its significance in organizations. Despite the many attempts to come to an agreement about one optimal model, the control of the decision making process remains a major concern, weighing heavily on an organization's leaders. Managers must respond to one critical question: "How, and on what basis, did you decide as you did?" Simply asking the question is likely to sharpen the awareness of the process and improve the outcome of decision making.

We assume, then, that there exists no 'pure rational' approach, just as there is no exclusive reliance on intuition or past experience, or on determinism. Thus, most of the models for decision making are aimed at improving decisions and can serve as a starting point for control of the entire process. The clearer and more reliable the model, the more acceptable and applicable it will be. With this in mind, we have determined the following eight stages in the decision making process. These comply with most normative models and can be used to serve the control and evaluation process.

Define the problem or issue. The way in which a problem is solved, depends, to a large extent, on how the problem is formulated. At the very beginning of the process, evaluation and control of decision making must focus on the participation and involvement of all relevant parties. Successful solutions depend upon an accurate understanding of the question. This accuracy is most likely if all points of view are raised and considered when defining the problem.

Recognize and deal with conflict. Have you ever been involved in an important corporate change that was implemented without any problems? implementation often will take longer than planned, will cost more than expected, and will generate resistance from some employees. The control function must determine if the decision maker has analyzed the potential for these conflicts and is prepared to deal with those that may arise in implementing the chosen solution.

Define the method of analysis. Every new issue calls for a different analysis, and therefore, a different data set. An organization may prefer to use a quantitative approach based on objective analysis, a qualitative analysis based on expert judgment, or a combination of both. Because the method of analysis selected will have a significant impact on the results, the decision maker must have carefully considered the approach to be used.

Collect relevant data. It is necessary to identify which information and data will be needed in the analysis. The sources required for its collection must be determined as well. Once this is established, the decision maker must estimate both the reliability of the data and the collection cost.

Analyze the information. Data can be converted into information by different methods, each of which can lead to different results and conclusions. While this may seem unlikely at first, a simple illustration is presented below.

> A bank manager is dealing with the question of productivity at the branch she directs. She has data available on the number of customers, the number of tellers working, and the number of tellers scheduled to work, for a given time period. The manager determines productivity based on the average number of customers served per teller's window.
>
> With the data available, the manager might calculate this figure by dividing the number of customers by the number of tellers who were scheduled, or by the number who were actually working. The first analysis of the information might lead to the conclusion that more tellers should be hired, the second might result in a decision to change the personnel policy regarding absenteeism. Thus, the control function should verify that the conversation of data to information is done with extreme care, professionally and objectively.

Develop alternative solutions. At this stage, the control system examines whether the decision makers have used relevant criteria in considering alternative approaches to solving the problem. Effective criteria for evaluating alternatives include such factors as a cost-benefit analysis for each plan, determining the relative applicability of each solution to the situation, and the likelihood that each alternative will be accepted by the parties involved.

The role of the control system, is to ascertain not only that a reasonable number of alternatives have been identified, but also that they have been compared by relevant criteria.

There are many models for analysis and assessment of alternatives, however, the following stages in the process are typical to quite a few:

a. identification and definition of relevant variables for evaluation of the alternatives;

b. determination of the relative value or weight of each variable for all the alternatives; and

c. adoption of the alternative that achieves the highest rating.

It is not always feasible for the control system to take a stand regarding the method of analysis and evaluation of the alternatives. It is possible however, and necessary, for the control system to establish whether a rational process is being used for the purpose of identifying the 'preferred alternative'.

Evaluate the feasibility of the preferred alternative. An analysis of the feasibility of implementing a decision must be an integral part of the evaluation of the alternatives. An alternative is not a relevant one if it is impossible to implement. The issue of feasibility deserves special treatment, for the following reasons:

a. In practice, rejection of an alternative is too often based on the claim that it is 'unfeasible', before the essential characteristics of the alternative have been carefully examined.

b. The extent to which a given alternative may appear feasible, is influenced by the personal experiences and attitudes of the decision makers. Therefore, the preference of one alternative over another, may be due to lack of experience, and not to a comparison of reliable information.

It is usually possible to examine practical difficulties by simulation of alternatives and in that way, to identify specific drawbacks that may hinder implementation. When an alternative is labeled as 'unfeasible', it may be the result of examining specific criteria, such as cost, performance time, or human resources. This very breakdown of 'unfeasibility' is likely to aid in locating the critical problems, which can sometimes be overcome, resulting in an improved alternative.

The decision: adopt the preferred solution. The final stage entails details of the preferred solution. At this point, the decision maker should have the implementation strategy for the solution fully discussed and clearly stated, coupled with detailed operational specifications.

Objective and subjective variables in control of decision making

In the process of decision making control, both objective and subjective variables are involved. While objective variables relate to data and information, the relative importance of these depends, to a large extent, on subjective variables such as the decision makers' approach and philosophy. As early as the initial point in the decision making process, the definition of the problem, the decision makers' approach is central. The same problem may be defined in different ways by different people; therefore, they may also reach different conclusions.

Two examples from different types of organizations illustrate the dependence of the decision on the perceptions of the decision makers. These examples also highlight the significance of control in this respect.

In the first example, a manufacturer of small appliances receives customer complaints concerning the amount of time they have to wait for repairs to be completed. If the complaints are dealt with by the service department, the problem will probably be perceived as 'finding a way to reduce response time for service calls'. If, however, the problem is submitted to top management, it might be defined as 'a negative impact on the company's reputation due to the high failure rate of its products'. The two definitions of the problem would lead to very different solutions.

The second example is quite different in nature: in a suburb of a mid-size Eastern city, a serious increase in the rate of juvenile delinquency had been observed. The problem was discussed by three independent groups involved in the issue: social workers, police officers, and religious leaders. Each group had access to the same data and information, yet the definition of the problem, and consequently the plans for dealing with it, were completely different from one another.

The social workers concluded that the socio-economic conditions of the neighborhood were the fundamental issue; the police emphasized the lack of correctional and rehabilitation institutions for juvenile delinquents; and the religious leaders made an unequivocal statement that the problem was the deterioration of moral standards, and the atmosphere of permissiveness. A team of representatives of all three groups however, reached an ethical and pragmatic definition of the same problem that differed from any of those reached by any of the individual groups; that is, that the young people suffered from a lack of neighborhood identification.

Despite the fact that managers often view the group process as taking too much time, it remains true that managers spend vast amounts of time in meetings. This is testimony to the belief that 'two heads are better than one'. The two examples above, clearly illustrate that, even if an organization adopts a binding, normative formula for decision making, it is essential that the control system ensure that those involved in the process truly represent all relevant points of view.

Three areas of focus in the control of decision making

Control of decision making focuses on three main areas: the decision makers; the relationship between the decision makers and the nature of the decisions; and critical factors in the decision making process.

The decision makers

All members of an organization can be defined as decision makers of some sort. This is true even though there are vast differences between the decisions made by an employee at the operational level and those made by someone at a managerial level. From the perspective of control, there are four questions that must be asked for all personnel, regardless of their positions, levels of authority, or skill in making decisions.

How clearly defined is the employees' authority to make decisions in various areas of their activities? In terms of organizational design and operational management, it is crucial that the definition of each job include the authority attached to it. This is essential to four parties: the position-holder, those holding parallel positions, superiors, and subordinates.

Lack of clarity regarding the authority given to a particular function leaves employees suffering from uncertainty. If an employee takes the initiative to decide, he may not have been equipped with the necessary information required to make the right decision. This can result in decisions that hurt him and others. By failing to decide, he may also harm the organization, and damage his own standing as well. Either way, from the point of view of control, this is a two-fold problem. It must be dealt with both in terms of decision making and in terms of the analysis of the job and its definition.

Who decides what? In defining areas of authority, it is important to reduce to a minimum, the number of areas for which there are no authorized decision makers, and at the same time, to prevent having too many decision makers for a single area.

Is the decision making authority being used effectively? It is not sufficient that a position is accompanied by authority; it is also essential to ascertain that this authority is utilized properly. The control system will occasionally discover that decisions are delayed, not because of uncertainty regarding who should decide, but because the person with the authority is not capable of fulfilling this responsibility. This is usually expressed either in frequent failure to make decisions or in numerous erroneous decisions.

Is the organization committed to development in decision making? Based on the assumption that the willingness and ability to make decisions can be improved, control must examine the organization's investment in human resources development in this area. Organizational decision makers need ongoing development of their skills. This philosophy can be applied to all levels of the organization, but there is a significant relationship between functional-hierarchical characteristics and the nature of decisions made. The significance of this is discussed further below.

The organization and its employees must know what authority is attached to each position in the organization, and management should know the ability of its staff. Those responsible for the development of human resources must strive to reinforce and improve the knowledge and skills of the decision makers. This triangle -- authority, skill, and development -- is of interest to control, and it reflected in the relationship between the nature of the decisions made and the decision makers.

The relationship between decision makers and the nature of decisions

The higher the position, the greater the responsibility, and the more deeply involved is the individual in the decision made. For those at the operational level, the dominant concern is implementation of decisions and maintenance of standards, while for senior management, the emphasis is on new decisions. 'Performance' at the top level is expressed primarily in judgment and assessment, and the typical output is decisions.

Here, we should recall the strong connection between policy and planning (the major outputs of the executive ranks) and decision making. policy and planning are present decisions concerned with future objectives; thus the quality of policy and planning is dependent on the quality of the decision making process. The strong connection between policy and planning, and decision making, can blur the fundamental distinction between them: *decision management is a process*, while *policy and planning are outputs*. There is, however, a strong tendency to deal with them together, especially in situations of high uncertainty.

From the perspective of the control system, the organization faces a difficult paradox: relative ease in control at the operational performance level, yet great difficulty in control of judgment and decisions at the top levels. This relationship is demonstrated by Exhibit 7.2. At the lower organizational levels, the outputs are usually clearly defined and thus lend themselves relatively easily to standardization and control. At the upper levels, where the future survival of the organization is determined, control is minimal and requires long term assessment in the form of a 'wait and see' approach.

Substantial investment in control and evaluation of decision making at the top levels of the hierarchy is essential for three main reasons.

These are usually strategic decisions, which dictate the way in which the organization will function. Errors in such decisions lead to organizational deterioration, even if functions at the lower levels are performed efficiently. A strategic error is immeasurably greater than an operational one, which is usually easier to detect and correct. At the same time, it is easier to make an error at the strategic level than at the operational level.

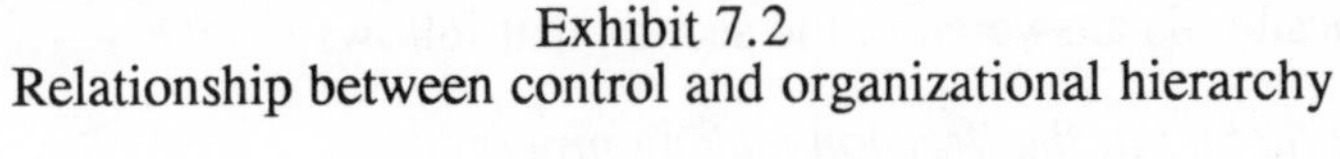
Exhibit 7.2
Relationship between control and organizational hierarchy

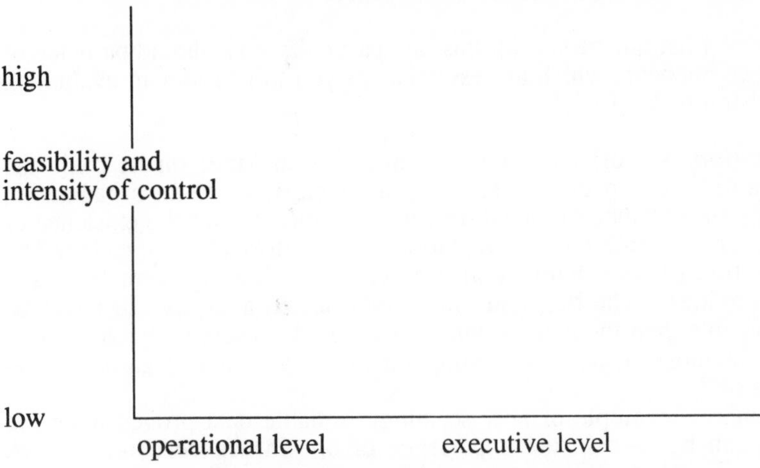

These decisions result in long-range outcomes, and therefore, by nature, require 'long term credit'. The common argument that the quality of a decision can be assessed by examining its outcome is unacceptable in principle. This would result in evaluation only at the completion of performance. In fact, control is most crucial at the pre-performance stage. It is therefore imperative to control the long term decision making process at the executive level.

The impact of the decision is greatest at this level. The higher the rank, the more organizational sectors are encompassed by the decision. For example, granting the right to be absent for a few hours is usually the authority of each unit manager in the organization; the decision to adopt a flex-time system, however, is undoubtedly an executive decision. This illuminates the significance of decisions made at the executive level, to which traditional control systems have devoted only minimal attention. Control has typically 'preferred' to concentrate on the lower levels, where comparison and evaluation is relatively simple, and has neglected the higher ranks, where control is complex.

A familiar issue in management literature focuses on the examination of the quality of decisions. It is, however, the decision making process that should be controlled. Even those who contend that the true test of a decision lies in its outcome, would have to agree that the better the decision making process, the better its results and implementation are likely to be. Following this logic, the control system faces a pragmatic question: What should be the focus of the examination of the decision making process, so that control is not limited to an evaluation of results? This question is answered in the section that follows.

Critical factors in the decision making process

In light of what has been said thus far, particular note should be made of several components which are essential for you to consider in evaluating the decision making process.

Information is a critical factor in decision making: on its basis the deliberators are expected to arrive at a conclusion. If an organization wants its staff to make rational decisions, it must ensure the existence of relevant and reliable data. Evaluation of the information inventory and examination of its reliability also serve as the starting point for many other activities. The best and most sophisticated analysis can never be more reliable than the data on which it is based. There is much wisdom in the mnemonic used in the computer industry 'GIGO'; garbage in -- garbage out!

A concrete example of how seemingly reliable data proved none too useful, can be seen in the experience of one insurance company. A computer based telephone system kept track of all calls coming into the company. The system was able to calculate how many callers were kept waiting, listening to a recorded announcement, before actually being answered by an operator. In addition, records were kept on the number of callers that hung up before ever talking with an operator, and how long the average wait was for these 'abandoned' calls. Managers determined standards of service and staffing levels by using the average waiting time, and the average abandon rate, for a given period.

Despite the use of a computerized data base, staffing patterns were not working out properly. It was not until the managers analyzed *hourly* statistics that the problem was recognized. The averages that had been used for decision making included data from evenings and weekends, when the company was closed. During these times, 'abandoned' calls did not represent poor service, because a brief recording had been instructing customers to hang up and call back during regular business hours.

The knowledge, willingness, and skill of the decision maker are central to the process. Creative thinking, intellect, practical experience, and the ability to make logical analyses, are all relevant to decision making. Conversely, if the decision maker is unwilling to decide, or willing to decide but lacking the necessary skills to analyze and decide wisely, the quality of the decision is jeopardized.

The degree to which all legitimate interests have been expressed and considered must also be examined by the control system. Have various relevant viewpoints been examined? Is the conflict between differing approaches and considerations incorporated into the process? Are factors that don't fit 'overlooked' for the sake of convenience? Is a mediocre solution arrived at because of the dominance of an individual perspective? Are less-than-ideal solutions arrived at quickly, without searching for better answers?

Inputs that contradict each other are likely to lead to constructive conflict, which can make an important contribution to the process of decision making. Foregoing such consideration for the sake of speed, or in order to avoid friction, is liable to constitute the sacrifice of vital essentials for the sake of immediate, pragmatic convenience. Yet, it is clear that in many organizations, expedience plays a major role in decision making. This is opposed to the 'inconvenience' of introducing problematic inputs that lengthen the process.

Delays in decision making may be an indication of an unwillingness of the organization to deal with problems as they arise. We are all familiar with the common tendency to avoid dealing with problems, particularly those that are complex, difficult to solve, or controversial. Yet, problems are seldom solved by delaying their treatment.

Delay may be caused by a number of factors. It may be conscious, based on considerations such as conflict avoidance and 'keeping the peace'. It may, on the other hand, be a result of an unconscious fear of the outcome. In either case, however, delay in decision making can be viewed as a decision itself, subject to all the rigors involved in evaluating any decision making process.

How the problem is defined, depends to a great extent, on the approach adopted by the decision maker. The determination of who will deal with an issue is itself an important, preliminary decision, having considerable impact on the orientation of the solution.

It is generally preferable to spend more time on problem definition through group discussion, involving individuals from different disciplines, than to save time by assigning one person to define the problem. This is because the same problem can look quite different, depending on whether it is defined by an economist, an engineer, or a sociologist, and whether it is dealt with by an individual or multidisciplinary team. It is often the practice to assign an individual to propose a solution to a problem without taking into account the intended decision maker's personal-professional orientation. This inclination has an impact on the way in which the issue is treated.

In summary, control systems must recognize decision making as a critical organizational function and dedicate far more energy to the evaluation of this component. Since it is problematic, it has generally been avoided, even though its effect on the survival of the organization is clear. Our position is based on a recognition of the extreme importance of pre-occurrence intervention. Decision making is a process, which the control system should examine and improve. The better the decision making process in an organization, the higher the quality of its output.

8 Operations control

The operational function is responsible for planning, operation, and supervision of conversion processes, and the introduction of changes to improve these processes. The term 'conversion process' refers to the way in which the organization transforms various resources, such as materials and labor, into desired outputs. Conversion processes exist in all organizations, whether they provide services or products. In this chapter, and elsewhere in the book, the term 'product' refers to either a tangible item, such as an air conditioner, or an intangible one (typically service), such as an insurance policy, or public transportation.

The soaring success of Japanese manufacturing and that country's attention to operations, has increased everyone's awareness of the importance of the operational function, and particularly of operational strategy. Developments in this area include innovations such as the Just-In-Time (JIT) method, by which inventory is reduced to an absolute minimum, and quality circles, which foster the participation of all employees in generating improvements in the organization's methods.

The operational function is considered difficult to manage, particularly because it encompasses so many aspects, including demand forecasting, methods and processes, work measurement, scheduling of employees, equipment, and material, and quality assurance. It should be noted, however, that examination of the operational function began long ago; it was first introduced by Taylor at the beginning of the century. Operations, or production management, is a field covered extensively in the literature (see, for example, Cook and Russell, 1980; Hendrick and Moose, 1985; Gaither, 1984; Butta, 1985; Chase and Acquilano, 1989; Monks, 1987).

Although the field of operational control is not new, it is not sufficiently developed in some areas, especially in the application of integrated criteria. In this chapter we review the performance criteria generally accepted in operations management, with particular attention to the conversion process and issues of logistics. Although project management is considered an operational issue, it is not covered in this chapter since it requires special attention and will be covered in the following chapter.

Typical criteria

Although every aspect of operations has criteria specific to that area, a number of measures are relevant to all of them. These measures reflect quality, cost, timeliness, and operational capacity. A failure in any one of these crucial operational dimensions, can bring the organization to a complete collapse. For instance, an organization with low operations cost and high quality but which can not meet deadlines, is likely to loose both present and potential customers. Here we discuss the criteria on which operations control is based, followed by a review of the two common levels of measurement in this context: micro (the specific situation) and, macro (the general or big picture).

Quality

To ensure that both the transformation process and the product meet specifications, they are tested according to relevant quality criteria. Necessary changes are then introduced to reduce undesirable deviations. Typical quality criteria include the reject rate (the percentage of items that do not meet specifications and can not be used), the rate of customer returns, the rate of complaints, and the response time for repairs.

These quality criteria apply to almost all organizations, but the relative importance of each criterion to a particular organization will vary. Therefore, before examining the performance of the quality control system, it is important to be sure that the essential quality criteria have been selected.

The effectiveness of quality criteria can be evaluated by means of a cost-benefit analysis, where you compare the cost of conducting the quality test to the probable savings derived from improved quality. Savings would be generated from decreased rework rates, decreased returns, increased sales, etc. Those of you who will be involved in the development of quality control systems should be trained in statistics and computers, and should be familiar with the operational aspects in which the quality system is meant to operate.

Traditionally, quality control has been based on the assumption that deviations and defects are bound to occur in any operational system. Although this approach is strongly reinforced by actual results, it has been opposed in the last twenty years by the *zero-defect management philosophy*. This approach assumes that defects in quality can be avoided and that deviations are not inevitable.

Proponents of this argument hold that defects are the result of some lack of professional knowledge. Because this knowledge can be acquired, the defects can be prevented. Accordingly, this approach concentrates on an analysis of the cause of defects, with the ultimate goal of zero defects. This attitude is clearly expressed in a recent article in *Fortune* in which the co-director of the Berkeley Roundtable on International Economy, Stephen Cohen says, "I don't believe quality is any cultural secret. I think there are learnable things to do to achieve it."

Alexander Trowbridge, president of the National Association of Manufacturers and former Secretary of the Commerce, believes that since World War II, "We were operating to some degree on a philosophy of planned obsolescence. In that sort of world, quality takes a back seat. Ultimately we got hurt by it." Indeed, studies show a steady improvement in output quality in recent years. Once, a two percent reject rate was considered an acceptable level of quality. Today, the standard in the electronics industry, for example, is down to only small fractions of a percent. (For more on quality control, see, for instance, Gryna Juran, 1980; Shetty and Verman, 1985.)

Cost

It is accepted practice to measure the cost of operations in terms of *labor hours per unit* or *dollars per unit*. When determining relevant cost criteria, it is important to remember that the operations manager may have decisive influence over the use of labor hours through method changes or scheduling, but often does not influence the wage structure. Another consideration to be aware of when using these measures, is that cost per unit is highly influenced by other variables, such as material and equipment costs, and the operations manager is not the only one to have an impact on these.

Measuring cost in terms of labor hours is popular, in part, because of the availability of work measurement techniques. These techniques allow us to determine the standard time needed for each task, and in this way, serve as the basis for calculating standard cost. This figure is important not only for budgeting, but also for operations planning and control.

Both direct and indirect costs are of interest to the control system. Direct costs are associated with inputs which are directly involved in the production process. indirect costs are not directly traceable to the particular product. indirect costs include such things as management salaries, advertising, or research and development expenses. Yet is has become increasingly difficult to differentiate between direct and indirect activities.

Many organizations use the *percent of indirect cost* as a criterion for operations control. This rate varies among industries; the more sophisticated the industry, the higher the indirect costs tend to be. In high-tech industries, indirect costs are often 75% of total costs. This phenomenon presents a professional challenge that has yet to be met: the development of an effective control system for indirect activities. Here, the common techniques of work measurement are not as applicable, because much indirect work is not of a regular or routine nature.

Productivity criteria are also based on cost. All productivity criteria employ a ratio of output to input, where every input can be expressed in dollars. In examining productivity, it is essential to analyze alternative inputs to reduce costs and improve output. Using this approach, less efficient resources may be replaced by more efficient ones.

For example, a photocopy department uses three old copiers, operated by three employees. The cost in personnel, machines, materials, and other expenses, is 9 cents per copy. The same work can be performed with two modern photocopiers, operated by one-and-a-half employees, at a cost of 6 cents per copy. In this case, replacing of human resources with equipment, improved the unit productivity. Of course, this change involves transferring and training employees, issues which are discussed in Chapter 13 on Human Resources Control.

Timeliness

The criterion of timeliness impacts all organizational subsystems. The ability of an organization to perform work on time is an expression of its operational efficiency and its profitability. Failure to adhere to timetables reflects the inability of at least one unit in the organization to complete its work as planned. If the process requires the input of more than one unit, coordination among units, including timing of each unit's tasks, is necessary.

Performance delays by any unit means that work may arrive late at the next unit, leaving the employees there idle, and delaying completion of the operation as a whole. In order to reduce delays and organizational idle time, it has become a common practice for inventory to be held in front of each unit. This method, however, leads to enormous waste. A large inventory in process means that capital is tied up in stock. In addition, a network of work stations loaded with work in process can not respond quickly to new tasks. As you can see, delays in the conversion process are a crucial issue for every control system.

Recognition of this is one of the reasons for the world-wide interest in the Just-In-Time (JIT) approach developed in the Toyota factories in Japan. This approach to inventory concentrates on the element of timing. The main principle of this method is to have items available no sooner than actually needed for the production process. In this way, inventory levels are reduced to a minimum. This approach does not stand alone; it is part of an entire management philosophy, which also includes approaches mentioned earlier such as zero defects and employee involvement through quality circles.

As controllers, another important reason for concern with a failure to meet timetables is the resulting short-term loss to the organization's profitability. Most organizations have customers that make payments on delivery or upon completion of performance. Delays result in late payments which can lead to cash shortages and the need to rely on expensive loans. In addition, if an organization is to blame for delays in a customer's ability to complete a job, the organization may be subject to fines. In the long run, such delays harm an organization's reputation and can certainly lead to a loss of customers.

In summary, a slide in time generally leads to a slide in operations cost. It is important to develop an effective control system to deal with adherence to timetables. Such systems employ techniques and aides such as GANTT tables and PERT charts in which schedules and the inter-relationships between tasks are displayed visually, for ease in monitoring. Exhibit 8.1 illustrates how these charts are used.

Some organizations have employed controllers, called expediters, solely for the purpose of monitoring schedules and initiating corrective measures when slides in time are detected.

Capacity

The concept of operational *capacity refers to the maximum output that an organization is able to perform per unit of time* (hour, day, week), for given resources and methods. The following are some examples of capacity measures:

restaurant	number of diners per hour
clinic	number of treatments per day
supermarket	number of shoppers per day
refrigerator factory	number of units per shift

In some cases such basic capacity criteria are not sufficient, because of the variety of customers and products. For instance, a diner who orders a light snack differs from one who orders a full-course meal, and a plant that produces a variety of products can not base its evaluation on the capacity for one product only. In these cases, it is customary to use an integrated capacity criteria such as dollars. For example, the capacity to produce 50 million dollars of sales per year.

Capacity can also be measured in terms of labor hours per unit of time. For instance, the capacity of an engraving unit might be 600 work hours per month, that is, the department can complete various combinations of work, as long as the hours required do not exceed 600 per month.

Organizational performance depends on its ability to adjust its capacity to demand. This is particularly true of service organizations, which cannot store their products (services) during slack periods in preparation for times of greater demand. A walk-in health clinic which is staffed by five nurses, when the present demand creates work for only three, cannot ask the other two to perform treatments on patients whors have the tools to adjust capacity to demand. To illustrate: the production capacity of an automobile manufacturer was 8 million cars in a certain year. It was estimated that demand for next year would be only 7 million

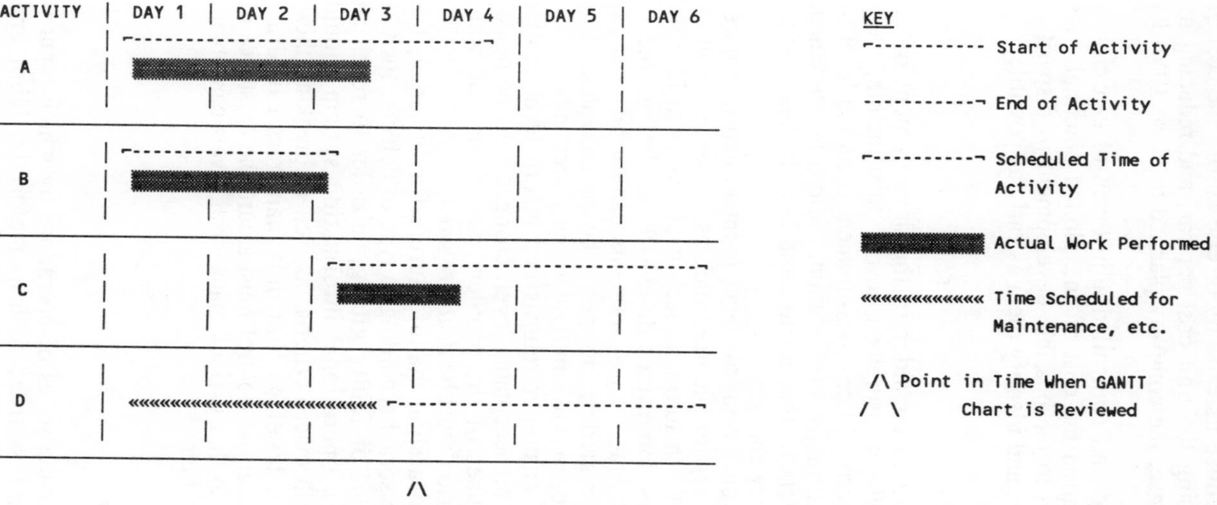

The following observations are made at the end of day 3:

- Activity A is behind schedule, as the shaded area does not reach as far as the dotted line.
- Activity B was completed on schedule.
- Activity C has advanced beyond schedule, as the shaded portion indicates that the work completed is past that which was expected for day 3.
- Activity D is behind schedule, as work has not yet begun.

Exhibit 8.1 GANTT chart

cars. The company had to reduce its capacity or else absorb the cost of the unused capacity, increasing the unit cost per car, and reducing its competitive ability. In response, the company planned to close 10 of its factories during the next year.

The process of planned and controlled adjustment of capacity to demand can save an organization the cost of unexploited potential. As controllers, you must be alert to the possible development of disparities between demand and capacity, and identify them as early as possible.

Micro and macro measures

An important factor for you to consider in the development of an operations control system is the measurement level. In principle, there are two levels, micro and macro. Micro measurement is on the level of specifics, for example at a particular work station. Micro measurement allows for detection of defects in that station and permits operational conclusions regarding necessary changes.

In contrast, measurement on the macro level is integrated in nature. Macro measures examine a bigger picture, such as a number of work stations together. Although the macro approach is also able to identify problems if they exist, it is sometimes done without being able to identify the specific cause. Macro measurements cannot be used for reaching specific conclusions regarding changes to be implemented. For this purpose, they must be broken down into micro measurements.

For example, the rate of customer returns is a macro level quality criterion. If the rate exceeds an acceptable level, changes must be made. In order to analyze the causes of the problem, and determine what changes are needed, the criterion must be *disaggregated.*

In the case of returns to a shoe manufacturer, for instance, the rejected merchandise must be sorted according to type of defects, such as weak seams, poor materials, or faulty gluing, in order to reach an operational conclusion. An operational information system should provide management with both macro criteria, as well as breaking these criteria down to the micro level so that unit managers can draw operational conclusions. Operations control must assure the existence of both levels of measurement, so that various managerial levels can obtain information that is relevant to them.

The transformation process

The transformation process is the series of operations by which input is changed into output, using resources such as materials, labor and equipment. Control of the process must address two major aspects: the process method and ongoing performance. *The process method* addresses the way in which the transformation is performed. It may take many forms, both technological and organizational.

Consider, for instance, a municipality that grants construction permits through a process involving 30 different stations. The controller must determine whether there is really a need for so many stations, as each one adds to both performance cost and response time. Similarly, a hospital controller would examine the policy of keeping patients overnight for surgery that could be performed on an out-patient basis. In another example, a controller must determine if a municipal garbage removal system should rely on city employees or on a subcontractor. It is clear, that for any transformation of inputs to outputs, alternative processes should be compared in order to ensure that the better choice is selected.

For instance, an organization provides lunch for 500 employees. The food preparation involves daily cooking and serving of the food by the organizational employees. Examination of this system and other alternatives has shown that this service could be provided using any of three alternative processes. These are: to maintain the present system; to institute the use of frozen foods; or the employ subcontractors.

For purposes of comparison, relevant performance criteria must be developed. Some of these will relate to objective aspects, some to subjective ones. In this case, for example, cost is an objective criterion, while the quality of food, the hygiene level, and the extent to which the organization is vulnerable to the delivery system, requires professional, subjective evaluation.

It is important to note that a controller who conducts such a comparison (objective and subjective) should not be expected to do so alone. The controller must obtain the assistance of professionals in fields relevant to the particular process.

Ongoing performance control examines the degree to which deviations arise in the transformation process, and also, the degree to which they are corrected before becoming serious. For instance, during the course of production in a bottling plant, the volume of liquid in the bottles is examined. Any unintentional change in this amount indicates a defect in the transformation process.

It may not be cost effective to perform examinations of this type on every item, but instead, at a certain frequency and randomly. Frequency describes not only how often the examinations are made, but also their intensity. For instance, it might be decided that for every 200 units produced (how often), 5 units must be thoroughly examined (intensity). The optimum frequency is based on a cost-benefit analysis using information regarding the cumulative damage likely to occur between examinations. The more frequent the examinations, the smaller the number of defective units, but the higher the cost of control.

In random control, the precise date of examination is not known ahead of time. This guarantees that the observed results will be as reliable as possible, because the person performing the operation will not know when the process will be evaluated. Random control is not necessary in cases of automated processes, since there would be no change in behavior patterns occurring as a result of being evaluated. In fact, automated processes can be tested at very regular intervals. For example. a machine might perform tests on a sample of 10 units after every predetermined batch size of 200 units.

Control charts are a widely accepted instrument for documentation and analysis of processes. These tools help the control system to monitor performance and deviations graphically and analytically. This makes it easier to spot deviations before they become critical. A typical control chart is demonstrated in Exhibit 8.2

Components of the transformation process

Technology

The level of technological sophistication of an organization has considerable affect on its control process. Technology refers to the type of equipment and know-how the organiza-tion uses in the transformation process: the more automated the equipment, the more technologically sophisticated the organization.

There is a high correlation between technological sophistication, the use of computers, and control. This is so since the interaction of a computer with work stations can also be used for *automated control.* For instance, the output of a work station, be it the transactions of a bank teller, or the production of an assembly line, can be measured automatically. High technology makes it possible *to incorporate the control system into the transformation process* and to ensure that it does not interrupt the functioning of the system in the same way that human control does.

The lower the technological sophistication of the transformation process, the more common is the use of personal or manual control. This makes effective control more difficult, as employees and middle managers frequently do not perceive control as an essential part of the ongoing functioning of the organization. For example, if a temporary shortage of employees arises, managers may be forced to transfer some controllers to operations. This may lighten the work load, but the quality of performance is liable to decline. The likelihood of deterioration of control diminishes as the level of technological sophistication increases, and as control becomes an integral part of the transformation process.

Inputs

Typical inputs in the transformation process are materials, know-how, human resources, buildings, and energy. Control of inputs is carried out on two levels: separate control for each input, and control of the integration of all inputs.

Exhibit 8.2
A quality control chart for percent of defects

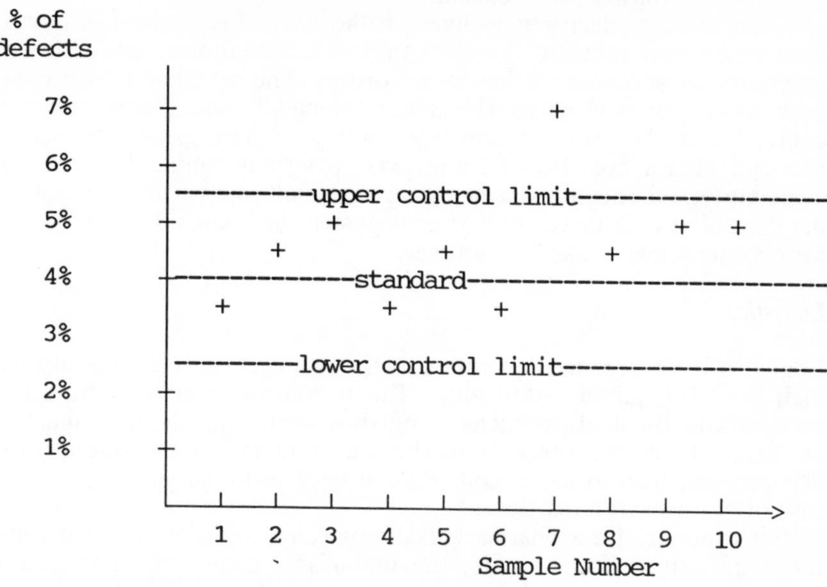

Control of each input examines whether the correct input is being used, and, if so, if the use is effective. For example, as a controller, you would ask, "Are we using the appropriate raw materials in this process?" and, if so, "What quantity is being used for each unit produced?" Similarly, you would ask whether suitable employees were assigned to a task and whether these employees were investing a reasonable amount of time in performing their work.

The transformation process can be performed using different combinations of inputs which affect the cost but do not change the nature of the final product. Because different decisions lead to different expenses, control should carefully examine the selection of resources. The following are a few typical examples of choices regarding use of human resources that might be confronted:

* using overtime,
* adding a second shift,
* hiring temporary employees,
* recruiting new employees, or,
* subcontracting.

The organization may prefer a leveling strategy, which employs a permanent staff, and produces an accumulation of inventory in times of low demand. This supplies employees with work during slack times and enables the organization to respond to demand in peak periods. An alternative approach to of the use of inputs would be to employ a minimal permanent staff and add overtime hours, part time workers, or a subcontractor during peak demand.

Other resource decisions include whether to rent equipment or buy it, how much raw material to keep in stock, whether to produce for inventory or according to customer orders, and whether to use coal, solar energy, or electricity. The choice among all these alternatives is an expression of the resources and input policy of the organization, which incorporates a cost-benefit analysis, pragmatic considerations of availability and feasibility, and managerial philosophy. It is the job of the control system to verify that management has policies and practices for choosing how to use its resources.

Logistics

Logistics in an organization refers to the management of materials and their flow to required destinations. This includes all materials, from raw materials to finished products. Logistics deals with the movement of materials from the supplier to the warehouses, to the operational departments, then to the customers, and back to the organization in the case of customer returns.

For example, for a pharmaceutical company, logistics would involve the acquisition of chemicals, the manufacture of medications, the packaging of products and finally the transport of the finished product to direct customers or to distributors. Exhibit 8.3 illustrates this schematically, indicating the relationship between the activities and the relevant information. Control is meant to examine this relationship as well as the integration of the logistics function in the organization's operations.

Logistics involves many areas in the operations of an organization and therefore, effective logistics is measured by means of an integrated criterion for all areas. An integrated criterion commonly used for logistics measurement is the time lapse between the acquisition of raw materials and the delivery of the finished product to the customer. Control must ensure that every area functions efficiently, and that they interact with each other effectively. Some of the areas noted in Exhibit 8.3, such as purchasing and inventory, are dealt with in other chapters. Here we deal mainly with distribution systems, which deal with the flow of materials or finished products to the customers and their warehouses. Distribution is critical to the organization, both as a consumer and as a supplier.

Management control must view distribution as an essential operational and economic factor. Typical performance criteria for evaluation of distribution systems are cost, response time, and quality of product service. The following list gives examples of decisions that must be made with regard to distribution:

* Is a single central warehouse preferable to several small ones?
* Where should the various warehouses be located?

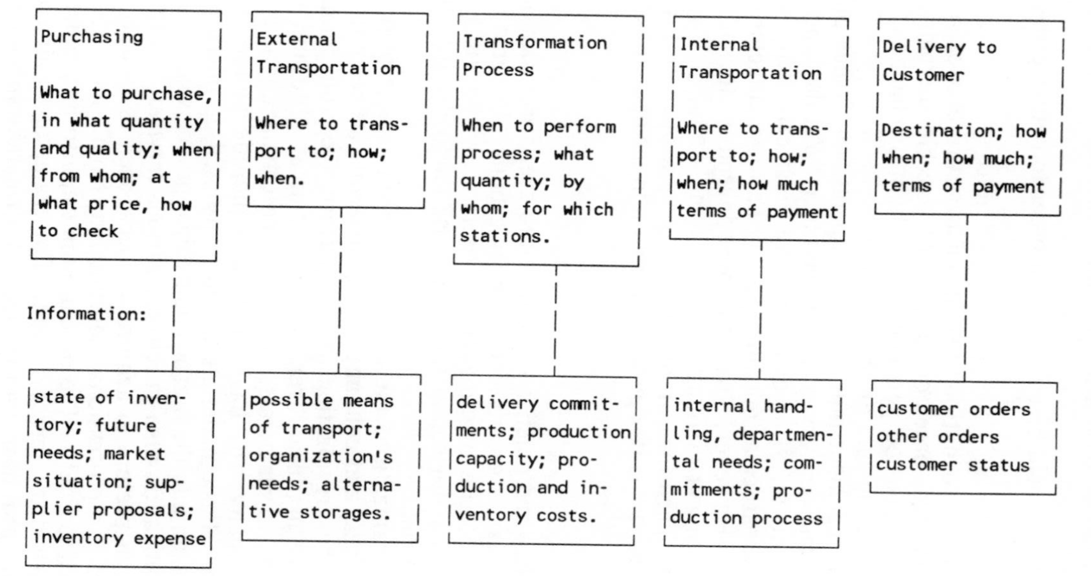
Activity:
Purchasing
What to purchase, in what quantity and quality; when from whom; at what price, how to check
External Transportation
Where to transport to; how; when.
Transformation Process
When to perform process; what quantity; by whom; for which stations.
Internal Transportation
Where to transport to; how; when; how much terms of payment
Delivery to Customer
Destination; how when; how much; terms of payment
Information:
state of inventory; future needs; market situation; supplier proposals; inventory expense
possible means of transport; organization's needs; alternative storages.
delivery commitments; production capacity; production and inventory costs.
internal handling, departmental needs; commitments; production process
customer orders
other orders
customer status

Exhibit 8.3 The relationship between activities and logistic information

* Should materials be transferred by truck, trains, plane, conveyor, pipes or some combination of these?
* Should a large vehicle distribute to a number of customers, or should there be several smaller vehicles, each handling one customer?
* What shipments should be combined in order to gain a volume advantage?
* What orders should be combined in order to optimize the delivery system?

Control of the distribution system must ensure that each of these questions is answered, based on analysis of possible alternatives. This analysis must be repeated periodically, in light of changes that might alter the relative advantages of an alternative.

Logistics management must consider operational issues on the one hand, and flow and delivery issues on the other. Yet these perspectives are often in conflict. For example, the most efficient method of production for a particular operation, might be to manufacture items in large lot sizes. However, this may cause inventory stockpiling in the warehouse, making it difficult to move items around and increasing inventory costs. Therefore, from the point of view of control, the test of logistics effectiveness is its optimal integration in the operational system.

Purchasing

Purchasing policy and practice is important to every organization, but its relative weight varies greatly among organizations. In some cases, the very survival of the organization depends on the quality of its acquisitions, while, for some, this aspect has relatively little functional or economic impact.

For most organizations there are three main aspects of purchasing: materials, services, and equipment. By *materials* we refer to the basic materials that the organization uses to perform the production process. For a furniture manufacturer, wood, formica, glue and nails are examples of basic materials; for a service organization, such as an insurance company, the basic materials include paper, pens, and computer disks. Basic materials are normally used up in the process of transforming them into the organization's final products.

Every organization also purchases various *services*. In many cases the organization prefers to acquire services, such as security services, cleaning, food and professional consultation, from subcontractors who specialize in these fields. The organization can also hire subcontractors to perform parts of the process itself. For example, an air conditioner factory might purchase motors from a firm that specializes in the production of motors, or a medical laboratory might purchase computer services instead of setting up its own unit.

No single organization is capable of functioning completely independently. Most companies spend large portions of their income on materials and services purchased outside the organization. A study of a sample of industries reports that 57.6% of production costs are spent for purchase of materials and services from other parties (US Bureau of the Census, 1978). This demonstrates the strong influence of purchasing on the ability of the organization to function. If the purchasing department improves performance by, say, 10%, this could lead to a savings of 5.76% of the total expenses of the organization; a figure high enough to move an organization from failure into a success. The potential savings from increasing the efficiency of purchasing increases considerably if we add the cost of the *equipment* acquired by the organization, including machinery, computers, and conventional equipment, such as office furniture and copy machines.

In order to plan effective control of a purchasing system, the principles of its operation, and the critical points of the purchasing process must be recognized. Even though the purchasing function acquires a wide variety of products and services, there is a basic sequence common to most cases, comprised of the following elements:

* identification of need,
* transmission of information concerning need,
* choice of supplier,
* preparation of order,
* follow-up of order,
* receipt of order,
* examination of order,
* examination of invoice, and,
* closing of order.

In order to ensure that each of these elements is performed effectively, the purchasing function must maintain continuous contact with other functions in the organization. The method of communication between purchasing and the other parts of the organization depends on the size and nature of purchasing, in particular, the dependence of operations on purchasing. Imagine the difference in this relationship for an electronic components assembly plant or a debt collection office.

Despite technological differences among organizations, the purchasing process is generally based on two main stages: the *request for purchase* and *the purchase order*. The request for purchase is submitted by the user, and the purchase order is placed by the purchasing department with the supplier. In companies with computer systems, all relevant data can be stored in a single file, so that each organizational unit can examine parts of the file relevant to it. The only paper work that remains is between the organization and the supplier, who may not be connected to the organization's computer system.

Main aspects of purchasing control

Relevant information. The control system must ensure that the information on existing inventory in the organization is updated. Has the purchasing department gathered relevant information on the item or group of items, before making an order? For example, there may be items in stock that can be substituted for the item to be ordered, or items may be back ordered and alternative suppliers might need to be considered.

Order size. It is very important to determine the optimum order size. Many suppliers offer discounts for large orders, but the purchase of an order which is too large adds unnecessary expense. The purchasing department should aim to acquire items at the price set for large orders and at the same time maintain low inventory levels. This can be achieved in various ways. For example, it is possible to sign an annual contract for delivery of small orders throughout the year, or to group a number of similar items into a single order, so as to obtain the cost advantages of a large order.

Supply sources. The control system must pay particular attention to comparison of potential sources prior to choosing the supplier of an item. This comparison is based on three central criteria: *quality*, *cost*, and *adherence to timetables*. It is important to make periodic comparisons of suppliers, even if the organization has worked with one supplier for a long time. Regular examinations will ensure that the permanent supplier continues to make an effort to supply appropriate services. For this purpose, the organization must approach a number of suppliers, usually in the form of soliciting contract bids. Experience shows that if suppliers suspect that the decision has been made before the bid, most will not submit bids.

In many cases, an organization must choose between producing an item itself, or purchasing it from outside sources. In these cases, large organizations generally call for 'requests for proposals', in which one of the bidders is a department or subsidiary of the organization itself. This process helps to maintain the organization's competitive ability.

There are three main reasons for an organization to decide not to perform all necessary work itself:

* The organization lacks the ability to effectively perform in areas in which it does not have expertise.
* The organization strives for a situation in which a certain percentage of its work will be performed by subcontractors, so that, in an industry-wide recession, it can reduce volume without layoffs.
* By using subcontractors, the organization can match its operational capacity to seasonal changes and produce according to demand rather than for inventory.

A completely different situation is created when an organization purchases a product on cost-plus conditions. Under this arrangement, the cost is determined by the expenses of the supplier, plus an additional payment. This makes organizational control more difficult since there is no strong incentive for the supplier to produce the product or service at the lowest possible cost.

A common control instrument in such cases, particularly in the case of serial production, is the learning curve. Learning curve theory anticipates performance improvement over time, or as a function of the batch size. The purchaser and supplier agree on the expected level of improvement, and therefore, on a reduction in the price of the product over time. This approach motivates suppliers to improve performance even beyond that decided upon because they get to retain any additional savings. This approach enables both parties to benefit.

Inventory. Policy and planning regarding inventory (raw materials, works in process, and finished products) are critical to the organization, be it a manufacturing company or a service organization such as a hospital. In this respect, control has an extremely important role to play, particularly as a warning and prevention system.

The determination of inventory policies in an organization involves decisions regarding inventory levels. These decisions require a variety of information, such as the demand per item, length of time needed to acquire and to convert inputs, handling and storage costs.

It is important to note that effective inventory planning and control requires extensive knowledge of the field of inventory (see, for example, Volmann, 1984). The central task in inventory planning is to determine the optimal inventory strategy for each item. Maintaining larger quantities of inventory than is necessary, adds costs in the form of frozen capital. This can even reach the point where an organization may suffer cash flow problems and be forced to take out high-interest loans.

On the other hand, when inventory is too small, resources such as employees and equipment may remain idle, waiting for required parts to be produced or purchased. In addition, customer satisfaction declines and customers are lost as the ability to adhere to timetables drops. Both these examples apply to service organizations as well. Hospitals, contractors, and universities, must avoid both pitfalls in order to have an optimum inventory policy.

It is important to note that optimal inventory levels change with time. These changes are the result of factors such as changes in demand, new processing methods, or changes in materials costs. Therefore, inventory levels should be evaluated periodically and on an ongoing basis.

The ABC approach

The number of items for which an organization has to plan inventory strategy may reach many thousands; therefore, it is essential to determine which items are a priority. This approach to inventory planning is called the ABC policy, the 20/80 Law, or Pareto's Law. Pareto, a 19th to 20th century Italian economist, found that a small group of citizens, 20% of the population, controlled approximately 80% of the national capital. In addition, he found that a much larger group,

50% of the population, had influence over only 10% of the nation's wealth.

We are able to generalize from this finding, and to say that in every population there is a small group (Group A), whose importance regarding a certain phenomenon is of highest significance. Conversely, there is a large group (Group C), that has relatively little importance (see Exhibit 8.4).

Exhibit 8.4
Pareto's Law

Group	Percentage of Population	Relative Importance
A	20	80
B	30	10
C	50	10

Pareto's Law applies directly to inventory policy, and is extremely important in the practice of inventory control, although the percentages presented in the exhibit, of course, are not rigid. Because of the importance of this approach to control, we describe its application in detail.

In order to control the inventory system by using the ABC approach, a list of items is drawn up, indicating their costs and annual volume. On the basis of this information, total annual investment in every item, and its proportion of total annual costs of all items, is calculated. Group A represents those items for which the relative investment is highest, while Group C is comprised of those in which the investment is lowest. Items may belong to group A, even if their unit cost is very low. This would be true for inexpensive items used in large quantity (see the example in Exhibit 8.5).

Exhibit 8.5
Annual and relative costs of inventory items

Item Number	Cost per Unit	Annual Consumption	Annual Cost	Percentage of Annual Costs	Group
1	40	80	3,200	1.2	C
2	50	30	1,500	0.6	C
3	20	2,500	70,000	25.0	A
4	250	70	17,500	6.5	B
5	5	6,000	30,000	11.1	B
6	10,000	5	50,000	18.5	A
7	20	200	4,000	1.5	C
8	30	70	2,100	0.8	C
9	150	600	90,000	33.4	A
10	60	25	1,500	0.6	C
Total Annual Cost =			269,000	100.0	

The exhibit shows that the annual cost of the items belonging to Group A is 77.7%; of Group B, 17.6%; and of Group C, 4.7%. The grouping of the data is very important for determining inventory policy as well as for controlling inventory. Once this classification has taken place, more frequent monitoring of inventory for Group A items should occur, followed by initiation of inventory changes, when required. Group B items need less frequent monitoring, followed by group C, with the lowest frequency required.

A change in inventory policy for an item belonging to Group A may have a critical effect on the cash flow of the organization. For instance, changing the supplier for item 9, in Exhibit 8.5, to gain a 20% discount, would lead to a savings of 33.4 x 0.2, or 6.68% in materials cost. Savings of these proportions might determine the fate of the organization. Attention to Group A items is important not only in seeking less expensive vendors, but also in efforts to reduce inventory levels, shorten waiting time for items in inventory, introduce incentives for cutting down waste, and to seek less expensive replacements.

The opposite is true for items in Group C; decisions on these items is a routine job. The guiding principle is to maintain enough inventory for regular demand of items, preventing shortages. This does impose some additional expense, but the extra cost is relatively small. Using the data in Exhibit 8.5 again, an addition of even as much as 20% in inventory volume for Group C, increases overall cost of materials by only 4.7 x 0.2, or 0.94%.

As noted earlier, Pareto's Law is applicable to many situations and can assist control in analysis of other problems. Imagine a situation in which a proposal was made to purchase land for construction of an additional warehouse, since the existing facility was filled. An analysis of inventory volume however, showed that a large percentage of space was occupied by a small number of items. Further examination showed that it was simple to reduce the level of inventory of a few items by ordering them more frequently, thereby making room for other items, and making an additional warehouse unnecessary.

Decisions related to inventory are generally quantitative in nature; how much to order and when to order. Mathematical models are often used for determining the preferred strategy. The control system must examine whether the best model is being used, as models differ in their effectiveness depending on the circumstances. (For some of the models typically used in inventory management, see, for instance, McLeavey, 1985; Tersine, 1982; Hax, 1984.) Another important aspect that control should evaluate is the accuracy of the values used by the models; using the proper model with wrong values for the parameters, will inevitably generate faulty results.

Just-In-Time approach

Organizations have been motivated to adopt the use of the Just-In-Time (JIT) approach because of the significant cost of maintaining inventory levels. With JIT, the ultimate objective of operations management is to have a situation in which an item reaches the work station only at the moment it becomes needed. Control of inventory flow and measures ensuring that each item reaches its destination only shortly before it is required, lead to a significant reduction of inventory cost and an increased demand for high quality inventory, either raw materials, parts, or finished products.

Use of the JIT approach requires a focus on the reduction of set up costs to the point that, in theory, it becomes worthwhile to produce entirely for demand, even if that means producing only one item per 'batch'. In this scenario, no inventory is accumulated at all. If management adopts a JIT policy, a significant task for the control system, is to ensure that the relevant subsystems are properly coordinated, and that possible failures are detected and corrected.

Modern management theory recognizes high inventory levels as a cover up for lack of managerial ability. Therefore, as inventory levels are reduced, problems are revealed. Since the JIT approach means controlled reduction of inventory, it requires a thorough examination of the problems that are revealed, careful attention to their correction, and continued reduction in inventory. Implementation of this approach requires a built-in control system, one that can ensure that diagnostic and corrective mechanisms function as soon as possible.

Another important aspect of inventory control is the physical storage of materials and products purchased or produced by the organization. The administrative aspect of this issue is the documentation of each item; its place of origin, its movement, and its destination. The inability to locate an existing item causes a double loss: purchasing cost of the item and interruption of work flow.

A well-managed inventory system is characterized by minimal discrepancy between the quantity of items on record and the actual quantity. This disparity, which is also called 'the shrinkage factor', is sensitive to the number of employees or customers with access to items. Organizations such as supermarkets maintain a standard for the shrinkage factor, for example, one half of one percent. Control over the shrinkage factor in such situations often involves rewards for employees when actual inventory shrinkage falls below the predetermined value.

In order to determine the rate of inventory shrinkage, physical inventory count must be compared to records. It is customary in inventory counts to use employees whose regular job is not in the same department. Since counting takes a relatively long time, it should be conducted during periods in which activity and inventory are relatively low; these are generally after seasonal peaks and before stocking up for the next season. inventory count is costly and is also liable to interfere with the routine functioning of the organization. It is therefore appropriate to use different counting techniques for different items, in accordance with their importance (an ABC policy); more accurate techniques should be applied to the more important items.

A typical example of the need for frequent counting and strict control, can be seen in the handling of medication inventory in a hospital. All medications are kept locked, and those employees with access to the inventory are required to sign for the keys. Narcotics and other controlled substances are counted by two licensed employees at the beginning and end of every shift. When any medication is used, the name of the patient and the employee removing the drug is recorded. Additionally, if it is a narcotic that is used, a separate, running tally is kept for each controlled substance.

Control findings can frequently lead the organization to establish a separate storage system for certain types of items belonging to Group A, and those that depreciate quickly because of fragility or a high shrinkage factor. The dependence of operations management on the quality of inventory management makes it imperative that operations control give ongoing attention to the strategy, planning, and maintenance of inventory.

Equipment

The present era is characterized by the widespread use of sophisticated machinery and equipment as a means of increasing productivity. This is made possible both as a result of the accumulation of technological know-how and because of a sharp decline in equipment price.

Technological know-how and automation were once exclusive features of the manufacturing industry, but since the 1950s, service organizations have joined this 'revolution'. For example, while banking transactions in the 1950s were all handled by tellers, at the end of the 1980s, more than 40% of money transactions in the U.S. are being performed by automatic money machines. The massive penetration of technology in organizations requires high quality control instruments because of the increasing dependence of organizations on this equipment. Thus, it is extremely important that the control system develop criteria for evaluation of equipment quality, productivity, utilization, and compatibility.

Machine production capacity represents the potential output of the machine when used by a skilled operator, and is often noted on the machine specifications. The actual output depends both on characteristics of the particular machine and the operator. Machine characteristics change over time, mainly as a result of wear. Nevertheless, it is possible to influence the rate of wear through appropriate maintenance policy, encompassing both preventive maintenance and repairs. For example, a regular 10,000-mile tune-up is preventive maintenance, while servicing required because of damage is considered breakage maintenance. In many cases, an equipment failure results from poor preventive maintenance; thus control of the maintenance strategy is very important.

The importance of maintenance control, however, changes in direct relation to the potential damage which would result from a malfunction. For example, control of airplane maintenance must be very strict because the results of a malfunction are potentially so enormous. This is not true, however, for a photocopy machine, where the risk to life is negligible.

A low level of preventive maintenance increases the risk of equipment failure. Similarly, an investment in preventive maintenance reduces failures of equipment. However, this does not mean that an investment in preventive maintenance is always more beneficial than a policy of breakage maintenance. Exhibit 8.6 illustrates that the marginal impact of investment in maintenance on the equipment failure rate is declining. In order to determine the optimal maintenance policy, the benefit from reducing failures must be compared to the cost of the preventive maintenance necessary for such reduction.

Equipment utilization refers to the time that equipment is used, relative to maximum potential time. For instance, a photocopy machine can produce 180 copies per hour. In a normal eight hour day, the machine can produce, 180 x 8, or 1,440 copies. In a particular company, the machine makes 500 copies per day; the utilization of the machine is therefore 34.7%, (500/1440). The greater the utilization, the less expensive its operation, as its purchasing cost and other fixed costs are then divided among a larger number of items.

Exhibit 8.6
Relationship between investment in preventive maintenance and rate of equipment failures

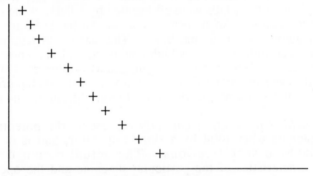

Imagine that your company is interested in reducing its operations costs. You realize that you must increase your company's utilization of its resources, up to an *optimum* level. Optimum equipment utilization is not necessarily synonymous with maximum utilization. A level of equipment utilization that is too high, can result in a decline in the level of service either to other sections of your organization, or to your customers. This does not seem obvious at first, but becomes clear quickly. High utilization means that equipment is in operation most of the time. This situation will mean that frequently your customers (or inventory) will have to wait in line for equipment to become available before they can be serviced.

An additional service factor to consider, is downtime. Maximum equipment utilization causes machines to wear faster, and increases the rate of equipment failures. For both reasons, an organization might decide on low utilization of some of its resources, so as to provide quicker service using these resources. Such a decision is, of course, affected by the cost of the resource relative to the cost resulting from waiting.

Low levels of equipment utilization can arise for a number of reasons that are not the result of optimum utilization decisions. These include such factors as; a lack of knowledge in using the equipment, faulty equipment, poor maintenance, or low demand relative to equipment capacity. The control system is interested in continuous examination of equipment utilization and must study the possibilities for improved utilization, particularly in periods of low activity.

Here is an example of an organizational change that contributed to increased equipment utilization. Two departments suffered from low utilization due mainly to equipment failures. Each department had a maintenance person who handled the department's equipment repairs. It was often the case that one of the departments would have a number of failures at one time. As a result, the equipment in that department waited to be repaired, while the maintenance person completed the other repairs. This took place often during periods when the maintenance person in the other department had no work to do.

A change was introduced so that the two maintenance people formed a repair team to serve both departments. This new organizational set-up, an outcome of control involvement in equipment utilization, led to a significant improvement in utilization in both departments.

Equipment reliability examines the frequency of equipment failures. Mean time between failures (MTBF) is a widely used measure in the examination of equipment reliability. To demonstrate the results of this kind of control, we use the performance of Automatic Teller Machines (ATM). A large bank, which owned 500 ATMs, instituted a special control system in response to a high failure rate among these machines. The criterion of average number of transactions between failures was used to represent the reliability of the ATM. The first set of measurements showed that, on average, there was one failure after every 3250 transactions (the results of the control records are illustrated in Exhibit 8.7).

During the 13-month period shown, the number of transactions between failures increased from 3250 to 7900. In other words, the frequency of failures dropped to less than one-half of the original rate. This was the result of identifying the most frequent sources of failure, and introducing changes to prevent them. For example the problem of customers using folded bills, was easily minimized by posting clear instructions explaining the way that bills should be fed.

Exhibit 8.7
Data for mean time between failures average
number of transactions between failures

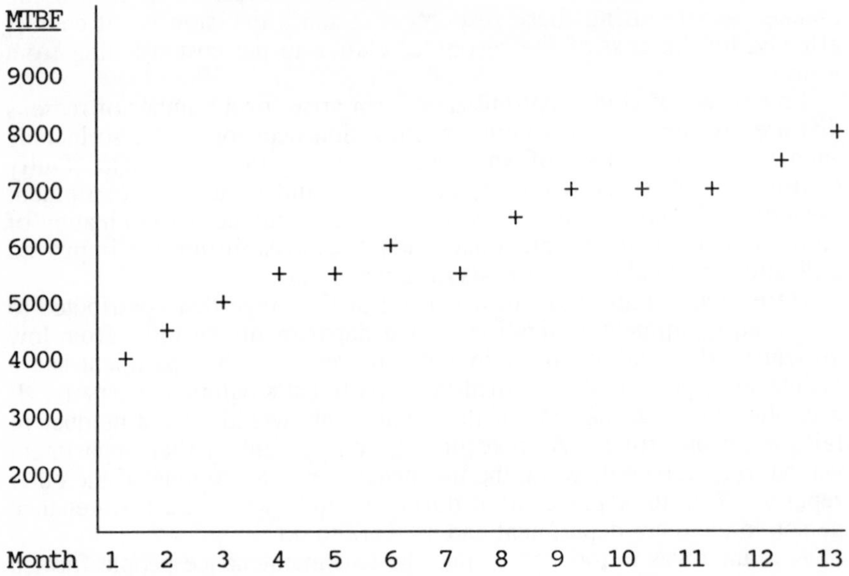

Equipment compatibility is a measure of the ability to integrate a given piece of equipment into other equipment systems so that they will function properly. This factor is becoming increasingly important as technology is growing more complex. Often an organization purchases one brand of equipment as well as items from other manufacturers, with the intention of combining them in a single system. This is particularly common with computers and communications equipment. In such cases, it is imperative that all the equipment purchased, meet certain standards, that enable it to function with other pieces in the system.

As a result of the growing importance of standardization of automatic equipment, various public organizations such as the National Bureau of Standards, have been established. These agencies are playing an increasingly important role. Their purpose is to formulate requirements for equipment specifications that will make it possible to integrate items manufactured by different companies.

The role of the control system with respect to equipment compatibility is seen in its involvement in the design of a purchasing policy and in planning. Control must ensure that organizational plans for the technological infrastructure (foundation) and compatibility of purchased equipment are taken into account when new purchases are made. Control should also be involved in evaluating the compatibility of the equipment to the personnel operating it. Characteristics of the equipment often dictate the way in which it is to be operated; some may require skilled personnel, while others may need only basic knowledge.

Human resources

Human resources are vital to the survival of an organization, and the quality of its functioning. Because of its importance and complexity, this topic is dealt with separately in Chapter 13, Human Resources Control, and given special focus in Chapter 14, Remunerations and Incentives. Here, human resources are discussed from the perspective of operations management, as one of the basic inputs in the transformation process.

Employees constitute a crucial factor in determining the quality of the process. In many companies, they represent over one half of all costs. In service organizations such as banks and insurance companies, the cost of labor may be as much as 75% of all expenses. The effectiveness of personnel functioning therefore, has a decisive effect on organizational performance, and human resources control is imperative to its survival.

The following example illustrates the influence of human resources control on organizational performance. In 1978, a law was enacted in the United States, requiring the development of performance-based rewards systems in the social security agencies. As a first step in this direction, a traditional control system was developed. This included evaluation through performance criteria such as the number of days between submission and completion of claims, and the rate of claims requiring more than 30 days to process. As soon as control-related methods were initiated, the claim processing time decreased, both because of operational improvements and employee awareness.

Below, we list a number of criteria that are widely accepted as essential to human resources control.

Utilization is the percentage of time during which an employee performs tasks that are part of his job. This may be measured by means of a multi-observation sample spread over a given period of time. The controller records the number of times a job related activity is observed, and this data is used to calculate the proportion of total time spent in each activity. An example of results of this kind of sample is shown in Exhibit 8.8 for employees in an assembly department.

The exhibit indicates that employee utilization is 64.3 + 9.8, or 74.1%. Potential utilization of employees depends upon the nature of their work. While an accepted utilization rate for office work is 90%, utilization for work that requires heavy physical effort may be 80% or less, because of the need for frequent breaks. Optimal utilization can be estimated by using tables indicating the percentage of time required for breaks as a function of the nature of the work. Organizations can achieve optimal utilization by motivating their employees to improve performance and by organizing logistics to support continuous work, reducing unnecessary delays and idle time.

Exhibit 8.8
Human resource utilization percent of time spent in activities for assembly employees

Type of activity	Operation	Percentage
Direct work	assembly	22.3
	welding	10.6
	soldering	31.4
		64.3
Indirect work	training	3.0
	assistance	4.8
	control	2.0
		9.8
Non-work	shortage of materials	8.4
	absenteeism	12.3
	smoking and others	1.2
	private activities	4.0
		25.9

Efficiency in use of human resources is an expression of the relationship between the level of expectations regarding performance and actual performance. For example, if standard output per work day is 80 units and an employee produces 88 units, the employee's efficiency is 110% (88/80). Similarly, if 60 hours are allocated for a given task, and an employee completes the task in 80 hours, the efficiency is only 75% (60/80).

A situation may arise in which an employee completes a task at an efficiency rate which is high, but at a low utilization rate. Let us give an example of such a situation. Assume a standard of 80 units per employee per 8 hour day. Imagine an employee who produces 88 units, but is involved in work related activities only 5.5 hours each day. This worker is producing at a daily rate of 110% efficiency, but his daily utilization is only 68.75% (5.5/8.0).

If you were to be confronted with a case in which an employee was able to perform 10% above standard, despite low utilization, you would most likely find one of two causes. First, the situation might be the result of loose standards, in which the standards are significantly lower than what is feasible. The second possibility is that the employee is so skilled, that he is capable of performing the work in much less time than the standard time. A full examination of these factors would necessarily include an evaluation of the quality of output, as high efficiency combined with low utilization can certainly result in faulty products.

Absenteeism measures the percentage of days that an employee is absent from work. In this section we deal with absenteeism from the point of view of operations only. Absenteeism causes longer waiting time for customers because of delays in completing work. Absenteeism leads to a lack of work in stations that follow the station where an employee is absent, causing additional delays in processing. This situation can seriously affect service and damage the organization's reputation. If only 3 out of 5 tellers arrive for work in a branch bank, it is reasonable to assume that a portion of the bank's customers will be dissatisfied with the service they receive.

It is customary to distinguish between planned and unplanned absences; most problems arise from the latter. Some organizations allow for a 'norm' of 6 to 12 unplanned absences per employee per year, even though the frequency of real illness is only a few days per year. Absenteeism is also handled in Chapter 13, however, we briefly mention four areas that are particularly significant to operations control:

a. Control of absenteeism requires a reliable, updated system of records, tracking individuals as well as departments.
b. Systematic analysis of absences and patterns, as well as follow-up, including frequency of causes, is essential.

c. Each organization should have a contingency plan for unexpected shortages of personnel.

d. Control of absenteeism should take into account all costs to the system, including equipment shutdown, material loss, loss of customers and income, and damage to the organization's reputation.

Occupational flexibility, or cross-training of employees, is measured by the percentage of employees who are capable of performing jobs other than their main job. Exhibit 8.9 illustrates job flexibility in an insurance company claims department.

Exhibit 8.9
Rates of occupational flexibility of employees

Main job	Secondary job A	B	C	D
A	100	15	0	20
B	100	100	15	0
C	0	0	100	0
D	15	0	25	100

The exhibit shows that 15% of those employed in Job A are cross-trained to fulfill Job B as well, while 100% of those employed in Job B can also do Job A. This is because proper functioning in Job B requires that the employee knows Job A, as well. In contrast, none of those employed in Job A is capable of performing Job C. Control should examine the implications of this situation, particularly in terms of limitations on job rotation as a method of coping with absences or changes in operational needs.

Improvement rate refers to rate of improvement in performance measures defined as essential. Improvement may result from technological and organizational factors, or it may arise from actions initiated by the organization's employees. Employees' ideas frequently account for improvements such as changes in work processes or product design.

Performance improvement has gained widespread attention, and is expressed through the use of learning curves. Learning curve theory assumes that individuals and organizations have the potential to improve performance over time as a result of practice, experience, and improvements in operations. These improvement rates can then be predicted for the purpose of performance evaluation.

Organizations in intensive competition, whose survival depends upon improvement, often apply the concept of improvement rates to all criteria. An example of this approach is illustrated by the case of a troubled restaurant chain, which has decided to improve performance by a fixed monthly rate, in three areas:

* growth in sales by 4%;
* reduction in food expenses by 5%;
* Reduction in use of overtime by 20%.

The control system would be interested in management's decision to execute the plan, including the specific improvement rates selected, and of course, in follow-up of the actual improvement.

Use of subcontractors is a very important element of organizational operations today. It allows considerable flexibility in the organization's functioning, reducing dependence on permanent staff, and the risk of high personnel cost when organizational activity is reduced due to market conditions. A decline in an organization's activity requires cut-backs in inputs; this is particularly difficult if operations rely heavily on permanent staff. On the other hand, operations which are performed by subcontractors can be reduced with relatively short notice.

Operational changes that alter requirements for human resources are easier to make with subcontractors working on short-term contracts than with permanent employees. For instance, a change in mail distribution to central neighborhood mailboxes instead of house to house distribution, considerably reduces the need for letter carriers. Post office employees would be likely to oppose such a change because they would feel that it would jeopardize their permanent jobs.

The use of subcontractors also helps achieve effective control in other ways. Subcontractors know that they can be replaced easily if they do not respond to the job requirements. Many municipalities have developed a combination of permanent staff and subcontractors, for activities such as garbage collection and gardening. This combination has many advantages, as the city can enjoy the relative benefits of both arrangements.

There are however, two major disadvantages inherent in reliance on subcontractors. An organization relying heavily on subcontracting may develop an overdependence on external parties which do not share the organization's interests. In addition, it is usually difficult to ask a subcontractor to perform jobs that do not exactly match the tasks agreed upon, and therefore a certain degree of flexibility is lost.

Determining the proportion of work to be assigned to subcontractors is a strategic decision of utmost importance. The central variables that should be considered in this respect are:

* the difference in cost between permanent staff and the subcontractor's services;
* the difference in technology between the organization and the subcontractor;
* special needs that the subcontractor can supply;
* changes in operations that would be difficult for the organization's personnel to make;
* the number of subcontractors that can compete for the assignment.

Control should continuously examine whether the optimal composition of human resources has been determined according to these variables.

9 Project control

Every organization, manufacturing or service, carries out projects. A project is a one-time operation that encompasses a sequence of activities with a defined beginning and end. The activities are carried out in a given order, determined by technological and logistical considerations. Examples cover a wide spectrum; upgrading a computer system, remodeling an office, constructing a building, moving to a new location, organizing elections, producing a new product, or offering a new service.

You can see what these have in common; each involves a single objective. Project management is aimed at an objective. Yet despite the fact that projects involve one-time operations, the operation might be repeated at another location or time. A hospital could upgrade the computer system in patient accounts and then later in purchasing. An electronics manufacturer might introduce a new product this year and another one next.

In recent decades, project management and control has gained increased attention at all levels. As projects have become more costly, and competition has intensified, project delays and the costs associated with them, can be devastating. The damage caused by poor project management may be beyond the organization's ability to recover. For example, an article on the downfall of Wang Computers in the late 1980's, attributes the situation, in part, to losses involving overly ambitious time schedules and new products which were not carefully planned (*Boston Globe*, 11/27/89).

Planning and execution of projects requires sensitive control, because the time frame for identifying and correcting errors is relatively short.

In this chapter we address issues applicable to control of project management in many areas. We will cover: criteria for control; project components and integration; organizational structure of projects; one-time projects; batch projects; and research and development projects.

Criteria for control

Three criteria are crucial in project control: time, cost, and quality.

The time schedule refers to the completion of a project by a predetermined date. Control must check the timetable at intermediate stages, in order to assure that the it is progressing as planned. Despite all the measures taken to meet schedules, you are all familiar with cases of 'sliding' during project performance. Projects often take more time than planned. Delays typically arise from poor planning, unanticipated breakdowns, and an ineffective control system that fails to detect and correct problems in time.

Project cost represents the total capital invested in completing a project, including all types of resources. The *Life Cycle Cost* approach (LCC), is an integrated way of calculating project cost. Using this method, all expenses, from conceptual development to delivery to the user, are added together. In this way, an organization might choose an alternative that is more expensive during production, but less expensive to maintain, because its LCC is lower.

Quite frequently there is a budgetary slide, a gap between the planned budget for a project and its final cost. Baker and Dalmer (1974) note that project expenditures exceeding double the original budget are not unusual. Their survey of 450 project budget officers revealed that the most common reasons for incorrect assessment of project costs were; lack of data, unclear definitions of project goals and characteristics, and lack of experienced personnel.

It has also been found that many government projects cost as much as triple the budget set for them (Goff, 1975). The extent of the slide from the planned project budget is usually related to the degree of uncertainty about the project. Models have been developed to assist managers in determining the required budget as a function of the preliminary budget and the level of uncertainty about project performance (see Martin et al., 1975).

Project control must ensure that there is a built-in mechanism throughout the life of the project so that slides in time and budget can be spotted early, and corrective actions can be taken. Slide indicators are demonstrated in the following widely accepted equations:

$$TD = \frac{BP-BS}{BS} \qquad (1)$$

$$BD = \frac{BP-AP}{BP} \quad (2)$$

where:

TD - slide in time
BD - slide in budget
BP - budget for work performed
BS - budget for all work that should have been performed to date
AP - actual cost of work performed

Example: The actual cost of work performed on a given project to date is AP = 100,000, while the budget for performing this work was BP = 120,000. A budget of BS = 160,000 was set for all the work that should have been completed to date. Using equations (1) and (2), calculation of the deviations yields the following results:

$$TD = \frac{120000-160000}{160000} = -.25$$

$$BD = \frac{120000-100000}{120000} = +.17$$

Since TD = -.25, the project is 25% behind in terms of time schedule. However, with BD = .17, the work completed has been performed with a budget savings of 17%.

Since the timing factor is critical, control must examine the coordination between the project schedule and timing of resources. A typical performance criterion in project control is: *the utilization of resources while meeting the project timetable*. Clearly, special attention must be paid to the implications of the time schedule on the total project cost.

The importance of timing is not unique to projects; it is relevant to the operation of every organization. However, different processes and outcomes require different techniques for effective time scheduling. For example, an organization that provides a service does not have precise information as to when its customers will arrive and what they will need when they get there. In the case of a project however, there is clear information about the activities to be performed and the desired time schedule.

Quality of performance is defined by specifications both for project inputs and for the final product or service. Sometimes quality can be measured quantitatively; in these cases deviations between actual and desired performance can be measured. In other cases the definitions are qualitative only, stated in terms of whether or not the specifications are met. Typical objectives in project quality control are; to determine whether the project is meeting specifications at particular time intervals, and, to recognize deviations in the processes that would lead to quality concerns.

Project components and their integration

For efficient planning, a project must be divided into its major work areas, with each work area divided into operations. It is essential to specify the order in which the operations are to be performed. For instance, it is impossible to install counter tops in a new office before the cabinets have been installed, and it is impossible to polish a part before the rough processing has been completed.

PERT networks

The more complex an operation, the more difficult it is to determine the order of its components and their integration in the project. This is one of the central issues in project control. There are various methods for describing the network of relations and sequence of operations. One of the most widely accepted methods is the PERT network (Program Evaluation and Review Technique).

Exhibit 9.1, is an example of the kind of PERT diagram that is frequently used in operations planning and control. It illustrates the sequential relationship between activities A,B,C,D,E and F. The number next to each letter denotes the time required to perform the activity, and the numbers within the circles denote the events. For example, Event 2 represents the completion of Activity A and the possible beginning of Activities B and C. The performance time required for Activity C is 2 units of time (for example, 2 days). Activity F may start only after completion of Activities D and E (event 5). Project completion time is determined by its longest path. In this case the longest path is A,B,D,F with time length of 19. The longest path is referred to as 'the critical path'. For more information on the use of PERT, see classical books on the subject such as Kerzner, *Project Management*, Third Edition, Van Nostrand Reinold, 1989.

Exhibit 9.1
A PERT network

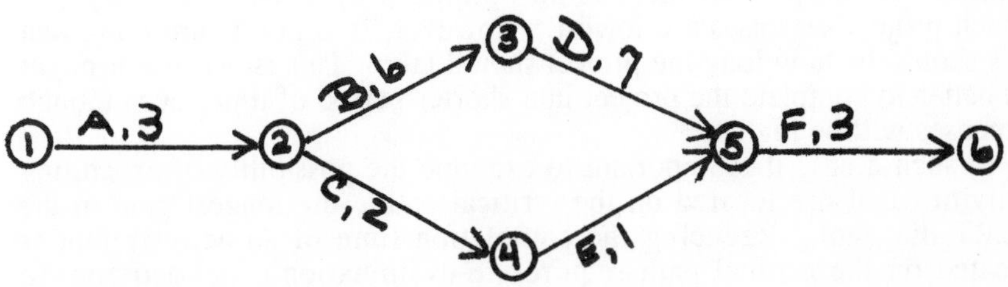

Resources are required to perform activities. In order to determine the optimum way to manage the project, the resources required for each activity must be established, after several resource combinations are evaluated. In addition, this assessment will allow you to determine the total resources needed and when they will be required. The decision about resources is, among other things, an outcome of resources policy and availability. These influence, and are influenced by, the sequence and timing of all the project activities. Control must assure that alternatives and interactions have been examined.

Just as there is a relationship between timing and resources, there is also a relationship between the time it takes to perform a project and its cost. The relationship between the cost components and project duration is shown in Exhibit 9.2.

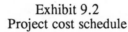

Exhibit 9.2
Project cost schedule

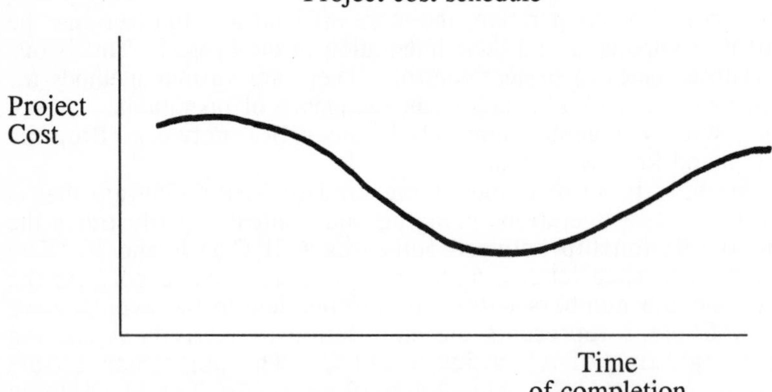

Indirect expenses are usually related to project administration, while direct expenses arise from the operational cost of activities directly related to the project. Loss of income may occur when project completion is delayed, resulting in lower profit or penalties.

Critical path method

The graph of expenses during the lifetime of the project depicted in Exhibit 9.2 shows that there is an optimal project period, 5 days, in which project expenses are lowest. However, it is not a sure thing that this should be how long the project should take. This is because it might be better to complete the project in a shorter period of time, even though expenses will be higher.

In such a case it is important to examine the possibility of expediting activities that are located on the 'critical path', the longest path in the PERT diagram. Reducing the completion time of an activity that is located on the critical path requires re-examination of all activities to identify which ones will be located on the critical path, or paths, after the change has been made. This type of examination has become very useful to the control function, and constitutes the basis for TIME-COST calculations.

Developing TIME-COST calculations requires some basic data, which is summarized in Exhibit 9.3. Using the data in the Exhibit, you can see that the time needed to complete Activity B under regular working conditions is 6 weeks, and the cost is $700,000. The activity can be completed in a shorter period of time, but it will cost an additional $100,000 for each week saved. Notice too, that it is impossible for the activity to take less than 4 weeks.

Under normal conditions, the cost of the project is $2,500,000, with a completion time of 10 weeks, since Activities A and D are on the critical path. It is these activities that would need to be shortened if the project completion time is to be reduced. In terms of cost, it is preferable to shorten Activity A rather than D, since it costs $50,000 to save a week on A, but $200,000 on D. It is possible to continue with this kind of calculation until the completion-time constraint does not allow further reduction. Remember, with each change in activity time, the critical path must be reassessed. (For further discussion of project costing, see Roman, 1986.)

Work breakdown structure

Project control should assist in dividing the project into a hierarchy of work units, or a work breakdown structure (WBS). 'Units' may be products, data, or services. They are defined by the ability to plan, perform and control them separately.

Exhibit 9.4 describes a WBS for an air defense system. The highest level, Level 1, represents the entire system. Level 2, consists of units that are subsystems of Level 1, and Level 3 includes the subsystems of Level 2. If necessary, and if possible, a fourth level may also be developed. For instance, with computer programs on the third level, a fourth level might divide them into types of programs.

According to the WBS approach, each work unit is assigned to a defined organizational unit, which is responsible for its execution. This requires the identification of organizational units that carry responsibility for defined work units. This is the *organizational breakdown structure*, or OBS. This model of reciprocal relations between WBS and OBS assists control in mapping the system, and serves as a point of departure for defining the organizational structure of a project.

Organizational project structure

A company that manufactures standard products requires a different organizational structure than one that is mainly involved in projects, such as a construction company, or even one that occasionally implements projects. Organizational structure has a significant impact on organizational performance. Control must be aware of structure alternatives

Activity in Weeks	Normal time of activity (thousands)	Normal cost of savings 1 week	Additional cost	Minimum completion time in weeks
A*	3	300	50	2
B	6	700	100	4
C	2	200	200	1
D*	7	800	200	3
E	1	400	—	1
F	3	100	150	2
Total		2500		

*Denotes activity is on critical path.

Exhibit 9.3 Data required for TIME-COST calculations

and see these as a function of the nature of the operations in general and of the specific projects in particular. Common organizational structures used for managing projects are the functional, matrix, and project-oriented structures.

Exhibit 9.4
WBS for an air defense system

Level 1	Level 2	Level 3
air defense	basic equipment	system assembly and integration sensors
		data processing
		computer programs
		data description
		peripherals
		training equipment (simulators)
		services (training programs, aids)
		structures (area, classes)
	system testing	test development
		examination of tests
		construction of simulator
		testing services
		testing equipment and structures

In the functional structure, every manager is responsible for a specific function in the organization, such as finance, marketing, production, engineering, or research and development. Considered the classic structure (Exhibit 9.5), it is designed mainly for routine work, and for short and simple projects. Such projects are integrated into the regular functioning of the organization, with no structural change.

When projects become complex and require very close monitoring, it is a general practice to assign a project manager, whose job is to ensure that the project is performed as planned. This manager promotes project performance with the help of individuals from different functions, without being in charge of the individuals themselves. This arrangement is the matrix structure (Exhibit 9.6).

Here, key functions are similar to those in the previous structure, however, organizational units are required to contribute to projects as needed, and there is a defined responsibility for project promotion. At the completion of the project, the project management unit is dissolved. This structure is particularly suitable for frequent projects, because of its flexibility. The organization is able to maintain a basic organizational structure, expanding and contracting in accordance with the addition or completion of projects.

The more frequently major projects are carried out, the more the organization's time and resources are invested in projects. The more unique the technology and research required for the project, the greater

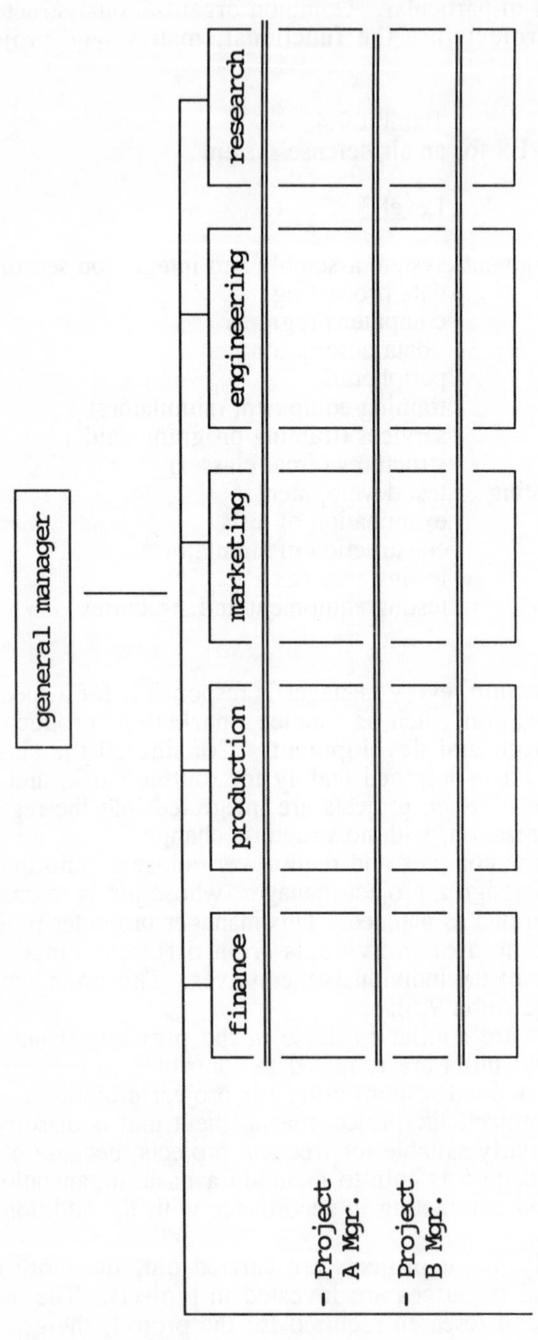

Exhibit 9.6 Matrix organizational structure

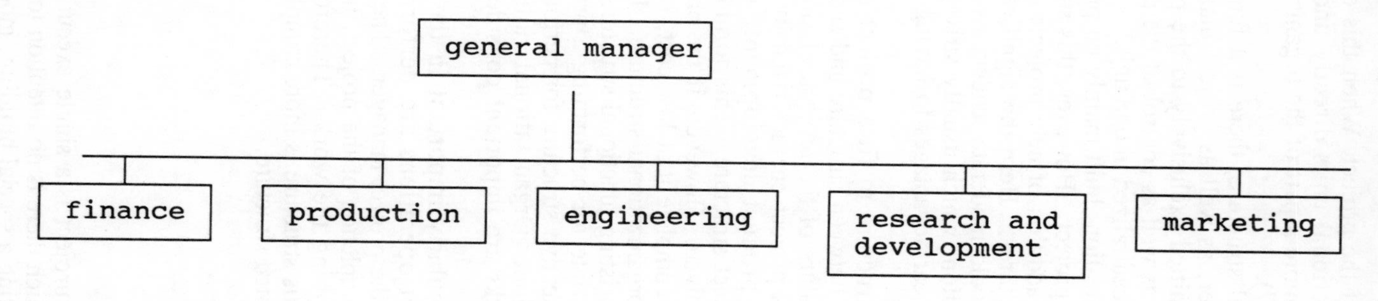

Exhibit 9.5 Functional organizational structure

the need for organizational autonomy of the project. When this occurs, the importance and power of the functional units directly under the general manager is reduced, becoming more a part of the organizational structure of the project itself (Exhibit 9.7).

Under project-oriented organizational structure, there is a functional staff subordinate to the general manager, as well as project managers. Each project manager has a staff committed exclusively to the project. This simplifies planning and execution, as well as control of the project, since the resources designated for it are centralized in one unit.

It is not unusual for a complex organization, built mainly on projects, to have an organizational unit for each project. However, this structure should be flexible enough to allow the addition of new projects and the elimination of completed project structures. Here the significance of control increases. In particular, it should moderate tendencies toward self-sufficiency of the project organization, which usually strives to be 'independent', even when there are clear advantages to having central units and services common to all projects.

The design of an organizational structure to fit a project may be crucial to its success. The relationship between structure and successful project performance, depends on the nature of the project. Exhibit 9.8 outlines this dynamic. For example, a project characterized by a high degree of uncertainty, such as new product development, will be organized most effectively under a project structure. This form enables intensive interaction between those involved. However, if the project is relatively simple and it is important to complete it at low cost, it would not be worthwhile to set up a special organizational structure. Instead, the project should executed within the existing functional structure.

The organizational structure appropriate for performing a project in one company, may not be the most effective structure for performing a similar project in another organization. Organizational culture and interpersonal communications networks are important considerations when designing project structures.

Effective communication is particularly important in the matrix structure, where most of the project operations are performed by employees who are not subordinate to the project manager. The project manager is responsible for effective completion of the project, but does not have authority over those performing the work. Therefore, the control of a project performed under this structure is more complex than for one performed under a project-oriented structure.

Types of projects

One-time projects

Just as its name implies, a one-time project is a single execution of a service, product, or complex event, which there is no intention to repeat. This would be the situation in constructing a special building, inoculation

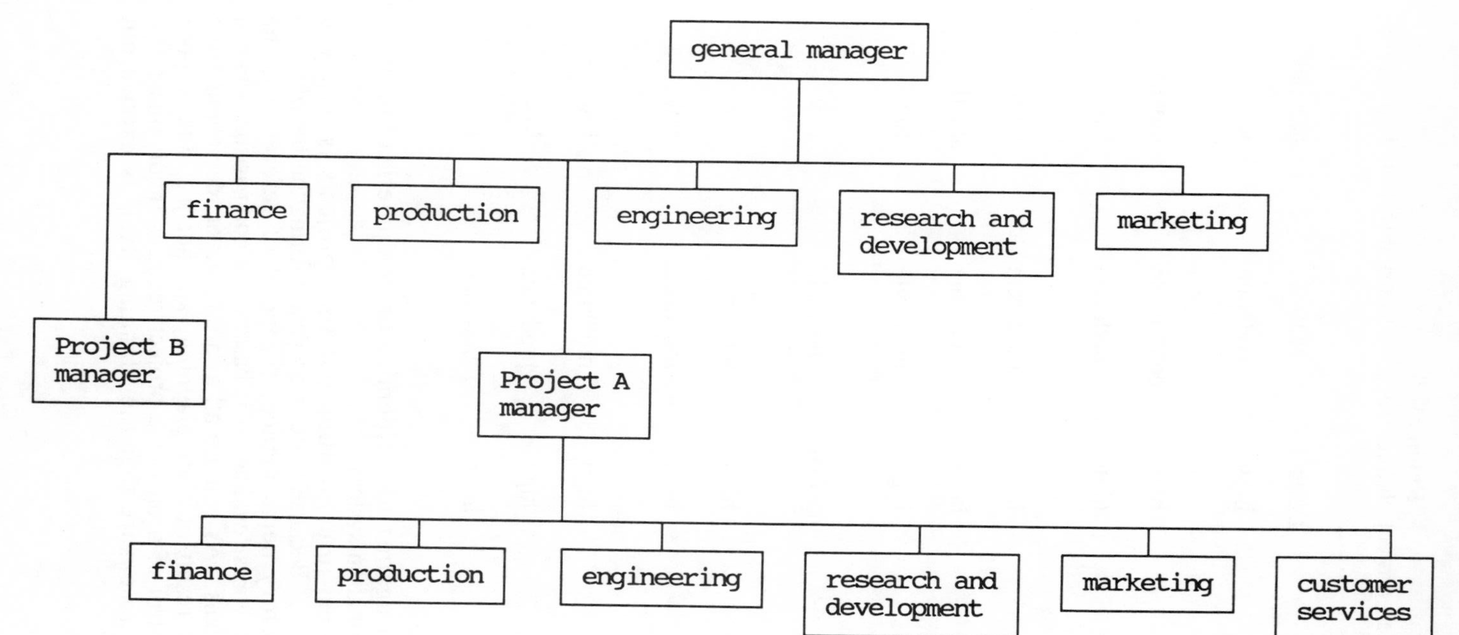

Exhibit 9.7 Project-oriented organizational structure

Exhibit 9.8

Relationship between project characteristics and organizational structure

Project characteristics	Project	Matrix	Functional
uncertainty	high	moderate	low
technological sophistication	new	complicated	standard
complexity of operation	high	moderate	low
project duration	long	moderate	short
scope of project	large	moderate	small
importance of project	high	moderate	low
customer specifications	special	normal	low
mutual dependence	high	moderate	low
cruciality of time	high	moderate	low
confidentiality	high	moderate	low
fixed costs	high	moderate	low
set-up costs	high	moderate	low

of the population against an epidemic, or computerization of an organization's information system.

A central problem in controlling one-time projects is how you evaluate performance. Because there is no past information by which to determine satisfactory performance, the point of reference is the planning. In other words, evaluation is based on a comparison between performance and plans. As you are all aware however, deviations from plans could be the result of poor planning, and not just due to poor performance. Control of a one-time project requires involvement at a very early stage, to ensure that the planning itself is carried out satisfactorily.

It is natural for project designers to prefer to exaggerate their estimates, in order to allow for wide leverage and flexibility during performance, and to reduce the possibility of 'sliding', in both time and budget. The outcome of this style of planning *is* performance according to plans, but performance could have been better than plans. This is true because there is a tendency for project managers to want to use all planned resources, for fear that better performance will lead to future cutbacks in resources. One way to overcome this inclination is to create incentives for maximum utilization of all resources, a concept discussed in the section on wage incentive systems in Chapter 14.

The basic principle underlying control of one-time projects is the examination of the differences between planning and execution, updating plans for future operations in accordance with past discrepancies. For instance, if past performance required 30% more time than planned, the plans for future operations may increase the time allotted by 30%. However, there is a danger that such an approach allows and accepts poor performance. As you can see, it is important to be aware that it is extremely difficult to evaluate operational performance of one-time projects, because there is little basis for comparison.

Another problem in control of one-time projects is the detection, and correction, of slides. The *process-oriented approach* to project control evaluates the project by breaking its processes into pieces. There are a number of possible control methods, and we will examine the three most widely used:

a. *Division of the project into activities*, involves determining what portion of the project budget each activity will take. budget adjustments are based on the actual cost of completed activities, with the addition of 50% of the planned budget for the activities that have been started but not yet completed. Exhibit 9.9 illustrates the use of this model.

Exhibit 9.9
Status of project activities and budget

Activity	Planned Budget	Status	Actual Cost
A	1,200	completed	1,800
B	900	begun	
C	800	has not started	
D	2,300	begun	
E	1,600	completed	2,300
F	2,000	has not started	
G	1,400	has not started	
H	1,200	completed	1,400
Total	11,400		5,500

The activities that have been completed are A,E, and H. The planned budget for these operations is 1200 + 1600 + 1200 = 4000. Their actual cost came to 1800 + 2300 + 1400 = 5500, that is a budgetary slide of (5500-4000)/4000 = 0.375, or 37.5%.

This data can be used to adjust the remaining budget for completion of the project. For instance, the initial planned budget for Task F was 2000. Therefore, its corrected budget should be 2000 * 1.375 = 2750.

In order to estimate the amount of work performed to this point, the values of the planned budget for those activities completed and those begun should be summed up. We add 50% of the budgeted cost of activities that have begun, to the total budget planned for the activities that have been completed. This sum is then compared to the total project budget. The data in Exhibit 9.9 yields the following calculation:

$$1200 + 1600 + 1200 + 0.5\,(900 + 2300) = 5600,$$

which is 49.12%, (5600/11400), of the total budget.

The estimation of the amount of the work performed in the manner described above is correct, as long as there is a linear relation between the budget, the time, and the work content. That is, the work required for an activity budgeted at 4000, must be twice that required for an activity budgeted at 2000.

b. *Use of milestones* is a method by which certain points are identified as indicators of project performance. The number of milestones affects the degree of precision of the assessment. If two milestones are designated, one in the middle of the project, and one at its completion, the average error in assessment will be 25%. This is because as long as a stage has not been completed, it can be assumed that the work is in the middle of the stage. In some cases however, the work will have just begun, while in others it may be almost complete.

The greater the number of milestones used, the more precise the control of the project progress will be. For example, let us imagine the construction of a building. Assume the project is divided into fifty milestones, each one representing a similar amount of work. That would mean that each piece would be 2% of the total project. In this situation, the average error in assessment of work would be half of 2%, or only 1%.

c. *Use of a central indicator* is possible when one element is continuously present throughout the project, and this element can be used as a measure of the rate of progress. For example, consider a drainage pool project, the central indicator could be the amount of land moved (relative to the total amount to be moved); or, the central indicator for a project where a warehouse is moved to a new location, could be the volume of merchandise moved, as compared to the total volume to be moved.

Let us illustrate the example of the drainage pool. Assume that the overall budget allocated for this project is $2,000,000, and that 20,000 cubic meters of land are to be moved. Within the first three months of the project, $600,000, or 30% of the total budget has been used, but only 4,000 cubic meters, or 20% of the land has been moved. That is, 30% of the budget has been used for 20% of the work. Clearly, performance is not progressing at the same rate as expenses.

It is important for control to assess this information to determine if a slide is occurring, and to correct the problems should they arise. It may be that the early stages of the project require more resources than the later ones. This can occur because of set up costs, or learning curves. Whatever the case, control based on a central indicator requires strict monitoring of performance, comparison of achievements to plans, introduction of changes in the course of the occurrence, and reduction of accumulated deviations.

Batch projects

In contrast to one-time projects, batch projects are ones in which the same, or a similar project, is repeated. This would occur with the production of a series of 40 mainframe computers, 50 planes of the same model, construction of 10 similar bridges, or building a residential neighborhood consisting of 20 similar town houses. The life cycle of a batch project can be viewed as a continuum of six stages, as shown in Exhibit 9.10.

On the time axis, the project stages are presented in order, and the vertical axis indicates the level of resources needed for each stage. This type of graph provides a normative description of resource requirements which change from project to project. In the following section, we discuss *central aspects of control* in each of the project stages, from the pre-project stage to project completion.

Pre-project operations. This is a decision-making stage in which possible future projects are compared in order to make a preliminary selection. Those that are selected should be discussed further, while the others should be rejected. The initial sorting is followed by more detailed analysis, including organizational capacity and project feasibility. As discussed in previous chapters, the role of control at this stage is particularly concerned with the decision-making and information collection processes.

In the last decade, there has been a great deal of interest in the analysis and assessment of projects, including techniques for project selection. In most cases, the alternatives are examined according to a series of critical control questions, which should include the following:

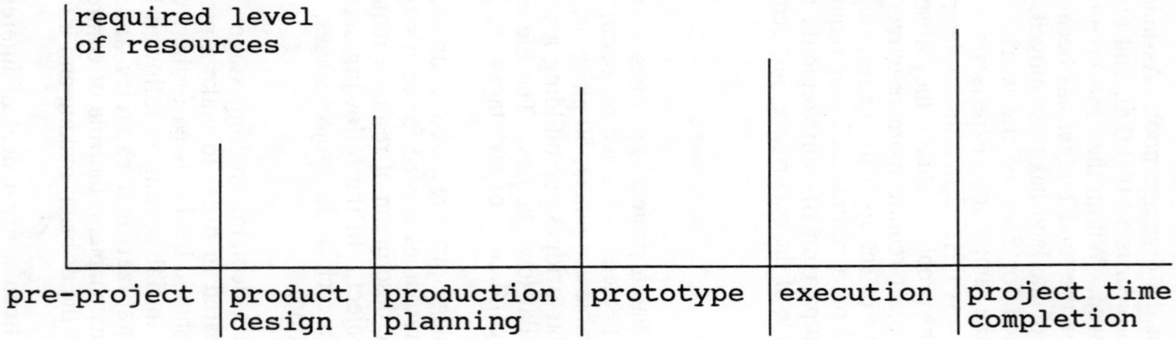

Exhibit 9.10 Life cycle of a batch project

- Are there serious limitations to obtaining required resources, such as information, knowledge, energy, materials, and equipment?
- Can the resources be obtained at reasonable cost?
- Does the project require heavy investments which the company may not be able get?
- Is the project consistent with organization policy and culture?
- Is the project consistent with the law?
- Does the project require substantial investment in development of resources that can not be used again?
- Does the organization gain an advantage over its competitors by approving the project?
- Is there a high probability that the project will be completed successfully?

Once these questions have been answered, and further analysis is indicated, more detail is required in three major areas, market, technology, and capital:

- A description of the market and types of customers, geographic location of marketing networks, relevant trade laws;
- An analysis of past demand and consumer tendencies;
- An assessment of the role and position of the specific project in the market;
- The technological implications of project performance including long and short-term limitations;
- An estimate of project cost, investments, and a financial schedule; and,
- The potential profitability of the project.

Selection and rejection of projects is usually based on a comparison of criteria such as profitability, size of investment, size of potential market, and, availability of resources. One of the central issues in such a comparison is the relative importance of various criteria. For example, there may be two projects, one that is highly profitable but not likely to open new markets, and the other with low profitability but likely to generate additional projects. Which project should be chosen? From the point of view of control, either choice is acceptable, as long as it is made on a sound basis.

Product design and production planning. In the product design stage, the organization must plan the product down to the smallest detail. This forms the product specifications that will be the basis for production planning.

Work process in a project is the same as in any operation. It involves the conversion of various inputs into a desired output. We note a number of issues that control must address in production planning:

- selection of work units to be performed by subcontractors, ensuring that the organization maintains overall responsibility for the project;
- determination of work methods appropriate for the project;
- selection of equipment and materials, and their delivery time;
- planning and follow-up of the production process.

Prototype. In some projects, planning can be evaluated by testing performance on a prototype, that is, a working model of the final product. For example, in research and development for a new product, a model is built, various experiments are conducted, and necessary changes are made. The construction of a prototype is particularly common in cases of batch projects, and less so in one-time projects.

The prototype analysis is a critical stage, and control's contribution may be significant. This may range from initiating minor changes, to deciding to cancel the project completely. Conflicts may develop between those interested in continuing the project and various control systems (which may be numerous, depending of the nature and size of the project). Such conflicts become increasingly common and severe as the number of people, and size of the investment, increases.

Arguments in favor of continuing a project must be given utmost consideration. Control must use reliable cost-benefit analyses, including those related to the qualitative aspects of the project. The arguments against a decision to cancel a project often include the loss of investments already made, loss of experience and skills, unemployment, and possible injury to the prestige of the organization. These all underscore the importance of control in the pre-performance period.

Execution. This is the stage where plans are implemented. Based on the results of preliminary tests, various steps must be completed before execution can begin:

- changes in project design;
- changes in production process;
- changes in equipment, material and staff.

Of course, control continues to examine these aspects during the course of operations, and deviations from plans are usually revealed. These will frequently result from a lack of information as to the actual time required for the project. In the absence of past experience with a similar project, it is only natural that some of the initial planning will be inaccurate. This is an important reason for ongoing evaluation and follow-up.

In a batch project, or a project with repeated steps, performance should improve from one unit to the next, and control must assure that this improvement potential is realized. This learning curve effect will depend upon the motivation for improved performance in the organization, and on the existence of information needed for improving the work process.

Project completion. Obviously, this stage is particularly significant to an organization, and an overall analysis and evaluation of the process and results is important to the success of future projects. This is especially helpful if the organization intends to repeat the same project at a later date. It is important that future projects be simplified by storing accumulated information and resources in a way that allows simple retrieval.

In almost all cases of project completion, the organization must decide which resources to keep and which to sell. These decisions depend on three central factors; 1) the chances of repeating the same or similar project, 2) the cost of keeping resources without using them, and, 3) the relative advantage gained over competitors by keeping the resources in the organization.

Research and development projects

The ability of an organization to develop new products and services, and to improve operational processes, is related to efforts made in research and development (R&D). R&D activities are typically unique; they are not repetitive. Therefore, an R&D unit can be considered a collection of one-time projects, generally performed in a single location. Although the projects may differ from one another, a few characteristics distinguish R&D projects from other one-time projects:

- they involve a high degree of uncertainty;
- there is a high failure rate;
- as a result, it is likely that some operations will have to be repeated more than once; and,
- many R&D projects never reach completion.

R&D projects are very important in high-tech industries, where there is a rapid rate of change. An analysis of electronics factories by Modesto (1984), revealed that differences between products that succeeded commercially and those that failed, could be traced in part, to the R&D process. Thus, control of R&D must focus on the analysis and evaluation of decisions made in the process itself. For control to focus on final results alone would be totally inadequate.

R&D projects can be classified into a number of categories. They are; basic research, applied research, product development, and product improvement. The optimal structure for a project, and the criteria by which its success is evaluated, will depend on the nature of the project. For instance, a basic research project can be assessed according to the number of publications and citations of its results, while a development project is evaluated by whether or not it is completed according to specifications, such as output, cost, and timing.

The literature on performance criteria for R&D is quite extensive. The most common approach is to develop during-occurrence and post-occurrence control systems. For example, one study (Schainblatt, 1982), is based on 11,000 subjects in 1200 research units. The during-performance criteria generally dealt with the characteristics of the research staff, the level of communication among staff members, and the administrative ability of the team leaders. Typical criteria for post-occurrence control were very quantifiable and included; the number of published articles and citations, patents and prototypes, reports and algorithms, and, invitations to lecture.

It is important to develop pre-occurrence and during-occurrence control processes for R&D projects. Examination of the stages in the development process is based on the principle of decision-making control: each of the initial stages is followed by a decision as to whether or not to continue the project. This is illustrated in the process chart in Exhibit 9.11.

The people involved in making decisions may change with each stage. This will depend on the importance of the decision and the knowledge required. The first stages might involve marketing staff who assess sales potential, while advanced stages will involve experts in technology and operations. R&D projects almost always include people from many disciplines. One of the most important functions of control is to make sure that interdisciplinary input is encouraged, since there is a tendency for organizations to attempt to avoid the possible 'complications' and delays which may arise when a variety of perspectives communicate.

The desire to avoid delays is particularly evident in the transition between stages, when it is sometimes necessary to repeat part of the previous stage. For instance, after a feasibility study has been conducted, it must be decided whether to continue or to stop the project. Discussion of the results of the study might reveal that some marketing data is missing. Therefore, a portion of that stage must be repeated.

Projects are often evaluated as a whole, according to performance criteria. Although these are difficult to use in the context of a project, because it is usually a one-time occurrence, indirect criteria may be used to measure the potential for performance improvement.

One such criterion examines the balance of resources used in performing the project: a perfect balance of resources means that the amount of resources needed for a unit of time remains constant throughout project lifetime. Since some of the activities in a project are not on the critical path, their scheduling, and therefore the need for certain resources, is flexible. Using the *earliest approach scheduling* creates a situation in which resources are allocated, and cash is needed, early in the process. This approach will reduce the risk of a schedule slide, but could result in cash flow problems. The opposite situation is true when using the *latest approach scheduling*.

Exhibit 9.11
Process flow chart of R&D activities required for a new product

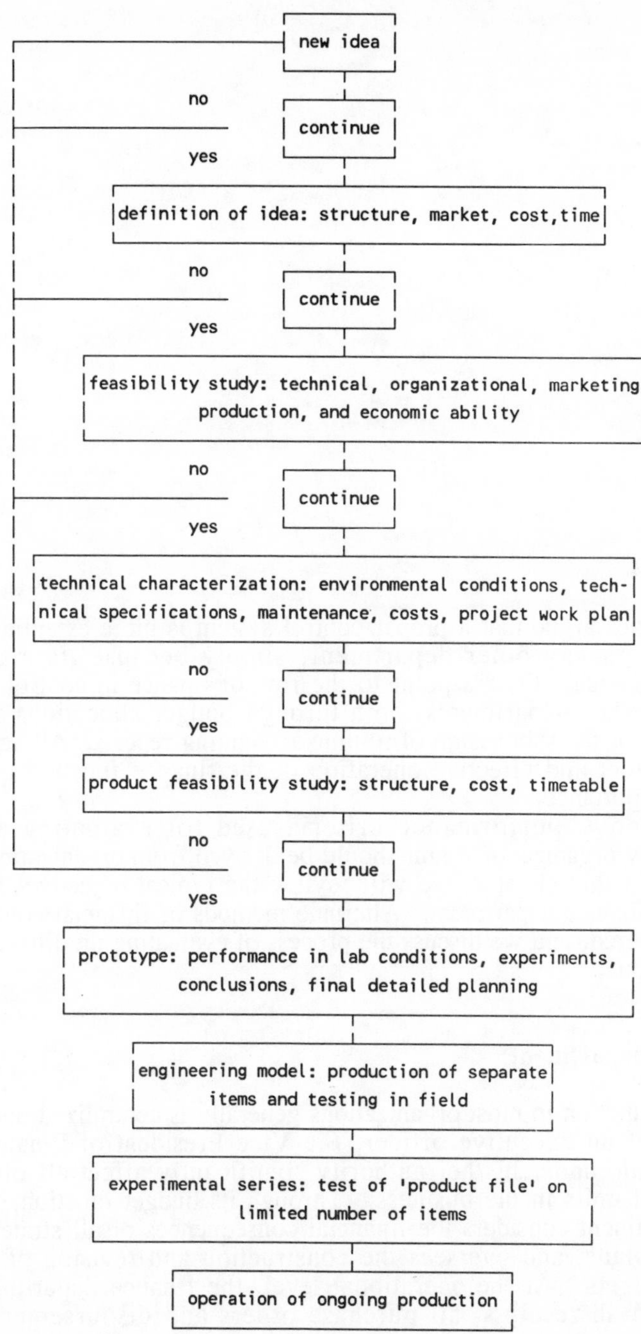

10 Financial control

Some authorities argue that a proper control system is more essential in finance than in any other department, simply because its major commodity is cash. Others point to the role of finance in controlling activities in other departments, both through budget allocations and requirements for the submission of routine accounting reports. All agree that the efficient and effective operation of the finance function is of paramount importance.

As you know, performance criteria used for evaluating and controlling any organizational unit should be derived from organizational objectives. In this chapter, we will review the typical objectives and duties of the finance department. Alternate methods of financial control will be considered, and we discuss the process of evaluating the financial control function.

The finance department

The finance function in most organizations generally is centralized under the control of an executive officer, the Vice President of Finance. Decisions made under his/her authority significantly affect all other organizational units in the business. Through its budget function, the finance department considers the financial consequences of all strategic and tactical plans, and oversees the construction and revision of all operating budgets. At the operational level, the finance department controls all cash receipts, all purchase orders and disbursements, evaluates capital-budgeting decisions, and supervises the corporate accounting function. Typically, the corporate Treasurer and Controller report to the Vice President of Finance, as shown in Exhibit 10.1.

Corporate financial strategy generally is established by the Board of Directors and the Chief Executive Officer. The Vice President of Finance has direct responsibility for articulating and implementing this financial strategy. In recent years, finance attention has focused on such issues as inflation and interest rates, the multiple financial impacts of federal deregulation of financial institutions, new strategies for maximizing shareholders wealth, social responsibility, and take-over prevention strategies. Both defensive and offensive responses to each of these issues continues to dominate strategic financial planning. In addition to these strategic and tactical planning functions, the Vice President of Finance exercises direct line authority over the Corporate Treasurer and Corporate Controller.

Treasurer's responsibilities

The Corporate Treasurer assumes direct management control over cash and marketable securities, designs tactics for achieving corporate financial structure goals, and assumes administrative control for developing operating budgets. Treasurers usually delegate to subordinates the responsibility for managing the credit, purchasing, and capital budgeting functions. Nevertheless, the Treasurer maintains line control over these three functions.

Credit. While most corporations would prefer to sell goods for cash rather than on credit, the pressure of competition forces most to offer credit terms. In fact, accounts payable represents the single largest category of short-term debt for the average nonfinancial organization, accounting for 40% of current liabilities (Brigham, 1986). The optimal credit policy depends on the firm's unique operating conditions. Credit policy consists of establishing the credit period, credit standards, collection policy and discounts for early payment. Once established, the credit policy must be continually monitored to ensure that the expected benefits from offering and using credit really materialize. For example, a company may decide to make late payments to vendors in order to stretch its credit. However, if this is done too regularly, these organizations would pay the price of being labeled as 'slow payers' and would loose favor with their vendors.

Purchasing. Policies concerning purchases of raw materials and components are designed to ensure that sufficient goods are on hand as needed. Such policies consider inventory ordering and carrying costs, safety stocks, credit terms and purchase discounts, and quality control. Purchasing activities must also be monitored closely. This area is discussed in detail in Chapter 8.

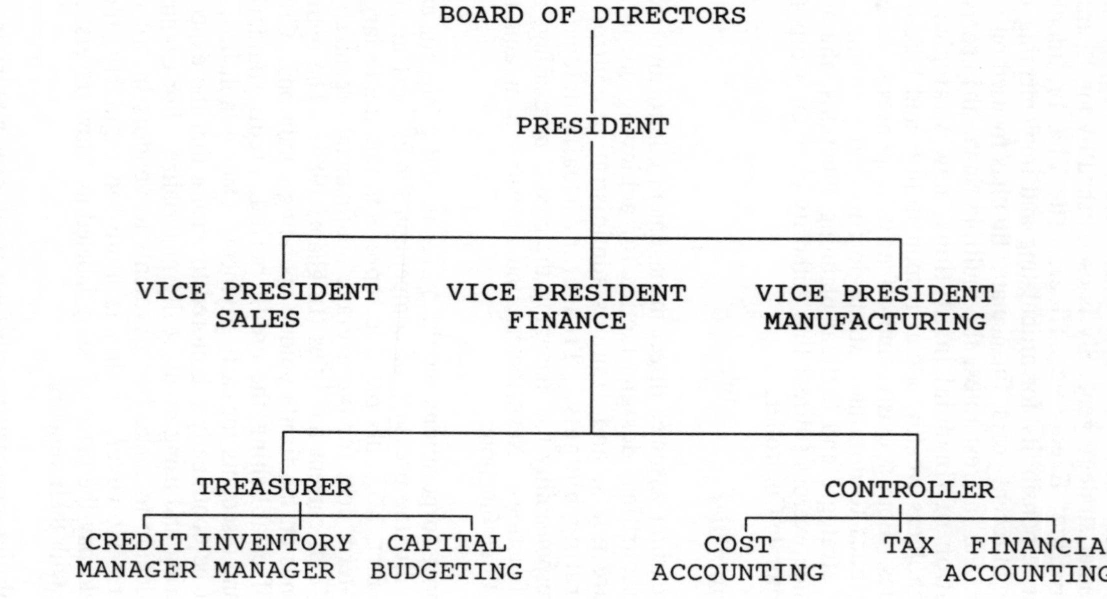

Exhibit 10.1 Typical organizational structure

Capital budgeting. The area of capital budgeting concerns the acquisition of property, plant, or equipment. Typically, such acquisitions require large expenditures at the time of acquisition. The benefits expected to be derived from these acquisitions come as a series of payments over long periods of time, or as a lump sum at the end the period. Generally the costs are known with some certainty, but the expected future benefits can only be estimated. Control of the capital budgeting function is designed to insure compliance with all company policies and procedures.

Controller's responsibilities

The Corporate Controller is the chief accounting official. Routine accounting procedures collect and process information about financial details of the whole organization. Information developed by accountants are intended to serve distinct reporting functions for both internal and external audiences. Accounting reports include financial statements for investors, performance reports and internal control reports for management, and tax reports for the IRS.

Accounting responsibilities within the finance department are rather broad. Four types of accounting functions must be performed, including financial, managerial and tax accounting, as well as internal auditing. In some organizations accountants also assume responsibility for accounting systems.

Financial accounting establishes a system designed to collect, classify, summarize, interpret, and report information about financial transactions. These transactions occur between the organization and its customers, suppliers, investors, employees, creditors, debtors, and taxing authorities. Relevant information about such transactions is recorded within six classes of accounts: assets, liabilities, equity accounts, revenues, expenses, and gains/losses. Summary financial accounting reports of corporate financial position, and results of operations, are routinely distributed to all stockholders and regulatory bodies such as the Securities and Exchange Commission. Top executive officers pay particular attention to these disclosures, since they are widely interpreted as indicating management's efficiency and effectiveness.

Managerial accounting is concerned with cash flow planning for new ventures and the control of the execution of those plans. Plans for repetitive operations take the form of monthly budgets listing expected inputs and outputs. Monthly control reports provide details about the budget expectations, actual performance, and the variance (difference between budget and actual amounts). Non-routine planning may concern capital budgeting for plant and equipment purchases; decisions concerning long term labor, capital, or financial needs; and other analyses of special situations.

Tax accounting is required because most companies are subjected to taxation from a bevy of federal, state, and local authorities. These include income, property and sales taxes, and quasi-taxes such as unemployment and Social Security insurance. In addition to tax compliance, the tax staff plays a significant role in structuring major transactions so as to minimize future tax payments. The tax staff in most companies is relatively small, and generally, they report directly to the corporate Controller or Vice-President of Finance.

Internal auditing functions have become established in most large organizations. This function is designed to ensure compliance with stated policies, standard operating procedures, and documentation to authorize or govern the conduct of business activities. The internal auditing staff in most companies is relatively small, and generally they report directly to the corporate Controller.

Accounting systems in most business organizations were developed and maintained by accountants before the computer age. These early systems concentrated on tracking three sets of parallel transactions: credit sales and accounts receivable; credit purchases and accounts payable; and labor hours and wages payable. As business acquired computers, these were among the first functions that became computerized. Once fully developed, computer based accounting systems require relatively little change.

With time, business experience with computers became sophisticated, computer data entry and retrieval was decentralized, and many new computer applications were developed. Currently, accounting programs in most large organizations represent a small fraction of total computer applications. Many large corporations reorganized all data processing under the control of management information systems (MIS) departments. Maintenance and revision of the accounting system in most large companies now rests in the hands of MIS specialists.

Traditionally, accounting information is heavily used by top management and significantly less by middle level operating managers (Lander, et al 1983). The enormous flexibility of reporting capabilities generated by computerized systems has made it possible to alter this trend and revise accounting reports to better serve managerial needs. For example, Copeland and Globerson (1986), describe how to apply cost accounting principles to operational measures and generate more meaningful information for middle managers.

In most organizations, managers do not evaluate the activities of their subordinates on a constant basis. The principle of *management by exception* evolved in order to assist managers in meeting the control responsibilities of their jobs. Using this principle, managers rely on reports in order to monitor the functioning of their departments. These reports highlight the *exceptions*, results that are different than expected. Accounting reports can be designed using principles of management by exception, assisting managers in recognizing those areas which require particular attention.

Typical performance criteria

As we have stated in previous chapters, relevant performance criteria are derived from organizational and departmental objectives. Although the objectives of the financial department are different from other departments, the performance criteria categories remain the same. That is, they cover areas such as productivity, quality, and timeliness.

The financial department is involved in both repetitive activities, as well as one time projects. Since repetitive activities call for a measurement system different from those required to evaluate project performance, both systems should be incorporated in the control function. The approach to project performance evaluation was discussed in Chapter 9. The guidelines discussed in that section are to be used for evaluating a variety of projects, including those in finance. The remainder of this section will be devoted to the evaluation of the routine activities performed by the financial department.

Productivity. It is not possible to identify performance criteria for every single activity, since information may not be collected on each activity separately. For example, labor hours spent per weekly payroll execution, is a relevant productivity indicator. This measure, however, is not likely to be feasible, since the specific activity is not usually separately logged. This difficulty exists particularly for productivity related criteria.

Although it is difficult to evaluate productivity per individual activity, it is of utmost importance to evaluate the *overall productivity* of the department. Such an evaluation may be accomplished by a criterion such as:

$$\frac{\text{percent of budget assigned to the financial department}}{\text{total organizational budget}}$$

That is, if the department is able to accomplish the same volume of activity previously performed, but with a smaller budget, then the department is more productive. The same approach is typically used to budget other departments and activities and the finance department should not be an exception.

Timeliness. Timeliness is a simpler domain to relate to. This criterion relates to the extent to which an activity is performed according to a specified time schedule. Typical timeliness criteria are the following:

1. percent of time an activity is completed when required -- "in 93% of the cases, employees were paid before the first of the month."

2. percent of time the completion of an activity requires more than a specified time -- "6% of monthly reports were not submitted within a week from their due date." or,

3. average time required to respond -- "an average of 1.5 days was required for issuing a special payment."

Quality. As we have discussed earlier, the most challenging measurement domain to deal with is quality. Although there are common quality measures that may be used in many circumstances, there are other important criteria which are situation dependent. The issue of quality is of utmost importance when dealing with the finance department, since frequently, it is this department which is responsible for conducting internal audits of the company.

Quality control of the finance department is crucial too, because this area can be a focal point for fraud. For example, an article in the 2/15/88 issue of *Business Week* reported on possible fraud activities by Rockwell International Corp. and Hertz Corp. in which the two companies overcharged their clients. Except in cases of very poor performance, this type of activity can not take place without the cooperation of the finance department. The issue of corporate ethics has gained momentum recently, and corporations are rushing to adopt codes of ethics. These codes must be a major concern of the finance department in developing and evaluating its reporting activities (NAA, 1983; Merchant, 1987).

There are two major categories of quality: *quality of design* and *quality of conformance*. Quality of design refers to the intention of the designer to include or exclude features in the product, be it a good or a service. This intention is manifested in the product specifications. For example, the product specification of a new payroll system might state that a difference of more than 15% between a previous and current payment should be brought to management's attention.

Quality of conformance refers to the degree to which goods and services conform to the design. For example, in the example above, this would address the percent of times that 15% payment differences went unreported. It should be clear that if a system is not designed for a certain feature, then it will not deliver it.

Performance measures of quality can be subjective. For example, evaluating the quality of internal auditing procedures will focus on its design and its ability to deliver results. In many cases, the quality evaluation will determine if the results are either adequate or inadequate, but may not lend themselves to measurement on a continuous scale. The same can not be said about a feature such as the percent of auditing errors resulting from improper examination by the auditor. In this case, the auditor's output can, and should, be treated in the same manner as any other output.

Objectives and control of the finance department

Internal control. Internal control is defined as "the plan of organization and all the coordinate methods and measures adopted within a business to safeguard its assets, check the accuracy and reliability of its accounting data, promote operational efficiency, and encourage adherence to the prescribed managerial policies," (Statement on Auditing Standards No. 1, AICPA, 1984). Internal control is so broad that it requires significant coordination of efforts and cooperation among all organizational units. In particular, promoting efficiency in the operational areas, generally requires technical insights beyond the scope of accountants. Industrial engineers, or operations managers, usually provide such insight.

Internal controls have both administrative and accounting components. The administrative component includes the plan of organization, standardized procedures, and a system of management authorizations. The accounting component concerns the reliability of financial records.

The finance department is responsible for designing and implementing financial control mechanisms for the entire organization. Internal auditing plays an important role in this regard. Internal auditing evaluates the design of control systems. Corporate strategy provides the focus for evaluating the appropriateness of control mechanisms regarding the areas to be audited, the performance measures used as criteria for evaluation, the measurement process, the reporting routines, and the response initiated for discrepancies between actual and desired performance.

Both internal and external mechanisms are needed for control of the finance function. Some examples of such controls are as follows:

1. The chief internal control officer must report to the president of the company, with summarized reports going directly to the Board of Directors.

2. The internal auditor must be able to initiate targeted audits at will, especially in response to requests from employees, management, stockholders, suppliers or customers, and government agencies.

3. The Board must play a major role in establishing strategic plans, reviewing finance reports and analyses of corporate performance, and exercising appropriate control over management's performance.

4. Both internal and external auditors must have free access to information throughout the organization.

Examples of external control mechanisms are:

5. Government agencies which are authorized by law to represent citizens' interests and to verify that the company is managed appropriately. For example, the Federal Aviation Commission investigates both aviation safety and the operational competence of air-line companies. The Security and Exchange Commission

is also authorized by law to intervene in company's activities and to initiate audits.

6. The stock exchanges which facilitate public disclosures of corporate information in ways designed to limit the ability of 'insiders' to use corporate information for private gain.

7. Independent financial analysts who have periodical publications used by present and potential stock holders. Although they do not have formal access to company's files, they are highly considered in evaluating company performance.

These mechanisms provide corporate financial information and/or constrain actions of parties in the finance department and the organization as a whole.

Financial reporting. The finance department is responsible for preparing annual financial reports. The financial reporting function in the United States falls under the institutional control of the Securities and Exchange Commission. All corporations subject to its jurisdiction must prepare financial statements that conform to the requirements of Regulation S-X.

Generally accepted accounting principles. Given the Regulation S-X reporting standard for large corporations, many other public regulatory agencies and private institutions (such as banks), have adopted similar reporting requirements for their constituents. Thus, financial reporting by corporate America generally is standardized, and financial statements must be prepared in conformity with generally accepted accounting principals (GAAP). Furthermore, these statements must be audited by independent Certified Public Accountants, who determine whether the accounting principles used by the audited company are in conformity with GAAP.

Unfortunately, some undesirable consequences stem from the universal acceptance of GAAP standards, and financial control must be aware of possible misinterpretations which could result. The names used on accounts in annual reports to designate assets, liabilities, equities, revenues and expenses, have both technical definitions as well as popular meanings. However, the technical definitions are poorly related to the popular meanings. For example, the term *current assets*, includes cash and other assets that will be consumed or turned into cash, within one year, or within the normal operating cycle of the business. On balance sheets for companies in the tobacco or distilling industry, this time period could be several years. *Retained earnings* do not represent actual resources of organizations. Reporting a large amount in the retained earnings account does not imply anything about the asset value of the company nor the availability of cash to stockholders. Ambiguities such as these can lead to misunderstandings and unclear interpretations of aspects of financial reports.

Valuation is another problem. All corporate assets are valued at the lower of cost or market. Yet the actual replacement value of net assets for most large businesses is several times larger than the corresponding accounting value. Confusion also occurs in determining the worth of corporate stock. In spite of the sound of the term, 'book value per share' provides little insight into market value per share. Another area open to misinterpretation is in determining cash flows. As you are all aware, income is not equivalent to cash, and in fact, corporate income is a poor indicator of net cash inflows from operations. Given these ambiguities, unsophisticated readers of financial statements are more likely to be misled than informed.

Historical reporting. Financial accounting information reports on historical events and, while this is certainly of concern to the corporate executive staff, relatively few other corporate personnel are directly affected by these reports. Although some employee benefits, such as bonuses, are based on actual yearly income numbers, typically, operating decisions are based upon budgeted expectations (of future events) rather than on historical events. Clearly however, one factor which contributes to the value of these forecasted budgets, is accurate financial accounting reports.

The internal financial reporting system must be tailored to fit the particular management style and need. The success of any reporting system is measured by the reports used to assist managers, at all levels, in operating the business. The various levels of reports must relate to each other logically. The summarized totals of the details contained in one level of reports, should become the detail of the next higher level. Items of interest must be highlighted. Exception items should be the first to be analyzed so that the situation can be corrected, or exploited, depending upon whether the variance is favorable or unfavorable.

Every effort should be made to format the reports so that they can be used for all divisions or groups within the company. An income statement or an inventory report should be adaptable, with only slight modifications, for all lines of business. It is important, particularly at the corporate management level, that the report format be consistent for each profit center.

The finance department plays a major role, not only during the routine reporting phase, but also during the report design stage, to ensure that the organization has the reports necessary to properly manage and control its operation. Therefore, quality evaluation should be related to both design and conformity.

If a financial report does not include a financial item of interest required for evaluating the organizational financial performance, it is the result of a poorly designed report. On the other hand, if the report itself is inaccurate, it points to a conformity problem. The error may be caused by the finance department or by another department. It is the finance department, however, which is responsible for reconciliation and verification all figures. Since organizational performance is evaluated via each of these reports, it is of utmost importance that the reports are designed to satisfy all possible users. The reporting system should be considered as part of the management information system, and as such, should be designed with input from all parties involved.

Maintenance of an effective procurement policy. The major control objectives for procurement are:

1. minimizing both material acquisition and holding cost;
2. establishing and maintaining reliable sources of material;
3. ensuring that procurement process is completed before payments are issued to vendors;
4. assuring ethical standards in procurement; and,
5. integrating procurement plans with broader financial and operational plans.

The purchasing department must identify multiple sources of supply, seek evidence about their reliability, and solicit multiple bids before the final vendor selection is made. Supplier reliability insures the company against wild fluctuations in material quality, a situation that will adversely affect production scheduling and product quality.

Thorough training of purchasing agents is essential to familiarize them with company policy and applicable state and federal statutes. For example, they must know that federal statutes prohibited buyers from knowingly inducing or receiving price advantages deemed to be discriminatory under law.

Purchasing department activities must be appropriately timed to meet the needs of other plans in the organization. Purchasing must accommodate production budgets, cash disbursement schedules, and other corporate goals established for the ensuing year.

The procurement process can be evaluated by monitoring objectives for purchasing management. On-time performance, quality performance, and standards conformance of vendors and suppliers, should be analyzed periodically, and the results made available to all procurement staff. The relative number of 'rush' purchase orders, orders with price variance from original requisition, and late deliveries, all provide information of importance in evaluating procurement effectiveness. Further discussion of procurement control is found in Chapter 8, Operations Control.

Maintenance of an effective accounts payable system. An accounts payable system must be able to facilitate timely payment to authorized individuals at low cost, with great reliability and with documentation sufficient to support retrospective audits. All liabilities must be recorded, prompt payments must be made, and documentation must support each payment.

Effective management of accounts payable will affect several other systems within the organization. Such a management system includes the following elements:

1. a method of vendor selection and approval;

2. a management philosophy governing quantities, prices, and terms of goods and services purchased;

3. routine performance audits of purchasing activities; and,

4. detailed procedures for documenting and approving liquidation of trade obligations.

The financial department should be aware of the most common methods of handling bill payments and monitoring the outputs necessary to measure the performance of the payable system. Disbursement accounts and funding techniques should be set up to serve payroll distribution. Certain outputs include zero-balance accounts, payable-through drafts, and remote disbursing. These allow the department to closely monitor, on an item-by-item basis, the validity of each payment.

The controller should also use, and monitor, the automated balance reporting systems developed by banks and third party vendors. The controller should be able to extract, in one report, the previous day's balance in each bank account, by early the next morning. Average available bank position should be calculated for the current month and compared to the agreed-to target level.

Maintenance of an accurate and reliable payroll system. The ultimate objective of the payroll system is to initiate periodic payments to the company's employees. The system also must be designed to accomplish the company's specific goals as they relate to employees, external interests, and internal needs, and to provide for a variety of contingencies imposed both by law and company policy. This function requires maintaining strict privacy of records that include personal information such as name, identification numbers, job title, pay rate, absenteeism, performance, and payment history.

Suitable segregation of duties is called for in the preparation of the payroll requests and distribution of payroll checks. Payroll operations are usually performed under the guidance of the controller, although the treasurer exercises ultimate control over payroll disbursements through validation and check-signing responsibilities.

Control objectives for payroll should be formulated for serving the following functions:

1. hiring and terminating employees;

2. setting, adjusting, and administering compensation and other forms of benefits;

3. recording attendance and performance; and,

4. accounting for labor costs, payroll taxes, employee benefits, and other related entries.

To ensure and maintain the system, most companies rely on authorizations and approvals, coupled with the distinct separation of physical handling and related record keeping. In addition, the internal auditing department constantly observes the payroll operation, ensuring adherence to procedure, but also looking for weaknesses in the system that could be exploited to perpetrate fraud. Maintaining good accounting controls over both input (an updated employee payroll master, pre-audit time attendance cards, etc.) and output files (auditing and pay instruments, documents, and reports), is essential for the proper functioning of the payroll department. All areas of the payroll system should be designated to reflect well-functioning accounting controls.

Maintenance of an effective accounts receivable system. A billing and collection system has three major functions. It must assure that all goods and services provided to customers are promptly and properly billed. The cost of goods and services provided must be established and recorded. Finally, customer accounts must be managed with both accuracy and integrity. Without proper accounting and management controls, the system may be vulnerable to irregularities such as misappropriation of cash, improper write-offs of doubtful accounts, and billing omissions.

The proper billing of customers and collection of payments, requires coordination among several departments within an organization. Its execution requires the design and maintenance of a well defined order processing system. Since this system involves the goals of both the organization and the customer, its implementation must consider both internal and external objectives.

The system should be designed to ensure rapid cash flow and minimize bad debt losses. Internal controls must effectively preclude the manipulation of accounts and the misapplication, misdirection, and misuse of remittances. The system should include the smooth flow of documents within the billing and collection, and other related systems. These documents include sales invoices, customer statements, the remittance advice, or the bad debt write-off listing. Controls over billings and collections should include matching shipping documents with sales orders, preparing and mailing sales invoices, preparing batch or daily sales summaries of billings, and accounting for prenumbered sales orders.

The order processing system is the bridge between sales and cash receipts. As a consequence, it is closely connected to the marketing system and the cash control system. It represents a very important interface between company and customer.

The most important element in evaluating collection efforts is the average age of the accounts receivable. Both a shorter age and decreases in age, are signs reflecting improvement. Certainly comparisons to industry standards will also provide insight. Effective management necessitates periodic monitoring four areas:

a. accounts receivable;

b. turnover;

c. age collection statistics; and,

d. problem accounts.

Typical effectiveness ratios are average daily sales per account, and total receivables to total debt.

Maintenance of an effective cash control system. This system should maintain control over cash, generate appropriate reports, and interact effectively with many other systems in the company (i.e. accounts payable, payroll, and collection systems). The major objective of the cash control system is to maintain adequate cash sums to meet the transactional needs of the organization.

To properly control and manage cash, the financial manager must monitor the cash balance, cash receipts, and cash disbursements. To achieve this goal, the design of the cash control system should include these objectives:

1. maintenance of proper cash balances;

2. maintenance of records; and,

3. internal controls over cash receipts and disbursements.

The cash control system should be triggered by sources external to the system. In the case of cash receipts, such impetus usually comes from customers, and disbursements are generated from accounts payable.

Only in rare instances do managers have opportunities to design a financial reporting and control system from scratch. Invariably some kind of system is in place. But how do managers evaluate the accuracy of these systems? They must ensure that preparation of the budget and corporate planning activities is continuous, that plans are systematically revised throughout the year. As new and more accurate information becomes available, these figures must be used in place of original estimates. Current operating results should be compared to original estimates to pinpoint the way to needed changes.

Accounting controls over cash are designed to safeguard this asset, and to aid in the proper and prompt recording of cash transactions. The basic control objectives for receipts are to establish control over all cash received and to ensure that it is deposited promptly in the company's bank accounts. Specific controls should be established to ensure that no one employee handles a transaction from beginning to end, and to separate the physical handling of cash from its record-keeping. Controls should specify that the function of authorizing payments and recording accounts payable should be separated from the function of writing checks, and that all cash disbursements should be made by check.

All organizations attempt to control cash. Corporate concerns focus on actual cash flow, budgeted cash flow, and a strategy to maximize corporate liquidity. Turnover ratios can measure the velocity with which receivables are converted into cash.

The *accounts receivable turnover* for example, measures the number of times that receivables are collected during a given period:

$$\text{Accounts Receivable Turnover} = \frac{\text{Sales}}{\text{Average Accounts Receivable}}$$

Increasing the rate of turnover reduces credit risk losses, and increases the pool of investable funds by decreasing the amount of funds that are tied up in receivables.

Controlling the accounts payable turnover is equally important. Payment should be made in time to take advantage of credit discounts, if any are available. Otherwise payments should be delayed until the credit-term deadline.

Inventory turnover measures the effectiveness with which the firm uses inventory in support of sales:

$$\text{Inventory Turnover} = \frac{\text{Cost of Goods Sold}}{\text{Average Inventory}}$$

The smaller inventory is in relation to cost of goods sold, the greater is the sales activity that inventory is able to generate.

Trends in financial ratios indicate long term patterns that can be evaluated relative to industry-wide or historical ratios. To enable management to get the most out of this information, it must be timely, and reliable. The data should be pertinent to the needs of management and, the system not so efficient, that it produces more information than is actually needed.

Assets management. Maintaining an effective fixed assets control system requires attention to issues such as the recording of new property acquisition, asset transaction, the safeguarding of existing fixed assets, and the maintenance of property appreciation and depreciation systems and records. The system should be designed to match the cost of the property consumed with revenues generated through depreciation. In the same way that there is a separation between the record keeping and actual handling of monies in payroll, the property accounting function is kept separate from the operating departments. This is an essential feature of control for every company and, an important factor in maintaining good internal accounting controls.

Property controls are necessary to safeguard these assets and to provide assurance that they function properly. Features such as the segregation of duties, proper procedures for authorization, adequate documentation and record-keeping, physical control over assets and records, and unexpected checks on performance, are all necessary parts of a well-designed property control system.

Assets management also involves decisions about a firm's asset acquisition, and this is perhaps the most challenging of all executive endeavors. Striking the balance between too much and too little capital investment is a difficult task. Proposals to spend any money must be scrutinized with comprehensive care. Management must make certain that a full effort has been made to bring together and evaluate all facts bearing on a proposed purchase.

Decisions to invest scarce dollars should never be subjected to the intrigue of front-office politics, or created in an atmosphere of favoritism. Planning and control of asset mix should be a pragmatic matter. Financial control must provide the following checks before determining its mix of assets:

1. ferret out investment opportunities;
2. determine the cost and benefits of each prospective investment;
3. pick and choose the most advantageous;
4. provide funds and channel them into the most productive outlets; and,
5. hold periodic post-mortems on investments already committed.

There should be a continuous search for ways to improve the assessment of asset acquisitions.

Assets management's responsibilities include the development of programs for the provision of capital, and the execution of these programs. The starting place for control is determining measuring ratios which concentrate management's attention on increasing the return on each investment. An important ratio to consider is fixed assets to net worth, which measures how much ownership funds are invested in assets with relatively low turnover.

Both responsibilities and target objectives need to be considered before assessing performance in determining the mix of current and fixed assets. The establishment of performance standards here will be an exercise in futility unless they can be reported upon regularly, consistently, and with relative accuracy. The end use must be kept in mind, and as always, standards could change.

Monitoring and evaluating the firm's financial position. Transforming financial data into a form that can be used to determine the financial picture of the organization is required of any financial system. This information allows an accurate assessment of needed financing for events such as increased production capacity requirements, new labor contract terms, or unexpected opportunities requiring capital expenditures.

A variety of financial monitoring techniques can be used to isolate variances from the norm. The most common methods include omparison reporting, ratio analysis, and multi-year trend analysis. Information is typically presented either numerically or graphically. For example, comparison reporting can be used to evaluate financial position in the following ways:

1. actual versus budget;

2. current period versus prior period;

3. actual versus forecast; and,

4. actual versus industry or competitors' statistics.

The proper tools must be selected to highlight significant variations and trends in an efficient manner. If too many monitoring methods are used, the results may become as difficult to interpret as the basic financial figures. The efficient use of monitoring techniques will allow the controller to isolate the areas which require management's attention, with a minimum of effort.

Design and implementation of the financial structure. Planning its financial structure is of critical importance to the organization of a new company, as well as to a going concern. The two major decisions to be made are the mix of short- and long term financing, and the selection of the individual sources of financing.

There are many factors which influence management's decision on the make-up of the capital structure. For short-term financing, the decision of the financial manager should not be based solely on interest rates. The financial manager must also consider qualitative factors such as the confidence of creditors and restrictions which might be placed on company operations. The final choice of financing should depend upon the objectives of management and the desires of the individuals or institutions that supply the funds. By affecting availability, the suppliers of funds help determine the capital structure of the firm.

Financial management excellence in well run businesses is maintained both by specifying explicit criteria for evaluation and by developing the structure needed to accomplish financial goals. Lack of such criteria and infra-structure may result in the finance department controlling the other departments in a manner that serves finance's internal interests rather than the interest of the company as a whole.

11 Control of information systems

Information systems can be thought of as a portion of control mechanisms designed to monitor other systems. This description applies equally well to simple home thermostats or complex national input/output models requiring mainframe computer support. Both use data to determine system status (heat, national economy) and to initiate action (turn on the furnace, increase interest rates). No control system is perfect, however, and information systems may malfunction. Prudent managers devise means to control their information systems, many of which support other systems.

System reliability

Often automatic control procedures are integrated within information systems to increase their reliability. Concern about system reliability is of paramount importance during three functions; data input, processing, and output. Management has the responsibility of identifying weaknesses in these three functions. While management bears the ultimate responsibility for all errors, there are some areas where predictable errors are accepted.

This chapter is largely based on Ahituv and Neumann, *Principles of Information Systems for Management*. The authors thank them for their contributions to this chapter.

Prudent managers do not and should not seek to achieve 'complete' control, except in a 'zero defect' environment. Control is considered in a cost/benefit context. In no circumstance should the costs of implementing and maintaining control exceed the benefits of having error-free data. Complete control is not economically feasible in many applications.

For example, consider *redundancy* as a control element. Redundancy occurs when one piece of information enters the system more than once. Redundancy reflects inefficiency in data processing. Redundancy consumes more storage space and increases the number of operations/ transaction needed to update data files. While many commercial computer programs tout the elimination of redundancy as a feature which increases efficiency, complete elimination of redundancy may adversely affect control.

Redundancy helps reconcile related balances, and it supports retrieval or recreation of information after a system 'crash'. As more control features are integrated into information systems, they tend to become less efficient. Selecting the optimal trade-off between control and efficiency is delicate choice.

The quality of information, its timeliness, accuracy and relevance, are all of concern to managers. However, not all managerial decisions require information of uniform quality. Information needs differ, depending upon the types of decisions under consideration. In the following section, we consider characteristics of information needed to support several types of decisions.

Strategical, tactical, and operational decisions

Corporate management is responsible for three types of decisions. Strategic decisions concerning corporate philosophy, objectives, and long term goals are, jointly made by the chief executive officers and the corporate board of directors. Of prime concern to these individuals are long term future expectations about the organization, its industry, and the national or international economy. Information needed to support strategic decisions may have relatively low reliability, since few executives can foresee the future, and fewer still can influence an industry or an economy. Estimates about future expectations may require constant revision.

Tactical decisions concern broad action programs, all of which are constrained by the strategic corporate goals. For example, consider a company with a strategic mandate to increase its production by 20% annually. The tactical planning team might consider such alternatives as overtime, instituting a second or third work shift, or subcontracting part of the production.

The time horizon for tactical planning is more immediate than at the strategic level. Tactical plans are more constrained by the availability of existing resources and new resources already on order. The information needs of tactical planners are more easily satisfied, because tactical plans are usually based upon existing resources, technology, and personnel. Since these decisions are more immediate, tactical decision makers can better identify how to obtain needed information. They can better assess the reliability of the information, and the expected costs of getting additional information.

Operational decisions are concerned with planning and executing current programs according to well defined time schedules. Information required to support operational decisions is typically generated within the firm, or obtained from established external contacts. Progress reports enable operational managers to identify specific problems and initiate corrective action.

A typical operational decision is one involving the scheduling of resources. Resource scheduling is usually a function of customer orders with known expectations regarding delivery time. Imagine your company had budgeted sales of 25,000 units per month, but you have only sold 15,000 units in the first month. The deviation between your plan and reality would be obvious. A geographical analysis of sales (relative to budgeted sales) could identify the deficient sales territory and even the salespersons who failed to meet budget. A variety of remedial actions (the process of control) could be initiated, based on the detailed operational information provided by a control system. Information available might suggest instituting incentives, hiring or firing someone, reducing prices, or increasing advertising.

Information characteristics

Quality of information reflects three characteristics; timeliness, relevance, and cost.

Timeliness

Timeliness is evaluated by measuring the period between the occurrence of an event and the point at which information about that event is available. Detailed operating information can be, and often is, collected and reported to first and second line management in a timely fashion. Foremen and department heads generally are well informed about their own operations. Most often, information is aggregated, both in terms of longer time periods and larger organizational units, as it is reported up in the organization. Information may be relatively old by the time it reaches top level management. in addition, it may be aggregated to such a degree that divergent trends, obvious at lower organizational levels, are no longer discernible.

Relevance

The relevance of information depends on the particular situation. To be relevant, the information must have the potential to influence the decision. The value of information is time-, place-, person-, and decision-specific. While a foreman is interested in information about the output of a machine being used by one employee during a specific week, the information, by itself, is of little interest to other managers in the organization. What distinguishes data from information, and gives it content, is relevance.

Information may be conveyed to users via several media, such as text or graphic report, video monitor, or audio recorder. Research has demonstrated that the medium does effect the message. A printed output may be superfluous in cases where information changes continuously and must be monitored on-line. The main problem regarding evaluation of format-related attributes is that they cannot be quantified through a simple analytic approach. One way to evaluate such data is ranking alternatives, and focussing on the extreme values.

Cost

Rational decision makers seek additional information only when the marginal cost of obtaining information seems to be lower than the benefit derived the knowledge. Information costs include systems design, maintenance, and those associated with the administrative process necessary to generate reports. The administrative process includes data collection, coding, printout, and distribution. Only necessary information should be obtained.

In determining what information is necessary, it is often helpful to see if the organizational structure is reflected in the structure of the information generated. For example, first line supervisors should receive information regarding the resources that are under their direct control, but second line supervisors need only receive summary statistics of performance. A regional sales manager needs detailed information on the performance of each salesperson, while the national manager needs aggregate performance information at the regional level.

Types of information control

Three categories of information system controls are discussed below.

Administrative control

Before the advent of computerized systems, bookkeeping usually was decentralized within each department of the organization. Since most business transactions involve more than one department, errors, or other discrepancies, were detected by reconciling accounts between various departments. For example, a sales transaction would be documented by someone in sales, warehousing, accounts receivable, and cost accounting. If a discrepancy was found in any one set of accounts, it could be traced back through related documents in other departments, and then corrected.

While computerized accounting systems can produce accounting reports that resemble those produced by non-computerized systems, much of the redundancy found in the mechanical systems has been removed. In addition, computerized data is less visible and concrete, than in manual systems. In order to access accounting data in a computerized setting, a terminal, extensive training, and a password are needed. This makes it more difficult to tell exactly what information is stored, which files contain the information, who provides authorization to retrieve it, and how to retrieve it.

Administrative controls of the management information system (MIS) are designed to promote efficiency and effectiveness while protecting the integrity of the system. Key elements of administrative control include the establishment of a clear organizational reporting hierarchy, segregation of duties, formal specification of plans, and systematic documentation of formal activities.

Concentrating all the data of an organization in a single computer installation creates an obvious risk. Satisfactory control may be gained by dividing the work among individuals who have access to data during capture, processing, storage, and retrieval activities.

Segregation of duties is accomplished by establishing work rules that prohibit one individual from participating in more than one of the following activities; system design, program writing, program review, system test and approval, and system installation. Applying this concept to operations prevents one employee from participating in more than one of the following activities; source document preparation, computer input preparation, reconciliation to source document, input error correction and irregularity inquiries, computer operations, file library, balancing inputs against printouts, output distribution, systems programming, database administration, and hardware maintenance.

Segregation is a preventive measure. It assists in detecting inadvertent errors as well as intentional tampering, since the work of any one individual is checked by others who have no interest in perpetuating the error. MIS must incorporate quality control into its daily function. Every piece of data that enters the information processing system must be screened for the prescribed quality control limits, such as accuracy, level of detail, and redundancy.

Exhibit 11.1
Accessibility of MIS functions to software libraries

MIS Function	Software Library
Development Function	Development Library
Quality Control	Test Library
Operations	Production Library

Another method of segregation of duties is shown in Exhibit 11.1. According to this framework, each function maintains its own software.

For instance, a project development team may have space on disks where all the programs under development are stored. When this system is ready for installation, the pertinent software is copied to a test library on which it will be stored for testing purposes until it is approved. Then the software is copied to the production library.

Only specified personnel are allowed to store or replace programs. In fact, development personnel are not permitted to access any program cataloged in production, and operation personnel may not access software under development. In bigger information units these restrictions are supported by means of passwords, logbooks etc., which serve as additional control tools. They are not foolproof, but they improve control. The procedure may cause delays in the pace of development, particularly when making minor modifications in existing systems; but that is a part of the price the organization must pay for proper control.

Segregation of duties is only one measure among many that constitute administrative control. In fact, every established procedure, in system development or operations, bears an element of administrative control. In development, administrative control includes the following additional elements:

* Formal reporting to committees
* Standards for system analysis and design
* Programming standards
* implementation practices and logbooks
* Testing regulations
* Change handling procedures
* Post audit
* Documentation standards

In routine operations, administrative control provisions include these items:

* Exact procedures for error detection and correction
* Operating procedures (in writing)
* Backup and recovery arrangements
* Routines for balance check and reconciliation
* Regulations for hard-copy storage and archive management
* Limitations on the accessibility to software libraries
* Limitations on admittance to the computer room, to the file library, and to other privileged places

These illustrate alternative ways to exercise administrative control. Their use will reduce the likelihood of system abuse. However, constant vigilance over development and operation is but one element in formal control procedures.

Built-in control

Most computer installations have integrated control features built into the hardware and software. Many of these features are automatically activated whenever the computer performs a relevant action (e.g. a parity check). However, there are some features whose activation is optional (e.g. password).

Hardware controls. Information processing equipment must have integrated control features to check the validity of various operations performed during data processing. Control features are installed not only in the computer and its peripheral devices, but also in off-line machines used for keying, communication, and other operations.

Most input media are equipped with control features. For example, duplicating input data encoded on optical reader forms, permits the optical reader to have two equivalent data lines to read. Even if one line has been damaged, the data can still be read in without human intervention.

More 'intelligent' input media, like diskettes, are usually mounted on programmable devices so control can be obtained by means of a software program. This is discussed in more detail later in the chapter.

Whenever input data is transferred from remote locations to a central computer, it passes through telecommunication networks. These are normally integrated with hardware features that check the completeness and validity of transmissions. Given various modes of transmission, each is characterized by different controls that affect data reliability. For example, the structural topology of a network can be designed in different ways. A certain topology may allow transmissions to be redirected through alternative routes once a certain link has been established. It is easy to see the vast possibilities for control given various proposed telecommunication networks.

Telecommunication networks can also be equipped with ciphering devices. These devices scramble all data flowing through the network so that only a designated station, equipped with a deciphering code, can understand the messages. Ciphering is very common in both military and commercial systems (e.g. electronic fund transfer systems).

Most central computer installations possess many control measures installed within the hardware. These unobtrusive procedures are not visible to the user. Some computer models will terminate a program when a calculation overflow is encountered. The overflow problem may be very important for scientific applications, and of less significance for business applications.

Control is also concerned with the tolerance of hardware equipment to fluctuations in temperature, humidity, and electrical power. Some models have more tolerance than others, and can be installed in less than desirable environmental conditions (e.g. in a production shop, on mobile equipment). Backup systems must be designed to accommodate these situations. For example, standby batteries or emergency generators may be required in certain cases. Such measures are costly, and management must assess the damage that might occur if they were not adopted.

External storage and output devices should also be considered in light of the degree of control they provide. For example, would it be better to purchase a fast laser printer, or two slow printers that perform equivalent work? The latter alternative provides better backup, but waiting time for urgent printouts may be longer.

Some very simple measures can affect control. For instance, magnetic tapes can be secured from undesired overwriting (i.e. destruction of current records) simply by securing a plastic ring on the reel. Computer terminals can be locked so that only authorized persons will have access to them.

Software controls. Software controls may improve the quality of programs through debugging aids and structured design techniques. Software features can also exert control over operations. Most operating systems allow users to be identified by confidential passwords, preventing unauthorized users from accessing the computer. Internal logbooks permit the tracking of each interaction with the computer. Many recovery routines are available for use after encountering a system failure, so programs need not be restarted from the beginning.

More and more systematic controls are being developed. Many operating systems maintain file catalogs, which contain the name, physical location, number of backups and other parameters, pertaining to data files. File catalogs facilitate the work of computer operators and file librarians. Automatic backups partially prevent premature deletions. Many database packages automatically record all transactions. This makes it possible to trace back updates and to recover after system failures.

Application control. Application control refers to those provisions employed to meet the requirements of a particular application. This may incorporate administrative, built-in, and ad hoc features designed to prevent, detect, and correct adverse events or conditions.

While control should be incorporated in every information system, alternate measures may be employed to accommodate specific traits of each application. For example, the control exerted over a monetary information processing system (e.g. cashier transactions) would need to be tighter than that applied to data collection for national statistics on the food industry. The likelihood of potential abuse is much greater in the case of the banking operation than in the statistics collection. In addition, the implications of tampering with cash transactions is probably more serious.

Common control measures

The following sections discuss some commonly used control measures. The descriptions parallel the data processing cycle as illustrated in Exhibit 11.2.

Exhibit 11.2
Data processing cycle

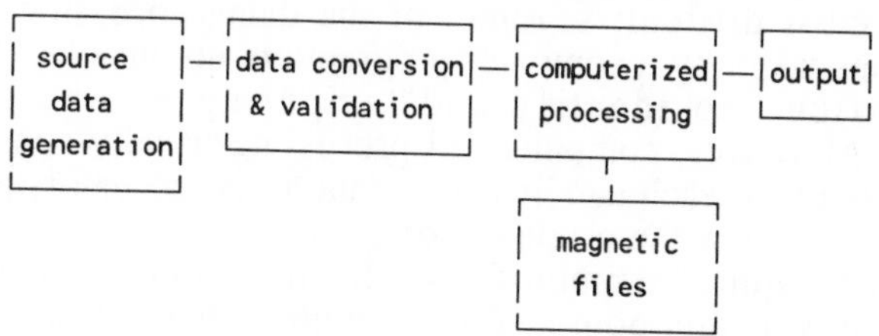

Data entry. Source data is usually created as a result of a physical transaction, such as sale, a payment, or a withdrawal. The description of the activity is recorded on a source document, a written transaction. Three types of control problems commonly occur during data entry:

Accuracy	-	How can we make sure that the recorded data is error-free?
Completeness	-	Have all pertinent transactions been recorded and forwarded for further processing?
Authorization	-	Is the person who initiates the transaction authorized to do so?

The design of a source document facilitates the ease of entry, level of accuracy, and flow of operations. Badly designed forms encourage mistakes, misunderstanding, and irritation. They may cause significant deterioration of system performance and control capacity. Several criteria commonly used to evaluate form quality include determining if they are self-explanatory, exhaustive, logically sequenced, non-redundant, easy to 'key in', and include only necessary information?

Data conversion and validation. Data conversion is the process of transforming data from a human-readable to a computer-readable medium, for example, keying in. Data validation is the process of error detection and correction, a crucial element in control.

In the past, off-line keying and batch processing, were separated from conversion and validation activities. First, the data was keyed. Later, a separate computer 'edit' program read the data and verified the correctness of some characteristics. Errors were printed out on a special report, which initiated clarification and correction activities. This resulted in repetitive keying and rerun of the edit program until the data was error-free.

Contemporary technology allows consolidation of conversion and validation activities, either by on-line keying on terminals attached to a central computer, or by utilizing programmable devices for off-line keying (e.g. diskettes mounted on microcomputers). In both cases, the keying operator communicates with an edit program that constantly monitors the validity of the keyed data and instantaneously signals errors.

Control over computerized processing. Computerized processing is probably the most difficult segment of the data processing cycle to control. Actions taken by a computer program are not visible. Mistakes are more difficult to identify and tampering can be cleverly camouflaged. Moreover, computerized processing usually consists of a sequence of programs, each handing over data to its successor, making it more difficult to identify the origin of some errors.

It is therefore, quite common for application controls to focus on external measures at this point. For example; maintenance of rigid programming standards, strict segregation of duties, and insistence on complete, detailed, and up-to-date documentation, reduces concern over potential problems in computerized operations.

Still there are ways to locate control measures within computerized processing itself. This is accomplished by adding control routines to operational programs. For example, if control figures are forwarded along the entire process, each program will accumulate record counts, control totals, and hash totals. These figures will be forwarded from program to program and reconciled with newly calculated figures. Validity checks along the process can also be inserted.

Output control. The primary control issues in output involve accuracy, completeness, and security. The cause of errors in output is most likely found during the input or processing stages. However, since output is normally more visible and concrete than intermediate steps, control options should be utilized as much as possible. These should include reconciliation of output data with previously produced control figures, such as totals and counts. In addition, scanning reports and screens can spot data that is unreasonable. Making comparisons between different reports, and between outputs and inputs, is another simple way to identify output errors and ensure completeness. Even a simple tool such as the consecutive numbering of pages is very effective in eliminating some output errors, and ensuring that documents are complete.

Security of on-line output, such as displays, is more complicated than that of printouts. This is because users may possess terminals at remote locations and it is difficult to make sure that only authorized personnel are in view of a terminal. It is most feasible to limit access to on-line output by means of frequent changes in passwords, identification requirements, and ciphering. Confidential data should be guarded and isolated from non-privileged reports. Output security should be regulated by clear policies and procedures, and maintained by competent and well trained personnel.

File control. Most file control measures are built-in, such as passwords, catalogs, and ciphering of stored data. A very common control provision preserves previous generations of master and transaction files. With these controls, each update of a master file maintains the input files that have been used to create the last version of the master file.

Another control measure is to place backup files in fireproof vaults, or offsite. Every new master file is immediately copied and the copy is taken to a separate location. Many of these provisions are administrative, and require control to ensure that appropriate procedures are established. Since the provisions are costly, they should be selected in the light of the specific application and the characteristics of the data involved.

Audit trail. An extremely useful tool is the audit trail. This allows the auditor "to trail an original transaction forward to a summarized total, or from a summarized total backward to the original transaction" (Porter, 1977). In order to use an audit trail, each transaction must be preserved along the processing cycle, and mutual references must be established between transactions and outcome aggregations. These rules apply not only to computerized data, but to hard data, such as source documents and printouts.

The audit trail concept shows clearly that application is often more of a problem of design than of operation. It is inconceivable to first design and implement an information system, and only later worry about controls on the existing system. Information analysts, system designers, and project leaders should be conscious of control issues, and auditors should take an active part in system development, to guarantee appropriate attention to control measures.

When auditors and system developers disagree on the degree of control necessary, the final decision rests with management. Management should be able to assess the cost of controls and compare this to the probable costs of not adopting certain measures. These costs not only include monetary outcomes, but also potential loss of goodwill, legal costs, and costs due to loss of individual and corporate confidentiality. As is so often the case, this involves a cost/benefit analysis, where tangible and intangible variables are intertwined.

Information system documentation

Documentation of the information system is an element inherent in the control process. In preparing documentation, system developers are forced to evaluate each segment of the proposed system before its structure becomes final. Prior to operation, documentation plays a key role in training information system employees, and facilitates clearing errors that are detected on-line.

Two approaches to developing system documentation are common. In many companies, the system is completely developed and only then is documentation provided. Once the system is installed, the designer and/or the application programmer are called upon to prepare the systems manual. They may however, consider this task to be an inappropriate use of their expertise. For them, documentation is the least creative task. In addition, they may not have skills in communicating with non-experts. However, when a technical writer is called in to prepare the systems manual, it may read well, but may be incomplete and/or technically incorrect.

A preferable approach is to create documentation as an integrated part of the development process. Extensive documentation is prepared at each step in design and programming progress. In this way, documentation becomes a by-product of the development process; in fact, development cannot proceed without supporting documentation. Many textbooks on system analysis and design provide sets of forms that can be used for system documentation (for example, see IBM-1975, Shelley-1975). Generally these ensure that documentation follow these principles:

* Consistency - Documentation must maintain consistency in labeling and reference to common terms and prevailing activities.
* Complete headings - All forms should contain complete headings which identify the system, the function being performed, the person responsible for developing that function, and the dates of all updates.
* Agreed set of symbols - All documents, particularly those containing data flow diagrams and flow charts, should use one set of symbols so that every person involved in a project will comprehend the documentation.

Proper maintenance of documentation is as important as its original development. Obsolete documentation may be worse that none, especially if it leads employees up false trails. For proper control, corporate policy should mandate periodic documentation review to determine that it is complete, current, correct, readable, and accessible.

Electronic data processing (EDP) auditing

Computers are becoming more complex. Many now have sophisticated multi-programming capacity, coupled with telecommunications links and a wide variety of new input and output devices. This means that another dimension has been added to the role of control. For example, in order for external financial auditors to fulfill their professional responsibilities, they must now perform a variety of tasks which, until recently, did not exist, or were not considered within the auditor's scope.

Once systems are placed in operation, auditors have a continuing responsibility to review both general controls and application controls. Such reviews are designed to ensure that systems support management policy, and produce reliable results. Auditors must determine whether the objectives of ongoing systems are being satisfied. If EDP accounting is not adequate, auditors may not be able to determine if the financial statements are prepared in conformity with generally accepted accounting principals. As a result, they must qualify their opinion. The financial and legal consequences of such an action are significant.

The responsibilities of modern EDP auditors are not limited to post audit concerns. Their duties include the following:

* They participate in reviewing the design and development of new data processing systems or applications, as well as significant modifications of the system.
* They review general controls in data processing systems to determine that; (1) controls have been designed according to management instructions and legal requirements, and, (2) the controls are operating effectively and reliably.
* They review application controls of installed data processing applications to assess their reliability, timeliness, and accuracy.

EDP auditors have a dual task: they must design as well as evaluate control systems. Participating in the installation of control measures is not the end of the road. Auditors have to be involved in the development and implementation of the information system to make sure that the control measures are operating. Auditors act as observers who remind developers of the audit requirements.

Auditors provide assurances that the clients' EDP systems and applications will:

* Faithfully accomplish the policies prescribed by management for the system.
* Provide the controls and audit trails needed for management, auditor, and operational review.
* Include the controls necessary to protect against loss or serious error.
* Be efficient and economical in operation.
* Conform with applicable legal requirements.
* Be documented so that the system can be maintained and audited.

Auditing approaches

There are two major auditing approaches. The first views the computer process as a 'black box' and analyzes the desirability of input-output relationships. This method is called 'auditing around the computer'. The second approach concentrates on content analysis of the process, and is referred to as 'auditing through the computer'.

Auditing around the computer

The basic concept behind auditing around the computer is that extensive examination of a system's inputs, outputs, and intermediate data, using controlled samples, will indicate whether the system is reliable. Three major criticism of this approach exist. Critics claim that it is superficial, and that it can not cope with applications involving voluminous data. In addition, they say that because it is based on intermediate and final printouts, the audit may not reflect what is really being done inside the computerized process. A final criticism involves that fact that intermediate printouts are not always automatically available. If the auditor requests ad hoc material, she is at the mercy of designers and programmers.

Auditing around the computer was most common at the beginning of the computer era when auditors lacked expertise. This approach was better than nothing. While the method has not been ruled out, it is accepted today as a compliment to more sophisticated techniques.

Auditing through the computer

Auditing through the computer is an approach that can be realized by various techniques. The principle here is that the auditor assesses the reliability of a system by running controlled tests and closely examining all the system's components, not simply the final outputs.

The simplest technique uses *test decks*, in which the auditor prepares test data, which encompasses every possible variation in the processing, including erroneous data. The test data is run through the information system while the auditor observes and analyzes intermediate and final results. These are compared to the expected results determined beforehand.

An extension to this method is the *dummy company* technique. The auditor creates a dummy company with dummy files, and channels artificial transactions through the real programs to see whether the process is performed as intended.

Another technique is *parallel simulation*. When using this technique, the auditor simulates the client's application by generating programs that are supposed to perform the same functions handled by the examined programs. The auditor may then run data (test data or real data) through both systems and look for discrepancies. This technique, however, is relatively costly.

There are many interesting methods of through the computer auditing which incorporate special software packages into EDP auditing (see Cash, et al, 1977; Will, 1978). These packages are specifically designed to aid the auditor in performing her task, particularly by having easy access to files and enabling interactive auditing.

Only a comprehensive examination can provide the auditor with enough evidence as to the degree of reliability of an information system. In addition to the responsibilities and areas already discussed, the auditor has to examine program and system flow-charts, program listings, operational procedures, backup/recovery procedures, and administrative provisions. (For a comprehensive text on EDP audit see Weber, 1982.)

Information system security

The need for information system security grew with the surge in decentralized access to information systems. Problems related to information security are difficult to resolve, since most information systems are normally built to facilitate data dissemination rather than to limit it. This section highlights some major risks and possible security measures.

Major risks

Threats to information system integrity can come from various sources, including nature, human intervention, or technological mistakes. Natural disasters such as fire, flood, and earthquake, can strike anytime and anywhere. Communication lines, computer facilities, and data files, can be damaged by whim of nature. The input of key personnel may be lost due to natural phenomena. Risks may be internal or external, physical and tangible, or intangible, such as loss of goodwill, or loss of data.

Employees, customers, suppliers, and others who interact with the firm, also pose risks to its information system. These threats may be either intentional or inadvertent. For instance, employees may make data entry errors; programmers may create software 'bugs'; hardware may be damaged, installed incorrectly, or otherwise malfunction. Information systems may be thrown askew by the activities of customers, suppliers, and other parties who obtain and/or provide goods or services. Unscrupulous competitors as well as criminals, pose threats to the integrity of the information system. Technology itself poses risk. A new piece of hardware can be unreliable; a new software package can fail to work properly; communication links can fail.

The following are major areas that should be reviewed in order to avoid, or reduce, exposure to risks:

* *Personnel* - Procedures for recruiting and selection, training, promotion, and terminating employment.
* *Physical environment* - Location of buildings, topographical and weather conditions, power supply, and access to the computer installation.
* *Hardware and software systems* - Internal and external maintenance, reliability, vendor support, documentation, and backup.
* *Communications* - Reliability, backup, security, verification, and control procedures.
* *Operations* - Backup procedures, data security, input/output controls, process controls, administrative controls.
* *Contracts* - With vendors and customers.
* *Laws and regulations* - Privacy acts, national security, and internal procedures.

Security measures

Security measures must focus on administrative, technical, and human elements. A senior official should be charged with the responsibility of developing information security policies and overseeing the security program.

Computer security specialists have been described as "a new breed of computer professions...who mix the technical knowledge of a programmer with the suspicions of an auditor and the sleuthing instinct of Hercule Poirot. The combination of the talents is rare, and good computer security experts are in short supply." (*The New York Times*, October 16, 1983). Similar to the EDP auditor, the security officer is responsible for a number of areas, including preparing an organizational security plan for information systems, implementing the plan, and supervising daily security activities.

The *information system security plan* will identify potential risks and assess possible damages. It will also specify measures which reduce or eliminate risk. A security system performs a number of functions, including the following:

Identification. The system should identify the location of each computer terminal, and the communication line that transmits or receives data. Passwords should identify both user and terminal, and a log of all transmissions should be automatically maintained.

Authorization. Access to the system should be limited, based on an established 'need to know' for each class of employment. The system should determine whether to authorize each request to access programs, files, or data from individuals, terminal, and transmission line. Any request that does not comply with an authorized pattern is to be denied.

Data security. The system should control the distribution of output and ensure that programs, data, or reports are not diverted to unauthorized locations. It should protect files and maintain directories. Obsolete data should be deleted from current files, though they may be maintained in backup files for one or two generations. Where necessary, ciphering/ deciphering capability must be maintained.

Communications security. All transmissions should be logged. The system should test the integrity of any line. If the integrity is questioned, the system should take action appropriate for ongoing transmission. On-line warnings should be given, and other appropriate actions taken. If abuse is suspected during sensitive transmissions, the transmission should be terminated.

Information to the security officer. The system must inform the security officer about exceptional activities, based upon predetermined criteria. Moreover, the system should automatically activate predetermined routines designed to minimize damage. (For more details, see Parker, 1981).

Security contingency plan

The security contingency plan must deal with at least three issues:

Emergency plan. This plan describes steps to be taken in case of a specific emergency, such as fire, flood, or sabotage. The plan should detail which materials are to be evacuated, and which rooms and facilities are to be secured. The plan should identify which individuals are responsible for specific tasks.

Backup plan. Unlike the emergency plan, which is rarely activated, the backup plan specifies routine arrangements made for other emergency situations, such as a system failure. These plans include file backups, computer backup, and training of personnel.

Recovery plan. Execution of the recovery plan generally follows an emergency or drill. Using backup files and backup equipment, the system is 'reconstructed'. The recovery plan sets priorities and determines the sequence of recovery activities.

All the components of a contingency plan should be subject to periodic drills, and modified when necessary in the event of changes in the organization and environment. The adequacy of untested plans can not be honestly evaluated.

Information is the basis for all managerial decisions and information control is crucial for efficient and effective operations. Management control over information systems is achieved by integrating audit and control mechanisms throughout all stages of processing, from data input to user access. Although the benefits of information control are hard to quantify, the potential damages caused by inefficient and ineffective information systems is readily apparent.

12 Marketing control

Market controllers at the 'Fast-Fix' Frozen Food Company, became increasingly concerned about a trend showing up in the firm's quarterly marketing reports. Although sales had grown slightly over the successive periods studied, Fast-Fix's market share had steadily declined from period to period. Yet figures showed an increase in market base industry-wide and increasing market share for several of 'Fast-Fix's major competitors.

A market analysis revealed that industry-wide increases were due to the rapid popularization of microwave ovens in domestic use. Market controllers at 'Fast-Fix' realized that certain adjustments to their product line would need to be made in order for Fast-Fix to increase its market share. They designed a plan aimed at product modification, which would include the following changes:

1. Product reformulation to reduce the need for browning, a feature commonly done by conventional ovens, but difficult to achieve in microwave ovens;

2. New inner packaging on sturdy 'plastic' plates, without the use of foil wrap, making the products suitable for heating in both conventional and microwave ovens;

3. New exterior packaging, as well as advertising and promotional campaigns, to inform consumers of the product changes.

Marketing does not operate on the principle of bringing goods to market in hopes of finding consumers. Instead, it operates in the reverse direction. Marketing must start with the consumer and work back to the production of *needed* goods, in the right amounts, and with the right specifications. Marketing management process can be viewed as an integrated sequence of steps, each of which will be discussed in this chapter: goal setting based on a consumer and competitor analysis, organizational considerations, strategy and planning, implementation, and evaluation.

Management sets goals which serve as intermediate steps in the pursuit of the organization's ultimate objectives. The consumer analysis assesses the needs and decision making processes of customers. The competitive analysis assesses existing or potential rivalry among firms selling the same, or substitute, products. Based on these analyses, a strategy and plan is developed and implemented. The marketing management process relies on the control function to continuously evaluate and give feedback on the results.

The marketing manager is responsible for the coordination of all aspects of the *marketing mix*, or the '4 P's':

1. Product (design and development);
2. Price;
3. Promotion (and advertising); and,
4. Place (distribution networks).

No part of the marketing mix is completely free from the need for careful control. Although the products offered by an organization are often relatively fixed, the desired mix of products and services which comprise the marketing program, is highly flexible. Customer acceptance of the product is even more flexible. Even though a product may not change physically, its image or reputation in the market may be drastically altered. The example of tainted Tylenol is a case in point. A significant drop in Tylenol sales volume resulted from isolated instances where the product had been tampered with on the drug store shelves.

The balance of the marketing mix is so involved with forces outside the firm, that change is common, and a strong program of marketing control is vital to the development of an integrated marketing program. Marketing control includes the continuous monitoring of results, such as sales, market share, customer returns, and other criteria relevant to organizational objectives. Rapid changes in the external environment require continual appraisal to ensure the suitability of the designed program. In addition, control must ensure that there is an analysis of deviations, an examination of their causes, and proposals for solutions.

Marketing goals and objectives

As was stressed before, any objective for a department must be derived from the overall objectives of the organization. Within that context, each department or subunit, will develop its own goals. For the marketing department, two goals must be paramount in developing and implementing its marketing plan.

Satisfying the needs of the customer is the starting place for marketing in any organization. Clearly consumers will not purchase products that they do not need. (The term 'need' here is used to denote real or perceived needs or desires.) Therefore, control must ensure that marketing decisions are based on a careful *consumer analysis*, identifying demographics, purchasing habits, needs, motives, and other dynamics of the prospective market. For example, as health conscious baby boomers have babies, companies like Gerber must ready themselves for changes in product line and increased demand coming after a long period of declining sales. Baby boomers, now in their 30s and 40s, will affect many marketing decisions in areas such as product offerings and target marketing.

Even an accurate analysis of the consumer market will not ensure success. Assume you have made a careful consumer analysis, and have launched a new product, for which you are sure there will be a demand. What would happen if an alternative to your product were put on the market? What if this product were less expensive, or of better quality, than yours?

The second marketing goal must be to achieve a *competitive advantage* in the industry. A *competitive analysis* must be part of the picture supplied by the marketing department. Control must ensure that the competitive analysis not only examines existing rivals, but also includes a study of possible substitutes for the organization's product. For example, the manufacturers of tennis rackets must not only compare their position to other tennis racket companies, but also to manufacturers of golf clubs, bicycles, and others who supply products for warm weather sports.

A competent analysis must continually assess the possibility of new entrants which might offer products with better technology, a lower price, or a new concept. For example, new and highly successful entrant into the previously mature tea market was Celestial Seasonings, which developed a line of herb teas designed to appeal to the increasingly health conscious consumer.

Marketing goals must be based on relevant inputs from all other organizational functions, such as operations and finance. There are sometimes inherent conflicts between marketing and functions such as production or finance. Production strives toward efficiency and cost containment. Marketing will find that this translates into a lack of product variety due to longer production runs, fewer product features, and lengthy intervals between product changes. Or, financial executives may lean toward limited inventories, fewer models, less money for promotion and research, and quick return pricing policies. The marketing manager must be aware of these potential conflicts, and understand that they are the result of sub optimization of the individual functions. Control must strive for a working environment where the interest of the organization *as a whole* directs the establishment of the functional goals.

Marketing strategies

Once an analysis is made, marketing must develop a plan to meet the goals of consumer satisfaction and competitive advantage. There are three typical marketing strategies, and control must ensure that each method is examined and that the most favorable alternative, or alternatives, have been selected.

1. The strategy of *product differentiation* aims to develop a product that is, or appears to be, different from others already on the market. This can be accomplished in many ways, such as offering a unique attribute or service, or even the perception of a unique quality. For example, a service station which offers limousine rides to customers whose cars are in for repair, differentiates its product. A Ralph Lauren tee shirt is differentiated from ordinary shirts by its designer label.

2. *Market segmentation* is another marketing strategy which must be considered by marketing managers. Here, the organization attempts to focus upon a specific sector of the market, such as a particular age or economic group. Perrier sparkling water is intended for a different market segment than is Diet Coke, although they are both products in the low-calorie, bottled drink industry.

3. Although all organizations attempt to keep costs down, all must consider *overall cost leadership* as a potential marketing strategy. The aim here is to achieve efficiencies which allow for high volume and low per unit profit margins. Successful cost leadership makes it difficult for rivals to compete on the basis of price, and discourages new entrants because low margins are disadvantageous to smaller, newer organizations. Marketing strategy is also highly influenced by the environment and the present stage of the product life cycle, as explained in the following two sections.

The marketing environment can affect goals and strategies

Marketing is a boundary system, interacting with many internal and external systems. As a result, the control function must ensure that marketing understands the environment in which a firm operates.

Marketing managers face an external environment that is subject to a number of powerful forces. These forces create and influence changes in consumer demand and public needs. The marketing manager must understand and forecast how key forces will affect the external environment, and must alter the marketing program accordingly.

There are a number of key factors that force changes in the external environment. They are social and economic factors, domestic and foreign competition, legal and political factors, technology, foreign governments, and demographics. For example, the changing political climate in France has forced one pharmaceutical company to dramatically alter its plans to market a new product, RU 486, or 'the abortion pill'. These forces have surely impacted marketing plans in other countries as well.

One of the most important factors in the external environment is social change. People's behavior and consumption patterns are influenced in part by culture. Marketing managers have adapted to America's changing life style by offering more variety and convenience in foods, more economical automobiles, and more outlets for physical exercise. Economic trends also play an important role. For example, during the inflationary period of the 1970s, marketers who hesitated to raise prices for fear of losing customers, often experienced severe losses in their own purchasing capabilities.

The devaluation of the dollar in the 80s has impacted many marketing decisions. Domestic firms are not the only ones vying for market share and profits in the U.S. The automobile, textile, steel, optical product, and banking markets, have been deeply penetrated by foreign businesses. By the end of the 1980s, imports of Japanese automobiles accounted for 20% of the cars purchased in the U.S., and Rebok's imports of shoes increased 52 percent in 1987 (*Business Week*, 2/29/87). These issues will be discussed further in the section on international marketing, later in this chapter.

The legal environment of marketing defines the parameters within which management must operate. Legislation, like other variables, tends to change over time, and new government regulations can require major changes in a firm's marketing mix. Control must ensure that marketing is adjusting to changes in legislation. The trend toward banning smoking in public places, for example, must alter the way that the tobacco industry does its business. Marketing managers must face two major sources of regulation -- federal and state. Most federal regulation of marketing activities is administered through the Federal Trade Commission (FTC). The FTC, unlike most other regulatory agencies, has broad powers, and its mandate from Congress permits it to regulate almost any industry.

Effects of the product life cycle

Products undergo a maturation cycle from the time that a new product is introduced into the marketplace, until the time that it is no longer profitable, and is taken off the market. This life cycle has significant implications for the marketing strategy.

As you can see in Exhibit 12.1, when a new product reaches the market, not only are sales low, but they grow at a slow pace. The task of marketing at this *introduction stage*, is to use advertising and promotion to increase consumer awareness and trust, and to stimulate sales.

Exhibit 12.1
Product life cycle

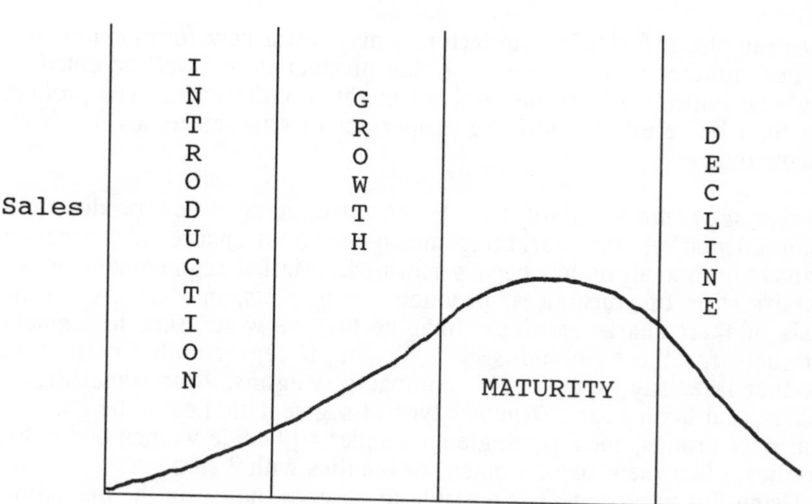

Assuming that the product is received well after its introduction, it enters the *growth stage* in which sales continue to increase, but at a more rapid rate. Here, marketing must ensure that consumer demand is met, and that other products which compete for this successful market, do not gain market share. Over the course of this period of *maturity*, all aspects of the marketing mix may be adjusted to maintain a competitive advantage.

At some point, for some products, demand begins to decline as consumers change habits, or technology makes existing products obsolete. During this period of *decline*, marketing must cut its losses, decreasing advertising, promotion, and development. The product may be withdrawn from the market entirely.

The marketing plan

Product

Test marketing. In the development stage, ideas that were once on paper, become products that can be produced and shown to the public. Test marketing should be considered for two purposes:

1. to judge the new product's sales potential; and,

2. to experiment with alternatives in the marketing mix.

For example, soft drink manufacturers may test a new formulation on a limited number of consumers. If the product is not well accepted, it might be reformulated or the package might be redesigned. The product can then be retested, until the proper set of characteristics has been discovered.

Market segmentation analysis. When introducing a new product to a potential market, the marketing manager should ensure that a market segmentation analysis has been performed. Market segmentation is the classification of consumers, products, or markets, into groups, on the basis of their characteristics. Imagine that we were asked to segment products for the auto industry. We might segment this market by product line, say, sports cars, compacts, wagons, four wheel drive, sedans, and luxury cars. Another type of segmentation could be done by consumer groups, such as, single men under 40, single women under 40, families, older men, older women, or families with 2 cars.

Using this approach, it is possible to observe 'holes' in the marketing pattern, or areas of unfulfilled consumer need. Exhibit 12.2 shows a hypothetical market segmentation analysis by product characteristics for apple drinks. This analysis would indicate a potential opening in the 'pure' juice/moderate price market. Of course, we would need to determine the level of consumer interest and our ability to cost effectively produce the product before going further into new product development.

In general, in order to apply market segmentation to one's product, there must be a detailed analysis of:

1. consumers and products based on group characteristics;

2. consumer values relative to the type of products, such as the importance of quality, style, or price;

3. how consumers would rate competing brands in the product category relative to your product's specific benefits;

4. criteria you will use to determine target market and product position.

Exhibit 12.2
Market segmentation analysis

NATURAL

*Nature's Own
*Good Times

*Jumping' Juicy

LOW PRICE

*Budget

HIGH PRICE

*Sweetness
*Apple-Aide

*Passion Fruit

*Good Enuf

ARTIFICIAL

*Brand names are ficticius and any resemblance to actual products is accidental.

With this information, segments with unsatisfied demands may be discovered. The new product can then be positioned so that certain qualities can be promoted, or advertising can be directed to certain consumer groups.

Product line analysis. Often, a company will realize that it has not met objectives, but the reason is not apparent at first glance. This is where *product line analysis* can be of tremendous assistance. The break down sales and profit figures by product lines is often the key to revealing quite unexpected results. product line analysis divides the sales of a particular product, or product line, by total company sales. The result is the relative sales contribution, or the percent of total sales contributed, by the particular product.

Using product line analysis, a company will find out that 20% of its products account for 70% to 80% of its sales (see Pareto's Law, Chapter 8). An awareness of this ratio will allow the marketing manager to make decisions concerning the product mix which will best allow the company to meet its goals. For example, it might be decided to concentrate marketing attention on lines with the greatest sales, or to drop slower, less popular lines.

Of course, careful consideration regarding the reason for any sales drop must be examined. Factors such as reduced market consumption, ineffective selling, and increased competition, are just a few of the possible reasons for changing sales. Product line analysis can be easily extended to show distribution by product type, size, price, or even packaging.

Price

In addition to offering new products, or altering existing product specifications, other changes in the marketing mix should be considered and monitored in order to achieve marketing goals. Typical pricing objectives are designed to:

1. obtain a satisfactory return on investment or sales;
2. meet and counter competition;
3. establish a target share of the market;
4. optimize profits.

A number of issues must be considered when pricing a particular product or service. A careful analysis of the *price elasticity of demand* is required. This is a specific measure of how alterations in price affect demand for a given product, and is defined as:

$$\text{Price Elasticity of Demand} = \frac{\text{\% Change in Quantity of Demand}}{\text{\% Change in Price}}$$

Changes in price can either increase or decrease total revenue. The actual result will depend on the elasticity function.

Another important factor to analyze is the pricing of substitute products. For example, the bottlers of Perrier have made a conscious pricing decision, aware of the position of alternatives such as club soda, seltzer, and other bottled drinks.

The pricing policy for a particular product can also have important effects on other products sold by the same company. For example, many restaurants serve meals at break even prices intending to make large profits on drinks. A firm's hierarchy of objectives, and general marketing mix strategy must be consistent and the pricing strategy of competitors should be understood and considered.

In establishing a pricing policy one should consider legal aspects as well. The United States tends to emphasize a free market system, but laws and state regulations do govern pricing policies in important instances. The FTC keeps a close watch on pricing practices. For example, the FTC is charged with enforcing the Robinson-Patman Act. This law forbids discriminatory pricing, that is, charging one customer a different price than another, for the same product, unless there are real cost differences associated with each customer. Consideration should be given to potential legal reaction by competitors, or regulatory agencies, that could be triggered by a given pricing strategy.

In order to arrive at an acceptable price, an analysis of the appropriate costs incurred in the production and marketing of a product must be determined. Several methods are used:

1. *The cost-plus approach* -- With this method, the price of a particular product is determined by adding an arbitrary amount or percentage to the unit's total cost, in order to produce a satisfactory profit. This approach is commonly used when working on new projects for the government and the military.

2. *Competitive pricing* -- With this approach, prices are set at the going rate.

3. *Market penetration pricing* -- Here prices are set below the competition in order to capture a share of the market. With market penetration pricing, firms are willing to underprice even to the point of sustaining a loss for a limited period.

4. *Market skimming* -- With this approach, the firm sets its price high, with the aim of either leaving the market at a later time, or lowering its price systematically over time.

A relatively new concept with a potential impact on the long range behavior of the marketing function, is the use of the *life cycle cost approach*. This approach calls for an analysis aiming to maximize total profit over the product life. For example, a company may choose to price a product very low, but earn a high return on the service contract. Using the life cycle cost approach requires a long term view of performance evaluation since the product cycle does not end when the product is sold.

It is important for control to ensure that the pricing strategy is consistent with the overall product strategy. For example, products should not be priced high at a time when the goal is to gain market share.

Place

In order to successfully market needed products, they must be accessible to the perspective user. The product must be placed where consumers can readily make the transaction from concept to use. Marketing helps create the need for the product by informing the potential customer of the availability of the product. It remains the task of the distribution function to ensure that the right product is at the right place at the right time, and for control to verify that this is happening.

The distribution function has two primary areas of responsibility. The first is concerned with physical distribution. Included in this is a mixture of all logistic components; location, transportation, inventory, communication, and material handling.

The second aspect deals with the selection of a distribution or marketing channel. The typical distribution channel involves a number of intermediaries who assist the company by performing tasks necessary to complete the final transfer of the product to the end user. Among the most important operational objectives of any channel management program is to provide a product, or service, of desired quality, when it is needed, where it is needed, and at the right price.

Territorial analysis. The distribution network is typically divided into territories, which are monitored separately. Often, a company is interested in studying the relative sales achieved in different territories. By using territorial analysis, companies will find that as much as 70% of total sales will be accounted for by only a few territories. Territorial analysis is obtained by dividing the total sales in a particular territory by the total sales for the country as a whole. The percentage can be easily compared to the same figure for industry competitors in the same territory. If a firm's territorial percentage figure is low in a territory where the overall industry figure is low, it can be concluded that low figures are the result of low product consumption, rather than ineffective company sales or increased competition.

Territorial analysis offers another measure of effectiveness. By multiplying total company sales by a general market index for that particular territory, the resulting figure gives some indication of the company's success in that region.

Promotion

The total promotional budget should be established at a level so that the added profit from each additional promotional dollar equals the marginal profit from using that dollar in the best non-promotional alternative. Exhibit 12.3a depicts a firm where the marginal profit from promotion justifies the expense, whereas Exhibit 12.3b illustrates a firm which should discontinue its promotion after $X is spent. Since promotion is only one of several ways to stimulate sales, companies face the question of whether promotional funds should be reassigned to other sales stimulators such as, marketing research, new product development, lower prices, or more customer service.

Members of marketing organizations have strong and varied feelings about the proper proportion of the company's promotion money to spend on different promotional tools. A sales manager might find it hard to understand, for example, how the company would get more value by spending $300,000 for a one-minute television commercial than by hiring and training three or four additional salespeople. Disagreement abounds, but organizational integration is needed. A product manager may be considering a spoon premium to boost sales, unaware of the fact that this premium recently bombed for another product. By centralizing and analyzing data on promotional efforts for a product, the company is in an excellent position to improve upon its promotional planning.

Deciding on the best mixture of personal selling and non-personal promotional tools is a complex problem. Personal selling is face-to-face communication, and while expensive, it is the most compelling medium available to a seller. Non-personal media put more distance between the seller and potential buyer. Radio, television, newspapers, fliers, and billboards are the most frequently used. Control must ensure that the relative merits of each approach have been analyzed before the final combination of methods is chosen. Clearly, the issue remains fluid in nature, and methods for evaluation and change must be in place.

Exhibit 12.3
Marginal profit of two different promotional campaigns

12.3a

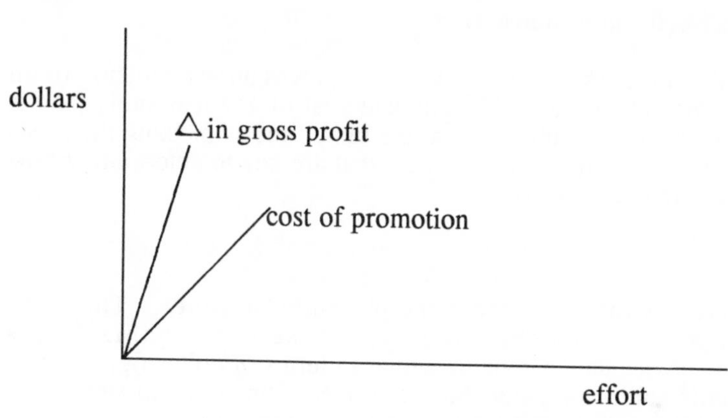

12.3b

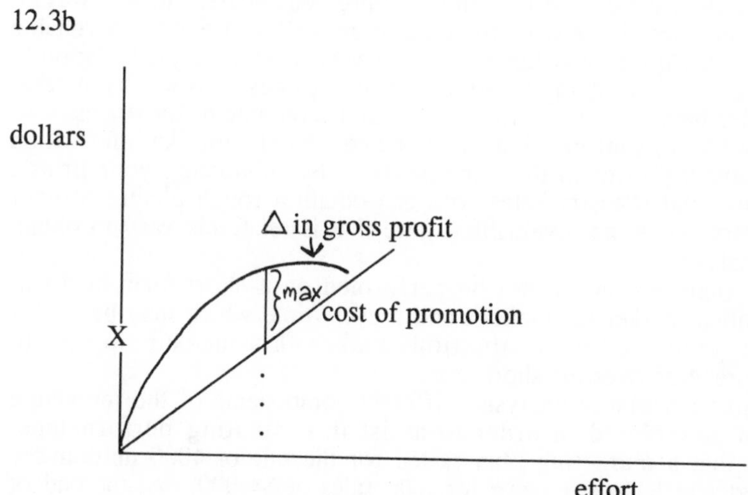

Effective advertising usually requires large sums of money, therefore, the less financially capable a company, the more is its reliance on the personal selling approach. For example, Coke and Pepsi have dominated the soft drink market, in part, because of their ability to advertise heavily. Proctor and Gamble spent $75 million in 1987 alone advertising just its Citrus Hill brand of orange juice. Advertising is usually extremely effective -- but it is also very costly. During the growth stage in the product life cycle, advertising is most effective. As previously mentioned, it is during the period of maturity that a company must be careful in its allocation of promotional funds. For instance, it would not make sense for IBM to spend a large percentage of advertising dollars to promote its old line of PCs.

Performance criteria in marketing

The evaluation of marketing effectiveness involves an examination of all areas of the marketing plan. The ultimate goal of any marketing plan is to achieve a competitive advantage at the same time as meeting the needs of consumers. There are several criteria that are key to determining how well a marketing plan is working.

Sales

In the marketing function, the principle output is *sales*. This is of utmost importance in checking the marketing organization's performance. Sales data can be looked at in terms of dollar figures or in terms of units sold, and often both are needed in order to supply the market controller with an adequate source of information.

More significant than absolute sales figures is an analysis which compares current sales with figures for previous years. In this way, a manager can see degrees of fluctuation as well as trends. A reliable index of *general* business fluctuations must be used during calculation to eliminate from company figures, those changes affected by market conditions, such as seasonal fluctuations and economic disturbances.

If possible, this information should be compared with like information from competing firms in the same market. By subtracting your firms's sales from total industry sales, you can obtain a rough picture of your competitors' sales, an invaluable figure that is relatively easy to obtain and to analyze.

Sales analyses should not be performed on a short term horizon. Uncontrolled market fluctuations and a cycle time which may be longer than the period under evaluation, makes this measure prone to misinterpretation over the short term.

By using a variance analysis, different components of the marketing plan can be isolated in order to assist in evaluating performance. Suppose that a marketing plan called for the sale of 4000 units in the first quarter at $1 per unit, or for total sales of $4,000. At the end of the quarter, only 3,000 units were sold, and these at an average price of $.80 per unit, making a sales total of only $2,400. The question arises -- how much of this under performance is due to the price decline and how much is due to the volume decline? The following calculation answers the question:

Variance due to price decline = (\$1 - .80)(3,000) = \$600
Variance due to volume decline = (\$1)(4000-3000) = \$1000

Since the total variance is \$1600, the portion of that variance which is the result of the drop in price is 600/1600, or 37.5%. The decline in sales volume however, is responsible for almost two-thirds of the variance, or 1000/1600, 62.5%. Making this type of analysis enables control to isolate the effects of different variables in the marketing mix.

Evaluation of the sales force

Several characteristics of sales force operations affect the nature of the marketing control process. Very often, organizational and physical distance between salespeople and management impose certain constraints on the nature of the control process. Often, the results of employees' efforts are not immediate; sales transactions are not executed at the press of a button.

A major difficulty encountered in the control and evaluation of sales force operations is found in the comparing process. For example, product acceptance as measured by market share differs among territories and can profoundly affect the level of, and change in, sales. Variations in the physical size of sales territories result in different sales efforts for the same sales volumes. Market growth and decline in a particular sector of the market, and gains of losses beyond the control of the salespeople, can result in favorable or unfavorable records which are unrelated to actual performance. For example, it wouldn't make sense to compare a salesperson in Alaska with one from New York City in the basis of miles traveled per week.

Exhibit 12.4 compares some commonly used performance criteria. The first column includes PC which suffer from the weaknesses mentioned above. The second column includes those performance criteria which are more linked to the efforts of the individual. By making an objective study of each salesperson's performance, and by comparing such figures to predetermined standards of performance, the marketing controller is made more aware of 'actual' versus 'ideal' ratios.

Exhibit 12.4
Effective and ineffective performance criteria used to evaluate salespeople

Effective:	Ineffective:
% change in sales	\$ sales
% change in new accounts	number of new accounts
% change in market share	number of calls
customer satisfaction rating	calls per order
calls per \$ of sales	

Market share

Another crucial marketing performance criterion is market share. This is defined as the percent of your company's share of sales in existing market. It is certainly true that this ratio can be affected by forces outside the control of the marketing department. However, if other factors have not changed, market share is usually altered by the market penetration which results from advertising and promotion. For example, we could deduce that the marketing plan is behind Rebok's increased market share if; there are no new entrants into the athletic shoe market, the quality and pricing of existing products remains stable, and Rebok engages in a large marketing campaign.

When using the criterion of market share, it is important to analyze the *reason* for changes and not just the changes themselves. Your company may recognize a drop in market share as a result of decreased sales. If the decrease in demand is industry-wide and demand for your company's product is decreasing at a rate that is significantly lower than that of the rest of the industry, you might consider changes in promotional activity and an adjustment in overall production schedules to respond to the situation. If however, your company experiences a drop in market share at a time when the industry-wide figures show a rise in demand, you might plan product adjustments and recommend increased expenditures for new product development.

In the analysis of sales and market share, several rules must be remembered in order to avoid reaching incorrect conclusions. Firstly, not all firms are affected similarly by mutual external environmental changes. The weakening of the dollar which occurred in the 80's had vastly different effects on leisure industries. While overseas travel, cruise, and hotel industries suffered, camping equipment and recreational vehicle sales rose.

Secondly, market entry of new competition does not necessarily translate into a drop in sales for existing firms. New entrants may increase *primary* demand for all products in the category and in that way, benefit existing products by increasing their sales (secondary demand).

Thirdly, certain policies adopted by firms might include intentionally reducing current market share in order to strengthen the company's position with a few of its most important customers.

Lastly, it must be remembered that not all market fluctuations have the same implications for all products in all territories. Low territory sales can be the results of a wide variety of factors, including;

- ineffective salespeople,
- increased competition
- reduced consumption rate
- low sales potential

- changing consumer buying trends
- ineffective distribution methods.

Evaluation of advertising efforts

There is no direct ratio that can accurately assess the effectiveness of advertising in producing increased sales. In fact, little is known about cause-and-effect relationships between advertising and sales.

The two most widely accepted measures of advertising effectiveness are *recognition* and *recall* tests. In recognition, a person is shown an ad and asked if they recognize having seen it before. With recall testing, the individual is given a small cue from an ad, and asked it they can generate information about the product. Opinion and attitude ratings, consumer inquiries, and of course, sales, are other measures used to quantify the effectiveness of advertising.

While these tests will measure the effectiveness of advertising, it is clear that the control function must assure that the company is not overspending to achieve results. Management can compare expense to revenue ratios to see which ones are growing out of control. For example, an advertising manager should pay close attention to the following:

1. advertisement cost...cost per thousand consumers reached by an ad;

2. promotional cost...cost per thousand consumers reached by each media category and vehicle;

3. percent of vehicle's audience reached by ad; or,

4. change in share of favorable attitudes following ad.

Marketing productivity

Unfortunately, most marketing costs are highly visible, while their links to output are less clear. Management needs a way of assessing how efficiently the marketing function is being performed. Such an assessment is required for effective resource allocation and performance appraisal.

Marketing productivity is a ratio of marketing output divided by marketing resources. The output of a firm's marketing effort can be thought of in several different ways, such as sales, market share, awareness levels, or repeat purchases.

Once your method of defining marketing output has been determined, the marketing resources, or input, required to generate this output must be established. While marketing expenses is the most appealing input measure, expressing marketing cost as percent of sales, allows the manager to measure the marketing output purchased for each percent of sales spent on marketing efforts. This approach allows us to observe how the portion of the firm's resources devoted to marketing is functioning over time. We will define marketing resources, or inputs in the following manner:

$$\text{Marketing input} = \frac{\text{Marketing expenditures}}{\text{Sales}}$$

By slightly altering the inverse of the marketing input ratio, we have a simple way to measure marketing productivity:

$$\text{Marketing productivity} = \frac{\text{Change in sales}}{\text{Change in marketing expenditures}}$$

If in a given year, your firm spent an additional $1,000,000 in marketing and realized $20,000,000 in increased sales, your marketing productivity ratio would be 20.

Looked at by itself, the value 20 has no meaning, but it does take on meaning when compared to other productivity values, such as last year's figure, or the productivity of your competitors. Changes in the marketing plan would be geared to increasing the marketing productivity figure.

It is important to realize that this measure can only be understood in the context of examining all other factors which might have affected sales. If not, the ratio as stated would imply that all changes in sales were the result of changes in marketing expenditures alone.

There exist many additional marketing ratios which can be implemented, reported and studied based on the needs of individual players in the marketing setup. Each can be used as a valuable tool in determining the marketing efficiency (Kotler, 1984). The marketing cost/profit ratio is a particularly meaningful productivity measure since it compares dollars gained with dollars invested in marketing.

Since this is one of the most important productivity measures, the following paragraphs will examine common methods of analysis using different categories, such as product groups, territories, customers, etc. The main objective of such a task is to examine specific and distinct areas where the company can make changes in order to improve marketing productivity.

In marketing cost analysis, there are three financial reports to be considered. Initially, the analysis of the basic operating statements, i.e. those which are prepared for general accounting purposes. Secondly, an examination of costs outlayed in performing particular marketing functions, and finally, a study of costs based on the purposes for which they were incurred.

In analyzing the basic operational statements, an analysis of expenses according to their nature is initiated. A company's profit and loss statements are examples of such documents. The marketing controller would break this information down into categories, for example, by territory or by product groups. The remapping of such expenses used to be tedious and cumbersome, however, advanced information system methods are of great assistance in recent years.

Exhibit 12.5 through Exhibit 12.8 illustrate the mechanical transformation of a simple profit and loss statement to a functional expense chart, an allocation of expenses by territory analysis, and finally, a profit and loss statement by territorial division.

Exhibit 12.5
Marketing accounting profit and loss statement

	Sales		40,000
	Cost of Goods Sold		19,000
	Gross margin		21,000
Expenses:			
	Personnel	6,000	
	Rent	2,000	
	Other	2,500	
			10,500
	Net Profit		10,000

Exhibit 12.6
Division of natural expenses into functional expenses

Natural Accounts	Sales	Promotion	Distribution	Other
Personnel	4000	1000	500	500
Rent	------	500	1000	500
Other	600	1500	400	------
Total	4600	3000	1900	1000

International marketing control

Engaging in international marketing activities is different from marketing products or services in a domestic market. Exhibit 12.9 highlights a few of the differences. It is important to recognize that such differences exist, for they must be carefully considered when devising an international marketing plan. The large domestic market that provided U.S. marketers with seemingly endless growth opportunities has, for many products, leveled off and even declined. This means that new market opportunities must be found if growth and profit rates are to be maintained.

Exhibit 12.7
Allocation of functional expenses by territory

Territory	Sales	Promotion	Distribution	Other
	Number of sales calls per month	Amount of advertising per month	Number of orders distributed per month	Number of orders placed per month
A	40	100	30	30
B	100	-----	40	30
C	60	400	30	40
Total	200	500	100	100
Expense per unit	23	6	19	10

Identifying and evaluating foreign market potential

Identifying specific markets, and placing a potential monetary value on them, relies heavily on estimates and forecasts. Five types of estimates and forecasts are common and useful:

1. Estimates of current market potential;

2. Forecast of future market potential, where economic, cultural, legal, and political factors, are carefully reviewed;

3. Forecast of sales potential and market value;

4. Forecasts of costs and profits; and,

5. Estimates of rate of return on investment.

This is a typical example where the function of control is primarily to evaluate the *process* by which a decision was made.

Tailoring the marketing program

Product. With available marketing research information, the marketer can decide whether to sell the same product abroad as at home, to modify it for the foreign market, or to develop an entirely new product. A number of product strategies exist to help adapt to foreign markets.

The simplest strategy is to offer the same product and message in all markets -- product extension. Pepsi, Coke, Wrigley's, and Levi's all follow this strategy, and they have been very successful. *Product adaptation* involves modifying the product to meet local preferences or conditions. Exxon modifies its gasoline to adjust to different climates.

Exhibit 12.8
Profit and loss statement by territory

	Territory A	B	C	Whole company Total
Sales	10,000	20,000	10,000	40,000
Cost of Goods Sold	4,750	9,500	4,750	19,000
Gross margin	5,250	10,500	5,350	21,000
EXPENSES				
Sales ($23 per day)	920	2,300	1,380	4,600
Promotion ($6 per adv)	600	------	2,400	3,000
Distribution ($19 per order)	570	760	570	1,900
Other ($10 per order)	300	300	400	1,000
Total expenses	2,390	3,360	4,750	10,500
Net profit	2,860	7,140	500	10,500

Exhibit 12.9
Characteristics of domestic and international markets

Domestic	International
One language, one nation-lity	Multilingual, multicultural
Data readily available	Data more difficult to collect
Uniform financial climate	Variety of financial climates
One currency	Different currencies and values
Monetary stability	Varying degrees of stability
Mature business rules	Diverse, changeable rule

Sometimes, a fundamental concept has to be totally changed to meet a market's needs and preferences -- *product invention*. For example, millions of people still scrub their clothes by hand, but only recently have companies attempted to develop an inexpensive manual washing machine (Kinnear). Although the opportunities for inventing new products are great, the response of firms so far has been small.

Place. To succeed in a foreign market, a firm must have an adequate distribution system. The three major types of intermediaries used by American companies to penetrate international markets are:

1. Resident buyers within the foreign nations who work for foreign companies;

2. Overseas representatives of foreign firms; and,

3. Independent intermediaries who either purchase goods and sell them abroad, or arrange to bring buyers and sellers of goods together.

Promotion. The ideal promotional message in any country depends on the characteristics of its society. Promotional campaigns may have to be changed because of language barriers or cultural differences. The medium used to convey advertising messages may also pose international marketing problems because availability differs considerably from country to country. In Sweden, for example, commercial television time is not available, and commercial radio in France is non-existent.

Price. Pricing decisions are made in a similar manner in both international and domestic markets. The cost-plus approach (discussed earlier) is generally used more in foreign than domestic markets. This approach, coupled with other international market cost factors (e.g. tariffs, shipping costs, and larger margins for intermediaries), can cause major differences in foreign and domestic prices for the same product. Some multinationals will attempt to sell their products at lower prices in foreign markets. This practice is called dumping, and is used to gain entry into the market. Dumping is not always looked upon favorably, especially if the foreign country offers competing products at higher prices. In fact, the US has set 'trigger' prices for steel products and will pose a special tax on countries which 'dump' products on the US market.

While international marketing is complex, it offers tremendous opportunities to many firms. Discovering these opportunities requires hard work, creativity, and bringing together the product and customer by applying the marketing concepts we have discussed. The role of control in this respect is to verify that all the required steps were taken to explore the international avenue, and to ensure that a system is in place to initiate new actions when needed. Once established, the same objectives, principles, implementation strategies, and criteria for evaluation apply.

In many cases, the control system uncovers internal sources of deviation from acceptable standards of performance. By using directive marketing management, forces can be redirected to fit more accurately within the framework of the current marketing plan. Such corrective actions might include:

* price adjustments
* changes of sales strategy
* personnel changes
* production changes
* redirection of R&D investments.

When deviations are in the external environment, it may be necessary to incorporate changes of a different nature. Needless to say, external changes, though more difficult to deal with, are not necessarily more troublesome than internal deviations. By reappraising the external climate, the effects of minor adjustments can be tested for viability over time. Such changes might include actions such as:

* becoming a member of a manufacturer's organization
* increasing communication with competitors
* lobbying efforts
* price wars between competitors.

Regardless of the outcome of the market control system, the key to successful application of change lies in the company's flexibility and ability to incorporate such change. Without both characteristics, a well designed plan is of little use. A firm having all the tools necessary to initiate change, but not flexible enough to use them, will remain exactly where it is. Similarly, a marketing organization with all the will and good intentions in the world, will have a hard time improving its marketing situation without the tools to measure results and assess the need for change. By combining good initial planning, good marketing control techniques, and the willingness and ability to perform necessary adjustments, even a seemingly unstable market plan can get back on track and be the key to success.

13 Human resources control

Imagine that you are a new employee in the Human Resources department of a company which manufactures electronics equipment. You have been asked to investigate a situation which has come up in your organization. A supervisory position had opened up in one of the production departments. The initial selection process had narrowed the field down to three candidates. After interviewing all three, the department head made his final selection. When the decision was announced, both of the candidates who were not promoted, independently contacted the personnel department, claiming that the department head had not been fair in making the promotion.

During your inquiry you learn that all three candidates have worked in the production department for some time, and have good work records. Mary Smith, one of the two employees not promoted, had been especially active on various committees and had come up with several new ideas which had contributed significantly to improving work methods and productivity in the department. Mary had recently become the chair of one of these committees.

In talking with Mary, you learn that during her interview, the department head, Mr. Goodfellow, asked her if she felt that she would be able to handle the additional responsibilities of the supervisory position, even though she had two children. Mary had told Mr. Goodfellow that both she and her husband had discussed the question thoroughly and that her children were in school most of the day, and were old enough to be at home alone. In addition, Mary told Mr. Goodfellow that her husband got off work early enough to be home by the time the children were there.

Bob Tran, the other person who was denied the promotion, was a Southeast Asian immigrant who recently completed his undergraduate degree in Business Administration, going to school at night. Despite working a full-time job, Bob graduated with honors and at the same time was one of the department's most productive employees. This had made him very well respected by his coworkers. After talking with Bob, you learn that he was surprised that he did not get the promotion. He felt his interview had gone well and that Mr. Goodfellow had been impressed with his work record and with the suggestions he had made regarding the role of the supervisor.

Tom Jones, the man who was promoted, had a family, like Mary. Tom had three small children. Tom's work record was good, but because he had not participated in any committees, he had not distinguished himself as being responsible for initiating new ideas in the department.

You learn from Tom, that during his interview, Tom had explained to Mr. Goodfellow that one of the reasons that he had not had time to do committee work, was because his wife was in school and, therefore, he had child care responsibilities. Tom felt that he had been able to assure Mr. Goodfellow that he was eager and energetic, and that he would be able to meet the demands of the job of production supervisor.

Mr. Goodfellow is an experienced manager, who has been with your company for 15 years. During that time, he has made many personnel decisions regarding promotion, hiring, firing and routine evaluation. The methods he uses in making these decisions are consistent with those recommended by the company.

When you meet with Mr. Goodfellow, he expresses concern about the situation. He is very willing to discuss his selection process with you, but explains that decisions of this type are usually difficult, and that often the individuals that are passed over feel that the process was not fair.

In talking with him, you learn that Mr. Goodfellow thought that all three candidates were qualified for the position. He was very impressed with Mary's leadership and creativity. In fact, he would have promoted her except that he was afraid that her family responsibilities would interfere with her ability to perform in a more demanding position.

Mr. Goodfellow was also impressed with Bob. He felt that Bob had learned a great deal in school that he was applying to his job, and his record was excellent. Mr. Goodfellow's hesitation in promoting Bob, centered around his concern that, as an immigrant, he would have difficulty in taking leadership in the department.

Although Tom was not as impressive a candidate as the other two, Mr. Goodfellow felt that he could do the job, and that he would make the easiest transition into the position. Mr. Goodfellow claims that he has made many other selection decisions using similar criteria.

You realize that Mr. Goodfellow's selection process is not only against the law, but that the most qualified candidate was not the one who was promoted. This is a loss to the department and the company. If this selection process is consistent throughout the company, serious legal issues arise and valuable human resources are being wasted at great cost to the organization. The control function is of utmost importance in this respect, as it serves to ensure that company policies conform to legal requirements and that personnel decisions are made wisely. The following section presents a brief outline of the regulations regarding selection decisions.

Guidelines on employee selection procedures

During the 1960s and 1970s, four major federal agencies began to tackle the problem of unfair personnel practices on the job. This occurred as a result of the passage of the Civil Rights Act in 1964, and of the civil rights and women's movements of the time. Each of these agencies issued separate sets of guidelines for employers to use in making selection decisions. Unfortunately, these guidelines occasionally conflicted with each other, and organizations which attempted to comply, were often frustrated in their efforts.

In 1978, the Equal Employment Opportunity Commission (EEOC) issued the *Uniform Guidelines on Employee Selection*, which became the law of the land, replacing any previously existing regulations (Federal Register, 1978). These guidelines included the following rules:

1. On the basis of Title VII of the Civil Rights Acts of 1964 and 1972, employers are prohibited from discrimination in employment decisions on the basis of race, color, religion, sex, national origin, age or physical handicap.

2. Employment decisions are defined as any process that leads to selection, hiring, training, promotion, retention or dismissal of employees. These include methods such as; written tests, performance appraisals, and interviews.

3. For discrimination to be present, it is not necessary for there to have been an *intent* to discriminate.

4. Discrimination is defined as an *adverse impact* on a group protected by the Civil Rights Act. Adverse impact is specifically defined by the *Guidelines*, and is explained below.

Adverse impact on the four-fifths rule

The four-fifths rule states that the selection ratio for a protected group must not fall below 4/5s, or 80%, of the selection ratio of the majority group. If the selection process results in a ratio of less than 80%, this is considered *prima facie*, 'on first view', evidence of discrimination. While this is not proof of discrimination, it is evidence enough to allow the federal government to scrutinize any procedure used in the selection process. Exhibit 13.1 shows situations of both adverse impact, and no adverse impact, in promotion decisions.

Exhibit 13.1
The four-fifths rule

<u>Situation #1</u>: All employees with at least 2 years seniority in a department are tested to determine if they are eligible for additional training and potential raises.

80 men have seniority	100 women have seniority
32 men pass the test	30 women pass the test
40% success rate	30% success rate

Impact Ratio = 30/40 or 75%

Conclusion: Since 75% is less than 4/5's, there is adverse impact, and therefore, prima facie evidence of discrimination.

<u>Situation #2</u>: 200 applicants have responded to an ad for a welders training program at a shipyard. There are 25 openings.

157 whites applied	43 Blacks applied
20 whites are selected	5 blacks are selected
13% success rate	12% success rate

Impact Ratio = 12/13 or 92%

Conclusion: There is no adverse impact.

Even when adverse impact does exist, if an employer is able to show that in the selection process, job related qualities were tested using reliable and valid measures (see Chapter 6), then there is no discrimination. Let's look at an example of such a situation.

A reliable and valid, job related proficiency test is given to all employees completing a training program required for transfer to another department within a company. As a result of this test, the selection rate for women to be transferred is less than 80% that of men. Because the organization can show that the decisions were based on the results of an accurate measure, the organization is not guilty of discrimination. This situation could occur, for example, if physical strength were a necessary requirement for successful performance in the position. It is likely that a disproportionate number of women would not possess that particular qualification.

The *Uniform Guidelines* are designed to protect employees from arbitrary, discriminatory, and prejudicial decisions such as the one made by Mr. Goodfellow in the example above. What was wrong with his decision making process, and the methods used by the company?

Mr. Goodfellow's selection process discriminated on the basis of national origin and sex. Mr. Goodfellow did not ask the same questions of all candidates. He asked Mary about her ability to care for her children if she were promoted, yet he did not ask this question of the two male employees, despite the fact that one of them was known to have small children at home. In this way, Mr. Goodfellow was giving two different tests for the same position, determining which test to give on the basis of the sex of the candidate.

Even though Mary had given much thought to the question Mr. Goodfellow had raised, had prepared for the additional work load, and had previously demonstrated her ability to handle extra work, Mr. Goodfellow none-the-less concluded that she could not assume the responsibility because of her commitments at home.

Bob, an obviously qualified candidate and a well respected member of the department, was denied the promotion on the basis of his national origin. Mr. Goodfellow assumed that Bob would be compromised in his performance as a supervisor, because of the attitudes of other employees. This was despite much evidence to the contrary.

You are concerned about your company's personnel practices. With the information you have collected, you realize that much must be done to ensure that your company is complying with the law and that it is utilizing its wealth of human resources to the fullest. What role can your department play?

The role of human resources control

Human resources control is of crucial importance to the organization for four reasons:

a. Human resources constitute one of the most expensive organizational inputs (about 70% in service companies and 50% in manufacturing), yet the behavior and results of this resource are less predictable than other resources;

b. The impact of human resources on the success or failure of the organization is crucial because the quality of the employees' functioning is critical to the quality of the product;

c. The atmosphere and culture of an organization is expressed most distinctly through human resource policies;

d. All human resource selection decisions are governed by federal regulations.

Organization policy and management style are strongly reflected in the *institutionalization* of the human resources function. Almost every book on management and organization deals at some level with human resources. This is even more evident when dealing with questions of control, where the human factor is a decisive element (e.g. Brown and Moberg, 1980; Rwe and Byars, 1986).

In research dealing specifically with human resources, focus is usually on the dual nature of control: the evaluation of both the functioning and achievement of employees; and the assessment of the quality of personnel management in the organization (Heneman and Schwab, 1986). In practice, control in this area is usually very intensive, but sporadic, used for occasional issues only. This intermittent control might have been the scenario in our example of Mr. Goodfellow's promotion procedure above. However, chance and fragmentary investigations, despite their importance, do not provide a reliable, overall view of the organization; at most they may provide some partial indication.

Issues related to human beings at work are complex and require a multidimensional analysis. In this area, control cannot suffice only with the analysis of statistical data related to past performance, nor just with employee attitude surveys. Human resources control requires the application of many methods and techniques for data collection and analysis in various areas of personnel activities. These methods include a wide variety of observations such as an examination of employee evaluation techniques, training procedures, grievance procedures, and benefits and wage policies. Only systematic incorporation of all control fragments in a single system is likely to provide a reliable reading of the human capital of the organization.

The nature of human resources control

One of the most difficult methodological problems in human resources control, is identifying a standard for measuring contribution in this area. No regular instrument, such as profits and losses, can serve as an adequate, single indicator of the quality of management and performance of human resources. Thus, a comprehensive and integrated instrument is typically searched for to measure the effectiveness of this function. There is growing attention being paid to this problem as the need for alternatives to the 'intuitive' method of personnel management is recognized.

The pertinent question in human resources control is: what are the criteria according to which standards can be set and achievements measured and evaluated? The answer to this question must contain two components. The first is an understanding of the *effectiveness* of activities or programs in the organization, that is, the extent to which one has achieved the anticipated or planned goals. The second component requires an understanding of the *efficiency* of operations, that is, whether the same degree of performance could have been obtained at a better input-output ratio (Nash, 1985; Willman, 1986; Ben-Yosef, 1985).

Performance in human resources, as in other areas, is evaluated by comparisons between existing and satisfactory levels of achievement. The evaluation of a person's achievements may take three alternative forms:

a. "He improved himself." In this form we mean that in relation to past achievements, the employee improved. In this case, the basis of comparison for present performance is the individual's past achievements.

b. "He is an excellent employee." Here we mean that in comparison to his coworkers, he is better than most. The standard in this case is the level typical of the employees in general.

c. "He could do better." Here we have a comparison between the individual's present level of achievements and his potential.

The goals of human resources control

The goals of human resources management can be covered under four categories in which the need for control should be emphasized:

a. institutionalization of human resources management;

b. the employment process;

c. employee attitudes and job satisfaction; and,

d. labor-management relations and negotiations.

In each item, the extent and depth of control is determined by managerial philosophy and using cost-benefit analyses. It is best to forego insignificant information and to concentrate on data essential to the functioning of the system.

Institutionalization of human resources management. The larger the organization and the greater the number of employees, the more complex becomes the problem of institutionalizing the treatment of human resources. Control must determine the extent to which the position and tasks of the function have been defined. Accordingly, five areas should be examined.

The organizational position of human resources management. There are several possible configurations for the human resources function in an organization: from the most centralized, in which the entire matter is handled by one central unit, to maximum decentralization, in which each unit deals with its own staff. The optimal solution is usually a combination of these: centralized in some matters, with wide decentralization where routine issues are handled by the operational units themselves. As a rule, it is expected that a central unit will determine the organization's human resources policy and planning, design the employment process, set procedures and standards, negotiate labor contracts; establish control systems, and conduct applied research in these areas. Individual units often establish training programs, hire, promote, and evaluate employees.

It is up to the control function to examine the position and status assigned to human resource management in the organization. For example, should the central unit be accountable directly to the head of the organization, or to one of his deputies? Should employee recruitment be handled by each operational unit, or by one unit for the entire organization? These types of questions warrant the attention of control.

The actual setup of the human resources function depends largely on the specific nature and needs of the organization, the needs of its subunits, the types of jobs being performed, and the number of people employed by the organization. In all cases there will be some organizational issues requiring the involvement of top management, and some that relate to specific units only. Thus, defining the authority and subjects handled by the various units is essential. The larger and more departmentalized the organization, the more important it is for control to examine this aspect carefully.

Traditionally, personnel affairs were handled at various levels of the organization. Today, however, the trend in large organizations is to manage this resource through a centralized, sophisticated, professional staff unit. It is because of the development of this autonomy within human resources management, that control must be alert to the quality of involvement of top level management. The approach of crisis intervention is not adequate. Indeed, one true test of top level management's attitude toward human resources is how regularly these matters are discussed in board meetings, in comparison to the 'first aid' treatment arising from crises.

Involvement of the human resources function in other areas. An important test of the effectiveness of an organizational function, is its contribution to other functions in the organization. Human resources management contributes to, and is influenced by, a variety of other aspects of the organization. However, the interaction of this activity with others depends on the prevailing management style and organizational culture in general. Human resources control must pay special attention to this interaction in four areas:

1. *The organizational policy, management style, and organizational culture* are all relevant to human resources, which is simultaneously a consumer and a supplier. Organizational intervention should not be made without studying its ramifications on the human factor.

2. *Organizational design* must include the input of those in charge of human resources. Control should examine whether such involvement exists prior to operations and staffing.

3. *Planning and development*, particularly in the early stages, are often carried out without any involvement of human resources. This input is often far more relevant than most planners and developers realize. Expansion, reduction, relocation of space, change in production processes, new technology or materials, or development of new products, are all matters related to employees. Such plans generally lead to changes in jobs, feelings of insecurity, and significantly impact on human resources.

4. *Evaluation methods* used by management also concern the personnel function. Even when workers' impact on the achievements of their organizational units is minimal, they are often blamed for poor results or failure. Even if particular sections have some unique problems, most are common to the entire organization. It is therefore natural that control examine the extent to which the central unit for personnel management is aware of the entire range of problems within the organization. Control must ensure that these are dealt with in a general discussion on human resources and are part of discussions in determining organizational strategies (e.g. Dyer, 1983; Manzine, 1986).

Work procedures. Institutionalization of human resources management includes procedures and normative arrangements for employee behavior and performance functioning. This requires attention to three areas:

1. identification of the issues appropriate for institutionalization;

2. determination of how and by whom these norms will be developed and disseminated;

3. determination of where responsibility for implementation and follow up will fall.

Examples for which normative arrangements and procedures are frequently used include; attendance records, lateness and absenteeism policies, working hours and break times, or the use of flex time.

Control should examine the extent to which routine issues are covered by binding, permanent procedures. No less important, however, is determining how and on what basis the procedures were established, and how effective they are. From control's point of view, the existence of a normative arrangement that is not followed, is no less serious than the absence of any such standard. Therefore, the institutionalization of proper human resources management requires a dynamic approach to work procedures; they must be constantly examined and altered in accordance with an ongoing evaluation of the needs of the organization and its employees.

Human resources records. The term 'organizational records', in its broad sense, refers to all data and information available to the system from the moment of their creation until their destruction. Generally expressed in writing or electronically recorded, this reflects the organization's memory (information) according to predetermined methods of classification (e.g. function, groups of issues, performance, etc.). The degree to which records are needed will vary among areas, as will the timing, frequency, and classification of this information. For instance, the human resources function needs completely different data than those essential to the marketing or finance units. Human resources records include personal and professional details on every employee and relevant data on past performance and salary.

It is usually agreed that information is the basis for evaluation, and the point of departure for planning and implementation of development management (Baird and Meshulam, 1984). The larger the organization and the more varied its information needs, the greater the significance of records control. It should be noted that in an era of sophisticated computerization, the temptation to computerize large and sometimes unnecessary volumes of information is great. From control's perspective, too little and too much data are two sides of the same coin.

The importance of control of personnel records lies not only in the cost of irrelevant or unnecessary data, but more importantly, in the need to ensure that necessary data is included in the records. An adequate test of the need for records is the degree to which they are used. Records that are not used are generally unnecessary.

Treatment of information and research findings. Human resources management, in its modern sense, is a relatively new concept, and is in a stage of accelerated growth. Its development depends largely on research and management philosophy. Control should examine this aspect from three perspectives:

1. *The degree to which the organization uses research findings and relevant information*, is an operative test of the justification of data collection and research done. For example: a study was conducted in response to complaints about the meals served in the factory cafeteria. Findings confirmed the employees' claims, but nothing was done. This is a common fate for many

studies ordered by organizations. Findings that are left without practical response represent a problem warranting attention. Information and research that is left without application, generates disrespect and lack of confidence, and is an obvious waste of resources. In the absence of a commitment to cope with findings, such activities are better not begun.

2. *The results of research conducted outside of the organization* could be an important input in an organization's life. From control's point of view, this constitutes a relevant source for comparison and sometimes a point of departure for improvement. The conscious effort to collect and use information and research findings for enriching human resources management, is an indication of the quality of this function in an organization.

3. *Exchange of views and ideas among executives*, based on their experience in personnel management, can be a source of enrichment. Control should learn how to take advantage of this accumulated experience and knowledge. This requires general application of an institutionalized method, rather than sufficing with occasional exchanges of views.

The collection and analysis of data and information, as well as its dissemination, are typical of a staff function such as human resources. However, it is less widely recognized how grave it is when the organization fails to respond to findings that indicate the need for intervention.

Control of the employment process

Human resources control can be viewed according to the various stages in the employment process. In this way the process is divided into three stages: pre-employment control, control during employment, and control of separation from the organization.

Pre-employment control. In recent years, business has begun to recognize the importance of careful recruitment and screening of employees before hiring. Organizations looking for workers with skill, energy, motivation and flexibility -- high performers -- realize that the pre-employment process can go far in assisting management in the selection process.

One such program exists at Diamond-Star Motors Corp. in Normal, Ill. Diamond-Starr, a joint venture of Chrysler and Mitsubishi, is looking for employees with good interpersonal skills, people they consider to be team players, willing to learn more than one job, rotate shifts, and take criticism. In order to aid in hiring appropriate candidates for assembly jobs, Diamond-Starr not only gives potential employees medical and drug tests, but a battery of written tests as well. About one quarter of the applicants do not get past the written test.

Even getting beyond that point in the selection process is no guarantee of employment, since another 40% of the group fails the rigorous training program that follows. Katsuhiko Kawasoe, executive vice president for administration and human resources at Diamond-Star says, "We believe the key to success is picking the best employees and training them well." (*Business Week*, 10/3/88).

An organization must constantly define its need for personnel. In accordance with these requirements, the organization may turn to the labor market. At the stage of pre-employment, control should examine measures taken by the organization before making a permanent relationship with a new employee. The emphasis is on five aspects:

1. *Human resources planning* relies on information in two main areas: the goals and needs of the organization, and its existing staff. It should achieve the organization's short and long term goals (see, for example, Sautell and Seweeting, 1975; Walker, 1980). Since planning is based on information about the organization's operations and functions, the quality of information will have a direct impact on the quality of planning.

2. *The analysis and development of job descriptions* is a technique for acquiring information about the work performed. This generally includes understanding working conditions on the job, as well as the characteristics and skills required to perform it (for extensive discussion of this subject, see, for instance, Heneman, et al., 1980).

Control should examine the organization's updating of job descriptions, and how well this information is utilized in human resources management. Of particular interest is the application of this information in activities like planning, recruitment, selection, wage determination, or training and development.

3. *Employee recruitment* should be examined by the control function to determine how well the organization succeeds in locating suitable candidates for vacant positions. Since generally only a few employees will be selected from a pool of candidates, it is clear that the quality of the pool will determine the quality of the candidate who is accepted. (For a general discussion of employee recruitment, see, e.g. Burack and Mathys, 1980; Wanous, 1980.)

It is important to realize that the *Uniform Guidelines on Employee Selection*, mentioned earlier in this Chapter, apply to decisions regarding recruitment and hiring, as much as they do to decisions pertaining to already existing employees. Human resources control must review the following areas in any evaluation of recruitment practices:

* recruitment methods (advertising, agencies, schools, etc.);
* the candidates (new recruits, previous applicants, existing employees);
* reliability of recruitment sources (the value of various recruitment methods, the quality of candidates with particular experience or education).

The employer and employee have a common interest; neither wants to make a mistake, the kind of error that is often difficult to correct. Ensuring that the right decision is made, is the purpose of the next stage in the pre-employment process. This is a process of mutual selection.

4. *Employee selection.* Recruitment is followed by selection. The organization aims to choose the candidate with the highest chances for success in the job, and with a potential suited to the future needs of the organization (for further discussion of employee selection, see Manese, 1980; Haberfeld, 1986; Schmitt and Schneider, 1983).

The selection process contains two variables: the requirements of the job; and the qualifications of the candidate. From the viewpoint of human resources control, this is a critical stage for the organization, as it involves long term, mutual commitments. It is more worthwhile and less expensive to invest in this stage, than to solve a problem resulting from incompatibility at a later stage.

Control of the selection process can be expected to focus on these questions:

* Is the selection based on a full understanding of the job requirements?
* Is the candidate's ability to perform the most demanding aspects of the job being evaluated?
* Are the methods and tests used in selection reliable and valid?
* Are the same methods used for all candidates, regardless of the sex, race, religion, origin, age, or possible handicap?
* Is care taken to present the candidate with both the advantages and disadvantages of the job?
* Do candidates undergo relevant medical examinations if necessary?

5. *The probationary period and induction.* The probationary period for a new employee completes the selection process. It involves seeing actual job performance rather than a best guess. In this sense, the probationary period has a dual purpose; it is the final stage in the selection process and the initial stage in the induction process. The goal of induction is to help the new employee get to know the organization and the job, and to integrate him into the work team as quickly and easily as possible.

Despite the obvious importance of the probationary and induction period, this subject has received only marginal treatment from the perspective of human resources control. Three points are central to control of this area:

* *Systematic evaluation of the new employee* during the trial period, involving organized exposure of the newcomer to several different situations and coworkers.
* *Formalized operational and personal assistance* to the new employee, usually by an experienced employee.
* *Decisions on permanent employment* based on evaluation reports and a summary interview with the candidate. Control will examine both the stock of relevant information and its use. At this stage, important details have been added to the organization's knowledge of the candidate, and the employee's knowledge of the organization and job. Control has a crucial task here; to ensure that unsuitable candidates are not employed.

The more systematic and professional the investment in the pre-employment period, the greater the chance that permanent employment and quality performance will result. This will permit selection of candidates who are *able* to perform the job and who are well *matched* to the position. A woman who has just graduated from nursing school, would be able to perform as a staff nurse on a hospital floor, but would not be able to assume the responsibilities in an intensive care unit. A man with a speech impediment might not be able to perform successfully as a telemarketer. A woman who likes to work outdoors would not be well matched to a sedentary office job.

Control during employment

Despite successful selection processes, during the active life of any employee, he is exposed to difficulties and pressures which will affect his performance. Control must give special attention to those problems that can be identified, evaluated, and corrected. Below is a summary of the most common of these.

Elimination of organization constraints on performance. Most often, poor performance is seen as the employee's problem. The possibility that the weakness might be the responsibility of the organization is rarely considered. Too frequently managers see the symptom and not the cause of poor performance.

For example, an assembly employee with a high percentage of defects may be working with faulty materials or machinery, a telephone operator with poor productivity may be working in a noisy area. Even problems thought of as 'behavioral' may be the result of organizational constraints. An employee who suddenly develops a habit of tardiness, may be frustrated with her job because an expected raise was not forthcoming.

Human resources control must be aware of the possibility that personnel problems may not be under the control of the employee, but instead, need to be corrected by the organization itself. Organizational constraints must be considered as a possible source of poor performance. Often it is the employees themselves who will uncover these areas, and therefore, control must ensure that necessary channels of communication are open to them.

Occupational health and safety. A particular form of organizational constraint can result from poor environmental health and safety conditions. Health and safety issues refer to arrangements in the workplace that affect the well being of the worker. Accelerated technological developments and increased use of new materials involve safety implications and increased health risks (for more on health and safety, see Osborne, 1983; Bagnara, 1985; Shain, 1986).

The extent and intensity of control in this area are affected by a combination of several factors, including; legal requirements and labor agreements, management and labor attitudes; and the possible risks and damages which could occur as a result of neglecting these issues. Health and safety has gained increased attention in recent years, and is the focus of negotiations of which control should be aware.

Employee development and training. In the wake of recent scandals concerning well known problems in purchasing policies at the Pentagon, Professor J. Ronald Fox, of the Harvard Business School, summarized a four year study he had completed on the subject, (*New York Times*, 9/4/88). Prof. Fox concluded that "...the most serious problem is that too many people assigned to key acquisition positions...are woefully unprepared for their jobs." His findings go on to say that, "...too many senior Pentagon officials hold the view that program managers...have no need of years of training and experience..."

In order to survive, any organization must incorporate an ongoing process of growth and adaptation to change. One expression of this process is continuous development of the organization's human resources through training.

Training is a planned, organized, and controlled activity, aimed at assisting employees to improve performance, prepare for different jobs, usually by furthering knowledge and skills. This field had developed greatly in the past decade, particularly in response to the vast investments organizations make in employees (see e.g. Yoder and Heneman, 1985; Bendon, 1985; Grippel, 1986).

Control is interested in the effectiveness and efficiency of training, and should concentrate on the following questions:

* Are the training programs based on a full understanding of the organization's present and future needs?
* Are the programs geared to the knowledge, skills, and potential of the employees?

* When an employee has completed a training program, is he prepared to function as was expected?
* Does the organization have consistent and effective policies regarding employees' requests for training, within or outside the organization?
* Are the channels for promotion and growth in the organization reflected in the training and development programs?
* Is it preferable to hold courses within the organization, on a regional or industrial bases, or to utilize external professional and educational institutions?

Usually, immediate returns on training cannot be expected; therefore the follow up and evaluation of development is an ongoing process. An employee who performs poorly because of inadequate training, is the victim of organizational constraints which could have been avoided.

Employee promotion. The term 'promotion' is used for different purposes, some of which do not express promotion at all. Changes in wage agreements leading to raises in salary are not necessarily promotions, in the sense used here. Not every salary increase is a promotion, although promotions are almost always accompanied by a raise in salary (for a general discussion of employee promotion, see Sonnenfeld, 1984).

Promotion, in terms of human resources management, is a change in role or in the content of the job, which usually expresses additional or different demands of the employee, in knowledge and skills, in responsibility and authority. Such a move generally involves a change in the employee's status, employment conditions and rewards, and is usually related to additional training, experience, or skills. Control will examine five promotion related issues.

Promotion policy. A positive policy of promotion means that suitable individuals employed by the organization will be preferred for vacant executive positions. Internal postings of position openings should precede, or at least, accompany, external recruitment efforts.

Promotion planning. Organizations should inform employees of the career paths for jobs or groups of jobs, as well as communicate the requirements necessary for attaining various higher positions. Long term commitment and loyalty to an organization can come when employees advance within that organization.

Relationship between promotion and training. Training programs outlined by the organization should respond to both the requirements of positions to be filled and the qualifications of employees. It might be unreasonable to announce a policy of promotion from within, and not provide the necessary training to achieve the knowledge and skills required by higher level positions. Control must ensure that excellent workers are not appointed to positions in which they will fail because they were not adequately prepared.

Fairness in promotion. It is essential that all members of the organization understand the legal requirements of nondiscrimination in selection. Control must monitor this essential aspect of human resources management. This not only ensures that the most talented people within the organization are promoted, but it fosters an atmosphere of trust in labor-management relations.

Employee services. In addition to wages and material fringe benefits, employees usually receive benefits that are not provided as payment per se. Part of these may be considered 'ongoing maintenance of human resources'. Fringe benefits that employees acquire are being broadened gradually, and may include on-site child care facilities, special terms for purchasing company products or acquisition of company shares, cooperative projects relating to housing and loans, children's education and summer camps.

It is customary to divide the benefits and services provided to employees into two categories: mandatory benefits and optional benefits (for more on employee benefits and services see Heth, 1985). Control will verify the execution of mandatory benefits granted by virtue of law, and examine the nature and implications of optional benefits and services that the organization initiated.

In this respect, control should ask the following general questions:

* What is the organization's policy regarding optional fringe benefits and services for its employees?
* Can these services be supplied at a lower cost?
* For the same cost, are there other benefits that would be more useful to the employees than some of those that are currently offered?
* What are the employees' attitudes toward management policy and practice in this regard?

Control of separation from the organization

Imagine yourself in a situation which recently occurred in a large New England insurance company. There are several entry level clerical positions currently vacant in the finance office. You learn that these positions have been filled in the past, but there has been difficulty keeping employees in these jobs. The manager of the department views this situation as a necessary evil, something that is in the nature of the job, or the employees occupying it. Is that the case, or is there a problem that should be corrected?

Understanding the process of employee separation from an organization can provide much information valuable to control. The analyses can be divided into two major categories, employee turnover and retirement. Termination of employment, whether through retirement or turnover, usually has significant operational and human consequences. A poor or frustrating process may leave its mark on an individual's record throughout both the active working life and retirement. A successful process provides for the well being of the employee, as well as information important to the functioning of the organization.

Employee turnover. In learning more about the clerical vacancies in the insurance company, you discover that most of these employees left to work in other organizations. Employee turnover is a central issue in human resources management, and particularly significant to control. The importance of employee turnover is threefold:

* high turnover leads to heavy losses in human capital;
* turnover generates significant operational problems;
* high turnover is an indicator of a low level of morale.

(For extensive treatment of this subject, see e.g. Price, 1986.)

Even though there are various methods for measuring employee turnover, the quality of the analyses depends to a large degree on the quality of records and data, and the size of the population. Since control is interested in comparisons of turnover for various periods, among different units and groups, the comparisons must be calculated on a consistent basis. Control must be aware of changes in external conditions when interpreting the data. For example, in a period of high unemployment, a low turnover rate is not necessarily an indication of high morale, because alternative positions are scarce.

The most common calculation of expected annual turnover (in %) is:

$$ATR = (ALFT/NEMP)100 \qquad (1)$$

where:

ATR = Annual Turnover Rate
ALFT = Annual Number of Employees Who Left
NEMP = Number of Employees in the Company

The analysis is enhanced by including an assessment of 'unavoidable employee turnover', that is, those who left or were dismissed for unavoidable reasons, such as serious illnesses or layoffs. While much can be gained from data collection, a detailed analysis can be conducted only in the case of significant numbers. If it is determined that the turnover rate in the organization or a specific department is high, two questions must be answered:

* What are the reasons for the turnover?
* What measures can be taken to reduce undesired turnover?

An employee who states she is leaving because she 'just wants a change', or is 'fed up', is giving the organization results rather than reasons. The use of a *separation interview*, conducted by professionals, or discussions with former employees who left the organization, are very helpful in identifying real causes. Despite the wide variety of possible reasons for separation from the organization, they will usually fall into six large categories:

* inappropriate selection of employees;
* poor occupational or interpersonal integration;
* dissatisfaction with wages, or benefits;
* difficult working conditions;
* lack of opportunities for promotion;
* lack of job security.

Separation interviews with the clerical workers leaving the finance office described earlier, revealed that there was serious dissatisfaction with working conditions. Specifically, each worker identified difficulties with the manager of the department whom, they felt to be autocratic and arbitrary. These interviews were conducted by the human resources department, which was viewed by the employees as an impartial body. In this case, the manager was provided with appropriate training, and the turnover rate did decline over time. It is crucial that control ensure that information collected and analyzed, is used effectively to improve the organization.

Retirement. A universal reason for completing an individual's active working life is retirement. Academic and pragmatic treatment of this issue has gradually increased, both because of a longer life expectancy enabling people to reach retirement age, and because of the expansion of social legislation designed for the third life phase. (For more discussion on retirement issues, see Palmore, 1985; Parnes, 1983; Rabinovitz, 1985.) Control centers on at least four aspects.

Institutionalization of retirement, voluntary or compulsory, is generally determined by legislation and collective agreements. However, there is room for flexibility at the organizational level, including separation standards and procedures.

Retirement planning requires reliable data on anticipated retirement and specifics regarding the particular individuals destined for retirement in the near future. The actual situation will usually have a significant impact on operations and on the organizational climate.

Preparation for retirement has increasingly become a concern of the modern organization (see, for example, Montana, 1985; Keith, 1982). What and how does the organization prepare itself and its employees for their gradual replacement? The better these preparations, the least costly they will be.

Systematic contact with retired employees is a relatively new concept. The concept of a permanent 'parting' between the organization and veteran employees is making way for varied forms of relationships between them, after retirement. Both can derive benefit from such systematic contact. The retired employee is a source of information, knowledge and skill from which great benefits can be gained. This includes consultation or advice and even partial employment in times of need. The retired employee, can in effect, become a public relations officer for the organization.

Employee attitudes and job satisfaction

Identifying employee behavior according to indicators of 'positive' or 'negative' attitudes toward the organization, will pinpoint issues that warrant attention. Phenomena such as complaints and conflicts, low achievement, unwillingness to invest special effort, and disregard for cedures, are often indicators of low morale.

Satisfaction indicators

Complaints and conflicts. In contrast to classic industrial relations which are generally foreseen in labor agreements, interpersonal and group conflicts are an expression of the quality of relations and of organizational culture. When general relations are tense, even a slight difference in views can constitute a basis for conflicts and misunderstanding.

A primary role of human resources control is to ensure that the organization is aware of, and carefully examines, the source and motives of tension. Common causes for grievances and interpersonal conflicts within organizations usually stem from four sources: faulty communications, poor leadership, unsuitable teaming, and conflict of interests (whether real or illusionary). In an atmosphere of frequent conflict, achievement tends to be low.

Low achievement. The source of low achievement in work is usually a combination of a number of interfering conditions: operational, technical, managerial, as well as lack of workers' ability or interest. High achievement is impacted by high morale. High achievement may be the result of purposeful organizational incentives or strong intrinsic motivation on the part of employees. In an organization with low morale, achievement will usually be low, in spite of sophisticated methods and equipment. It is control's function to ensure that trends and motives for achievement in the organization are being evaluated.

Unwillingness to invest special effort. There are inevitable deviations that may require special effort and extra hours. Expected worker response will be positive when morale is high. This is not so when morale is low. Control is interested in tracing this phenomenon through evaluating organizational needs for additional effort (e.g. overtime), and employees' willingness to supply it.

Disregard for procedures. Low morale and dissatisfaction is expressed in various forms traditionally thought of as discipline problems. These include; disregard for work hours and procedures, disrespect for instructions of supervisors, and failure to care for equipment and materials. In contrast to tardiness and absenteeism, it is more difficult to quantify factors such as disrespect for instructions and procedures.

Diagnosing employee attitudes

Attitude surveys can be considered both an expression of management philosophy and a pragmatic approach to human resources control. The assumption is that there is a significant relationship between employees' attitudes and their behavior and achievements on the job (Lawler, 1986; Neff, 1985; Ventura, 1985).

Attitude surveys are also known as morale surveys. Long term, low morale or dissatisfaction among employees, will have a negative impact on the organization's output, and in extreme cases, even on its very survival. Herein lies the rationale for control of this aspect. In this area, 'objective' evaluations do not exist; it is the subjective reactions of the employees that we are seeking. While it is impossible to provide all that employees feel is necessary, their attitudes should be seen as a dynamic indicator, and should be examined on an ongoing basis.
An attitude survey is usually intended to solicit reactions of employees in three major areas:

* *The employee and his work*: attitudes toward work and job interest; growth and promotions; working conditions, etc.
* *The employee and the organization*: the extent to which employees are satisfied with the organization, with management attitudes and those of direct superiors, etc.
* *The employee and employment conditions*: attitudes toward such issues as wages, benefits, overtime, etc. These issues are usually part of management-labor agreements and customs of the organization.

Two groups of tools, usually used in attitude surveys, are the questionnaire and the interview. *Questionnaires* are popular for several reasons:

* it is relatively simple to design a questionnaire of reasonable reliability and validity;
* a questionnaire can be administered to a large and dispersed population, simultaneously, and at relatively low cost;
* questionnaires can be easily and quickly processed.

Interviews represent a widely practiced instrument for collecting data from employees on their attitudes and the level of personal satisfaction at work. This method requires a number of conditions:

* the interview must be personal and face-to-face;
* the interviewer must be skilled;
* the interview must be representative;
* the interviewer must be seen as impartial;
* a uniform method must be used for recording responses.

The use of the interview for employee attitudes has both advantages and disadvantages, and is usually more appropriate for a relatively small population. (For further discussion of interviewing methods, see Hornik, 1986.)

Organizational ombudsman

The organizational ombudsman, although not yet common in the private sector, is of great potential in enhancing employee satisfaction and informing management of issues needing attention. The role of the ombudsman is to enable people in the organization to raise complaints whenever they feel offended. As such, the ombudsman may not only help to solve individual problems, but can also serve as a channel for feedback to management and an aid to control. Thus, it is likely to benefit organizational culture, while also offering an additional tool for human resources management (for more on the organizational ombudsman, see Caiden, 1983).

Understanding the need for an organizational ombudsman lies in understanding the concept of alienation, and the frustration that can result when employees find difficulty in obtaining a desired result using existing procedures. The ombudsman needs general recognition as a representative of 'organizational justice' or fairness.

Organizational justice cannot be guaranteed unless there is an appropriate mechanism for preserving it. One fundamental reason why the ombudsman is not more widespread is management fear that, by virtue of its existence, the position might encourage baseless or trivial complaints. The organizational ombudsman is liable to be seen by management as a threat to its authority.

In dealing with employee grievances outside of the hierarchical channels, the ombudsman strives to reach three important goals:

* making the organization more humane by providing an additional channel for communication, and thereby granting the individual access to the 'conscience' of the organization;
* controlling the emergence of unacceptable standards; and,
* minimizing conflicts by providing appropriate measures for early detection and resolution of them.

In this spirit, the purpose of the organizational ombudsman is generally defined as, "to supply the employee with effective measures by which to raise his concerns before a neutral person with investigative authority...a person -- appointed or elected -- whose sole or main role it is to investigate grievances of employees independently" (Silver, 1967).

It is in the interest of human resources control that the organizational ombudsman be effective. This will depend on the presence of three conditions:

* *Independence* -- The higher the rank of the ombudsman, the wider his authority and the greater his independence, the more influential and effective he will be.
* *Access* -- There must be direct and convenient access to the ombudsman, for every individual; the ombudsman should enjoy direct and convenient access to the various organizational units and all levels of management.
* *Dissemination of the ombudsman's activity* -- The existence of the ombudsman and the results of his interventions must reach those who may need his services.

An organization with an internal ombudsman will consider ways to integrate that role with other human resources activities as well as with the entire control system.

Human resources accounting

The concept of human resources accounting, used in a limited form for over twenty years, is both an approach and an instrument. The economic-accounting approach to human resources strives to express investment in human resources in a quantitative, balance sheet form. Human resources accounting is understood as the measurement, in monetary terms, of the ability of the human factor in an entire organization (see, for example, Meshulam, 1980).

This approach is based on the notion that the employee has a value that can be measured and expressed quantitatively, as can other assets. The rational is that only when human resources are expressed quantitatively, and included in the balance sheet, can decisions be made on the basis of the real situation of the firm.

In regular accounting statements, personnel is usually expressed in terms of wages, salary, and fringe benefits, which appear as production costs or expenses. There is no expression, for instance, of the accumulation of experience and investment in peoples' growth, the impact of age, and the balance of estimated active years in the organization.

The basic principle exists, however, that the human resources of an organization should be calculated as part of the organization's capital. Initially, such instruments were used mainly in relation to training, but later (influenced by the University of Michigan project of the 1970s), a more comprehensive approach emerged. This included additional aspects, such as recruitment, induction, absenteeism, training, mobility, turnover and declining competence ('burnout').

Despite the agreement in principle, on the need for human resources quantifications in monetary terms, there are still no adequate and universally accepted methods for expressing the human asset in financial reports. Two approaches that have gained the most recognition are the cost approach and the values approach.

The cost approach recommends that the asset be assessed according to the cost -- historical or real -- invested in its creation or acquisition. All expenses related to employee recruitment, selection, induction, training and development, are added together and deducted from the value of the work anticipated from the employee. When the employee leaves the organization, the balance that has not yet been deducted is recorded as a loss. The *values approach* determines the 'value' of the employee to the organization, expressed in terms of wages, anticipated years of work, and work experience. From the viewpoint of human resources control, the attempts at systematic accounting in this field may contribute to creating 'hard' criteria for otherwise relatively 'soft' elements.

Labor-management relations in unionized organizations

Labor-management relations in an organization are crucial to human resources management. In this context, human resources control should concentrate on five main aspects: the quality of these relations; the institutionalization of labor-management negotiations; negotiation topics and agreements; grievance procedures; and the communications network between management and labor representatives. (For an extensive discussion of these issues see Karp, 1985; Flanagan, 1984; Barbash, 1984.)

The quality of relations

The quality of labor relations can be determined by assessing several key factors:

* Do both sides honor the agreements made between them?
* Do conflicts erupt during negotiation periods?
* Are conflicts settled effectively?

This type of assessment can be made for past periods in the same organization and for other organizations in the industry, and comparisons can be significant indicators.

Institutionalization of labor-management negotiations

Control should examine the network of procedures for prenegotiations, negotiations and agreements, and settlement of conflicts during the contract. Key questions for control in this respect are:

* How much does the organization prepare itself for negotiations?
* Does it identify problems and crystallize positions?
* Do procedures and schedules exist and are they honored prior to and during negotiations?

Institutionalization requires the determination and maintenance of a schedule, from the opening of negotiations to the signing of a contract and grievance settlements.

Negotiation topics

The specific subjects included in a negotiation between labor and management depends on numerous variables. These include factors such as:

* The management philosophy, that is, management perception of the subject as appropriate for mutual discussion and determined by mutual agreement;
* The position of the union, which sees the subject as relevant to the employees;
* The willingness of the parties to negotiate on the subject and to reach an accord through compromise;
* Past experience, within and outside of the organization, regarding the results of other negotiations;
* The prevailing value system and social legislation.

It is easy to understand the considerable differences among organizations, industries, and regions -- not to mention countries -- regarding the issues included in labor-management negotiations. Nevertheless, the are certain groups of issues that are commonly included in agreements by most organizations and industries in most countries:

* stipulations about labor negotiations and agreements;
* wages and social benefits;
* promotion patterns for individuals and groups;
* work discipline;
* health and safety;
* settlement of labor disputes.

Labor disputes

One subject that has been most extensively researched and dealt with is labor disputes, in particular, disagreements between the parties during the contract period (for an extensive discussion of labor conflicts, see, e.g. Kochan and Barocci, 1895). Frequent labor conflicts and the consequent damages to both sides, will gain the attention of control. The dispute itself, however, is generally symptomatic; if the underlying causes are not identified and treated, it will probably reoccur. Control can contribute in three major areas:

* *Analysis of labor conflicts* -- Identification of the typical characteristics, as well as direct and indirect costs of conflicts, is a primary contribution of control.
* *Resolution of conflict* -- Control should examine the stage-by-stage treatment of conflict, with the aim of identifying those factors that created difficulties or discovering alternatives that have been overlooked.
* *Limitation or avoidance of future conflict* -- Control is interested in learning whether all reasonable measures were taken to avoid the conflict.

Every organization needs to find ways in which to avoid future conflicts. It is generally accepted that it is not within the assignments of control to know and suggest to management methods for preventing dysfunction. Control cannot be expected to become a multipurpose 'expert' in all aspects of the organization. However, control should know how to solicit the aid of relevant experts in the organization and from the outside.

Labor-management communications

This area will focus on three aspects: the partners in communication; substantive content and specific issues; and the communications mechanism.

The partners in labor-management communication are generally representatives from both sides, authorized to conduct discussions or negotiations on all subjects or on predetermined issues. These may become permanent or ad hoc forums. Intensified labor-management communication is growing through a number of joint forums, sometimes composed on a parity basis, such as joint production councils, committees for health and safety, joint welfare projects, and quality circles. The success of such groups relies not only on the standard of the participants, but also on the nature and mode of group operations.

The content and issues that labor and management decide to deal with, either as opposing interested parties or as partners, affects the nature of communication. The quality of communications depends greatly on its substance and the way in which the issues are handled. The degree of competence and authority of those communicating, significantly affects the outcome of the process.

Communication procedures are essential to successful communication. Control will evaluate the nature and effectiveness of meetings; the distribution of agenda and background material for discussions; suitable reporting to employees and management groups; and follow up of implementation of decisions. It is not the task of the control function to take over the role of a staff unit assigned to labor relations or communications. Its job is to ensure proper functioning in this area as part of human resources and general management control.

14 Wage and incentives control

It remains a fact that financial compensation is the most important reason for working, and universally recognized as an excellent motivator and an effective incentive for improved performance. Despite this, the control of wages and financial incentives has traditionally focussed on technical and bookkeeping factors rather than being seen as a substantial issue of business strategy.

The terms wages, salary, income, remuneration, compensation, reward, incentive, profit sharing, bonus, and fringe benefits, have become common in our language. In this chapter we will discuss wages, by which we mean guaranteed periodical financial compensation; and financial rewards, which are any additional financial compensations given for better performance. Both are payments that a person receives for his work, in the form of money, or that can be measured in monetary terms. (Non-financial compensations such as satisfaction, meaningful relationships, or the opportunity for self-fulfillment, were discussed in Chapter 13, Human Resources Management.)

Wages and financial rewards satisfy not only material needs, such as food, shelter, and clothing, but also higher level needs, such as self-esteem and self-fulfillment (for a discussion of intrinsic and extrinsic needs, see Herzberg, 1959). One's wage level (absolute and relative) often constitutes a standard by which a person judges his own worth and that of others. (For more on the relationship between wages and status, see Piore, 1973; regarding wages and self-worth, see Vroom, 1970.)

In this chapter we will concentrate on the following areas: the parameters of an organization's freedom of action regarding wages and remuneration; wage and remuneration policy; wage structure; and methods of setting wages. Particular attention is devoted to the control of financial reward systems.

Parameters restricting the organization

Every organization is subject to external rules and limitations (on the impact of external forces on organizations see, in particular, Miles, 1980; Stephen, 1983). This principle holds for organizations in totalitarian and democratic nations alike. It is essential to become familiar with these restrictive forces and their implications for your organization. An individual firm or organization is not an independent entity; it is subordinate to external, normative values, and must consider them as a point of departure.

The impact of external organizational factors is particularly prominent in the area of wages and remuneration because of interventions and restrictions (see Granovetter, 1981). Management control should be aware of the exact parameters within which it can maneuver. The four areas to give particular attention to are: those related to the political and legal system; those dictated by socio-economic legislation; those that emerge from labor relations on the industrial and national level; and those dependent on the labor market.

Political and legal system

Social values and ideology are expressed in the nation's constitution and its laws. These impact many areas, including a wide range of normative arrangements regarding labor relations and wages. The United States Constitution and Bill of Rights are the foundations for these laws and customs. However, both are open to interpretation, respond to changing ideology, and are subject to further clarification at the state level.

For example, Civil Rights Legislation has had a profound effect on wage relations in this country, where a two-tiered wage structure had been the norm. Proponents of the Equal Rights Amendment recognize that there remains a difference in the wage structure for men and women. While that constitutional change has not been passed, there are individual states which have instituted legislation requiring 'equal wages for equal work', mandating a change in the existing normative relations. (For more on the determination of normative arrangements, see Hellriegel and Slocum, 1979.)

Socio-economic legislation

Socio-economic legislation is inspired by the ideological system, the nature of the administration, and the power relations between political parties and trade unions. These become binding norms for employer-employee relations and dictate requirements such as minimum wage and social benefits, which determine the organization's labor cost. The 1989 increase in the minimum wage represents a compromise between the ideology of labor, the Democrats, and the Republicans.

This subject has become significant on an international level, given the increasing number of multinational companies. Since socio-economic legislation varies from country to country, its impact on total labor cost must be evaluated. Some socio-economic legislation is common to many countries. Many countries have a minimum wage law. Similarly, legislation often prevents discrimination in wages and social benefits. The law may require that employers pay for health insurance, or disability benefits. (For a detailed discussion of social benefits, see Bergel and Shamir, 1980.)

Socio-economic legislation dictates the inclusion of various components in the wage structure, on the national and organizational level. It is one of the parameters that organizations must work within and that draws the attention of the control system.

Employer-employee relations

This subject must be viewed on both the external and the internal levels. On the external level, we are dealing with the nature of labor relations between employers' and employees' associations, both nationally and within an industry. (For more about employer-employee relations and trade unions, see, Freeman and Medoof, 1985; Shirom, 1983.) The internal level deals with relations within the organization. The larger an organization, and the weaker the trade union and employers' organizations outside of plant, the more powerful the impact of the internal relations. The inverse is also true: the stronger the workers' and employers' associations in a given area, the more significant their impact on labor relations and wages on single organizations.

Institutionalization of labor relations and labor agreements generally serves as a restrictive framework for the single organization. In most cases, collective labor agreements are hierarchical: the national and industrial agreements serve as a point of departure for the single organization's negotiations with its employees.

Despite the wide variation in content and strength of this parameter in restricting the maneuverability of the single organization, it is quite common to find industry-wide agreements relating to a number of general issues, such as:

* flexible work hours and work week;
* wage levels and professional-functional ranking;
* professional competence and promotion tests;
* retirement terms.

The more successful the industrial trade union in attaining nation-wide achievements, the more control it asserts over its shop unions. This naturally diminishes the relative liberties that organizations would take in the absence of an industry-wide agreement. Therefore it is imperative that such external parameters be taken into account when planning management-initiated measures.

Control can only operate on two levels in this respect: it can verify that the organization is aware of the implications of the parameters, and examine the degree to which the organization's internal arrangements conform to them.

Labor market

In a liberal economy, the labor market has considerable autonomy with a minimum degree of direct government intervention. However, indirect intervention occurs through many avenues such as grant funding, educational assistance, and budgets. Labor market conditions have an impact on the supply and demand of employees, as well as on the nature of the relationship between the organization and its employees. Shortages of workers may force an organization to reduce its activity or to offer additional incentives in order to attract employees. On the other hand, when there is unemployment, the organization can find workers who will accept wages and social benefits below the accepted level, providing that there is no legal or contractual restriction. (For more on the impact of the labor market on the organization, see Reynolds 1982; Althauser and Arne, 1981.)

Since the labor market parameter is a major factor affecting operations and labor costs, control should verify that an organization takes it into account, in particular in the following areas:

* labor market trends;
* use of part-time workers;
* top level wage structure;
* subcontracting;
* training and human resource development.

Wage and remuneration policy

One of the most important steps management can take to develop healthy relations and minimize stress and conflict among organizational members, is to maintain a policy of wages and rewards that is perceived as fair and acceptable to all parties (for extensive discussion of wages and incentives, see Henderson, 1982).

It is not the role of the control system to determine this policy, but it must ascertain that such a policy exists, and examine the process by which it is formed, just as it evaluates the decision making process in other areas of the organization. Control must assure that special attention is focussed on three central issues related to the formation of a wage and remuneration policy; equity, wage structure, and confidentiality.

Equity

Wages satisfy various needs, from financial security to social status and self-fulfillment. The significance of the same wage for different people will vary depending on the employee's peer group, his dependence on his group for identity, his financial needs, etc.

In recent years, particular attention has been paid to the *perceived equity approach* to wage setting, developed by Adams (1977). This approach deals with a relative view of wages and with social comparisons. It provides the theoretical basis for widely accepted concepts in wage and labor relations, such as equitable wages, reasonable standard of living, and wage discrepancy. The equity approach is based on the model of social exchange: injustice exists when the individual perceives that the relation between his inputs and the rewards he receives is different than someone else's. The perception is subjective, that is, the inputs and rewards are perceived by the person making the comparison.

The inputs that a person invests in his work are varied. They include achievement-related characteristics such as education, experience, training, skill, and willingness to make an effort, as well as attributive characteristics, such as age, and gender. The rewards that a person receives for his work include monetary payment and other material benefits, as well as professional status and nonmaterial rewards.

The rationale for the equity approach is that a person strives for a balance between his inputs and rewards and the inputs and rewards of other employees with whom he compares himself, that is, his reference group. Because the basis of the equity theory is subjective, it is necessary to know the employees' value systems, and to recognize the real difficulty in defining inputs and rewards on an objective, quantitative basis. Moreover, the context for comparison is a dynamic one, changing with society and reference group factors. The importance of factors such as material possessions, promotions, and titles, will fluctuate, just as an individual's response to a lack of equity will vary over time.

Because of its subjective nature, empirical application of the equity approach and identification of tools for comparison are difficult tasks. It is also difficult to deal with the question of what should be compared with what. Should this be an internal, self-comparison, or one comparing co-workers, or friends outside the organization? Below we discuss four bases of comparison, which control should be aware of, if it adopts the equity theory in principle.

Self-comparisons are those that a person makes with himself, regardless of the input-output relationship of others. He uses past experience and past and present status, his aspirations for the future, alternative jobs and occupations, commitments, etc.

Interpersonal comparisons (within the organization) usually involve employees in the same or similar jobs. The individual compares the group to which he belongs with others in the organization. This basis of comparison is particularly significant in organizations in which there are large differences in wages between groups, such as between maintenance workers and pilots in an airline, or tellers and managers in a bank.

Interpersonal comparisons (outside of the organization) are made between individuals and groups such as friends, neighbors, colleagues in the same profession, members of the same union, and so forth. The more powerful the group, the more it will strive for comparison with high-income earners outside of the organization.

Comparisons between reality and expectations (within the organization) are based on a psychological contract between the individual and the organization at the time of employment. Expectations cover the anticipated relationship between input and reward. If the employee perceives a gap between the actual situation and what he felt was expected, he will interpret this as an injustice toward him.

The standards used for comparison will vary depending upon the employee's position in the system. This is particularly noticeable with regard to wages: the higher the position of an employee, the more he tends to compare himself with higher levels. The tendency to compare with lower levels is rare. Control tends to use statistical analyses to study equity in the organization. However, it is critical to be aware of the fact that individual employees tend to compare themselves with other individual employees, and not with statistics.

Wage structure and criteria

The remuneration policy of an organization is expressed in its decisions regarding the wage structure and the criteria used for matching jobs and individuals within it. Determining a specific wage system is a policy decision. (For an extensive discussion of wage policy and systems, see Steers, 1984; Lawler, 1981; Kochan, 1985.)

For what is a wage paid? As we mentioned earlier, in the section on restrictive parameters, the organization does not have full autonomy in this respect. However, there is a wide margin of freedom. Will material rewards be based on variables such as job description, professional ranking, seniority in the organization, and education, or will wages be determined according to results and achievements in work? It is likely that the wage system will be based on some combination of four elements; job requirements, position and role in the organizational hierarchy, achievements, and personal factors.

Lack of a clear policy in this area leads to arbitrariness and inequity, which in turn generates negative reactions and results. Therefore, control must address the formation of the policy of wages and rewards, and not simply concern itself with the maintenance of an existing system.

Confidentiality

What is the organization's policy regarding the confidentiality of information on wages and benefits? Is this open information, regulated by a normative framework, or is it based on confidential individual contracts, enabling two workers in the same position and with the same level of achievement to earn different amounts? Often, organizations maintain a policy of confidentiality concerning wages because it serves to decrease the bargaining position of employees and to hid problems of inequity.

The control system should assist management in determining the equity policy. Decisions in this area reflect the combination of management philosophy, organizational culture, moral and ethical values, and pragmatic considerations. Control should examine and evaluate these decisions in terms of their long term implications, and in light of the importance of trust in this area.

Wages vs income

It is essential that control distinguish between the nominal wage and its buying power. This becomes particularly important in times of inflation. In response to a reduction in buying power, various mechanisms have been developed for compensation of employees (generally in the form of cost-of-living raises, discussed later).

Another distinction that must be made clear, is the difference between wages and income. Wages are payments received by an employee based on his position, while income includes additional rewards paid in return for overtime work, shift work, various bonuses, and so forth. Even if the wage remains stable, income may increase or decrease, depending on the employee's achievements, the organizational situation, the labor market, the economy, and the results of collective negotiations or personal arrangements.

A distinction is also made between direct and indirect wages. Direct wages are those paid in return for actual work, while indirect wages refer to fringe benefits such as sick days, paid vacation, pensions, and insurance. The relative proportion of fringe benefits to total income rises steadily, for the following reasons: (a) an attempt to avoid shocking the economy by reconsidering wage agreements, which often result in difficult organizational problems or industrial unrest; and (b) intentional disguise of high incomes for groups and individuals through secret benefits.

Wage structure

The wage structure is greatly influenced by historical circumstances which were once valid and rational. Wage levels were assigned to given professions and jobs as a result of labor market supply, occupational prestige, and economic need. The wage structure is also affected by current factors, such as political, economic, and legal influences, as well as power relations among the partners in the labor relations network.

Discussion of this topic involves three levels: national, industrywide, and organizational. The issue of wages at the national level has been analyzed by current theorists in labor economics (for instance, the fundamental work of Ehrenberg 1985). However, the integration of sociological, psychological, and political factors along with negotiations and power relations between the negotiating parties, demonstrates that theoretical approaches provide an inadequate view of the wage-setting process.

The more wage negotiations tend to be left to the organization, without government or union intervention, the greater the interorganizational, intraprofessional, personal, and regional differences. In contrast, when negotiations are held at the industry level, between employers' and workers' organizations, the wage differences will be relatively smaller.

In organizations where management is free to develop its own wage policy, two parameters are particularly salient:

1. *The organizational situation*, which refers to its ability to pay employees, its dependence on employees and specific skills, and its tradition and culture. An organization that customarily pays low wages will find it difficult to convert quickly to high wages, even if it needs to attract workers, and is financially capable of doing so.

2. *The labor market* and the supply and demand of workers is a significant factor in wage setting. The existing wage level in similar organizations or professions, and the wages in a given region or industry, influence the wage policy of every organization.

Management control must examine the organization's wage policy not only according to its financial capacity, and in light of its past and customs, but also in terms of specific jobs, and on an industry-wide, regional, and national level. Remember, we are concerned here not only with nominal wages, but with the total compensation package, and see adjustments not only as a response to trade union pressures, but to organizational initiatives as well.

Among the mechanisms employed for dealing with the reduction in real wages due to inflation, two are particularly common: (a) periodic collective negotiations including changes in wage levels in light of price increases; and (b) tools such as 'cost-of-living increases' and 'indexation', which automatically increase wages and maintain their buying power. (For more on this subject, see Knobel, 1983; Liviatan, 1985.)

The first method is suitable when inflation is relatively low and there is no need for frequent adjustment to avoid a severe drop in buying power. The second method is used to avoid the drastic impact of rapid inflation the purchasing power of wages. A mechanism such as the cost-of-living increase is intended to maintain wage agreements in inflationary times, avoiding frequent negotiations of new contracts. It is the job of the control system to avoid unnecessary shocks in organizational functioning.

In practice, it has been found that countries in which inflation is high and the standard of living is low, employees are left with severely depleted real wages and strained labor relations follow. In contrast, in developed, industrialized nations, mechanisms have been established to ensure a maintenance of real wages, generally in the framework of national or industry-wide agreements.

Wage systems

From a relatively small number of basic methods for wage setting, a wide variation of formulas can be derived. Control should determine that various alternatives have been considered before the specific system is chosen. Below we will examine the five most common bases for wage systems.

Units of output (piecework)

Using this method, wages are directly and exclusively related to volume of output, or outcome. The higher the output in a given time period, the higher the income. Under this type of system, the employee has significant control over how much he earns. There is a clear, and usually immediate, incentive to increase output. It is relatively convenient for costing calculations.

The disadvantages of the piecework method lie in the risk of worker exhaustion, and the potential decrease in quality in favor of quantity. In addition, there can be resistance by employees to technological change because they perceive these as potential sources of wage reduction.

The piecework system is increasing less popular in organizations where trade unions are active. However, this is often the basis for wages when subcontracting is involved. Piecework wage systems usually lack social and employment security, a major reason for their lack of popularity.

Unit of time

Under this system, wages are paid in return for work for a defined period of time, regardless of output. The unit of time might be an hour, day, week, month, or in some cases, even a year.

The advantages of this method are that the worker has a fixed income and the organization has control over the physical presence of its employees at work. Its major shortcomings are a lack of control over output. In a sense, this system neutralizes or even reduces incentive for output achievements.

Incentives

Wage systems based on a combination of units of output and time, allow additional payment for output that exceeds a given standard for a defined time period. Proponents of the wage incentive system claim that it incorporates the advantages of the two previously-mentioned methods and avoids their shortcomings. This they feel is true, because the majority of incentive methods guarantee a minimum wage, with bonuses paid for exceptional output. The practical application of incentive systems has given rise to a number of difficulties, including problems in measurement, the need to determine norms, and the need to calculate bonuses in a variety of jobs and occupations. Since the issue of incentive is so important, and common to many other wage systems, it is discussed in much more detail later in this chapter.

Job evaluation or occupational analysis

In the job evaluation approach, wages are set based on the relative value of occupations to the organization. (For an analysis and evaluation of occupations in general, see Wexley, 1984; Ash and Levine, 1983; Wanous, 1980.) Job evaluation does not depend on the personal characteristics of the employee who completes the task, but to the task itself. It is defined in terms of the qualifications required of the individual who will occupy the job. At the basis of occupational evaluation lies the principle of attaching a wage to a position and not to an employee.

Because there are various methods for evaluating jobs for the purpose of wage setting, control must confirm two essential elements: the selection of a method suited to the organization; and monitoring the implementation of the method, and updating the process. Since it will not be the responsibility of control to deal with the technical details of job evaluation, we will only mention the basic methods here. (The interested reader will find more information on the subject in, Baird and Beatty, 1982.)

Ranking, which is subjective in nature, involves rating the occupations in an organization in order of their relative importance, as determined by the person or persons who do the ranking. Linking wages to occupations is done according to measures of relative importance on the scale, and the wage range (minimum to maximum) is predetermined.

Ranking according to *key occupations* selects a small number of representative jobs which are placed on a scale from the least to the most important. Each key occupation is assigned a wage level based on industrial and regional averages, thus providing a wage range related to each specific occupational level. All of the occupations in the organization are then fit in among the key occupations, to get a continuum of occupations and respective wages.

Factor comparison is similar to the key occupations method. Here, however, a number of factors are used for all existing occupations. For instance, a simple classification of occupations using five factors might include intellectual demands, skill requirements, physical requirements, working conditions, and level of responsibility. A monetary value is attached to each factor, reflecting its relative weight in the occupation, resulting in a scale that relates occupational demands to monetary rewards. Each occupation is then compared to the others in terms of the five factors, and placed accordingly on the scale.

The point system is similar to factor comparison, except that each factor is assigned a value expressed in points according to its relative importance. The total points for each occupation determines its relative wage level. This system has various forms, which enable setting minimum and maximum wages for every occupation in the organization. A wage range, expressed in points, is determined for each occupation.

The more complex the occupations in question, the more difficult the analysis and evaluation. The need to use criteria such as creativity, initiative, and administrative skill, make the results of analysis questionable. It is therefore more difficult to determine the commensurate wage for such occupations. Despite the importance and contribution of occupation analysis and evaluation, control must examine its suitability for the specific positions in question.

The control system must be aware of how occupations change as a result of new technology. Positions emerge requiring changing skills and knowledge. These changes are more frequent in the era of automation and computerization. For some occupations new requirements will develop, brand new occupations will emerge, others will become obsolete. The effectiveness of occupational evaluation depends on its being up-to-date, and gaps in this area remain one of its most prominent weaknesses.

Personal characteristics

This refers to differential payment of employees based on personal characteristics. The choice of these characteristics is generally an expression of an explicit intention to encourage a given characteristic in the labor force. An example of this approach is a system that grants differential wages according to seniority in the work place, regardless of achievement, position, or other characteristics. Giving the decisive weight to seniority is an expression of a policy aimed at preventing employee turnover.

Wage systems according to seniority, or according to family status, have been popular in various countries. In several countries, particularly in the Third World, wage systems in which the dominant variable is education are common. This is a policy intended to encourage higher education. This system exists in this country as well. Managers with MBA's may automatically start at a higher rate than those without the degree. Nurses with diplomas traditionally earn less than those with a BS. As discussed in Chapter 13, it is not always clear that the particular educational differences make these individuals better qualified for the positions in question.

More extreme examples of personal characteristics systems are those where different wages are paid to men and women for the same work and achievement, or different wages to specific ethnic groups, nationalities, or religions. This is, or course, illegal in the United States.

In general, wage systems based on personal or group characteristics are becoming less common. However, it is justified in some situations, such as using wages based on seniority as a mechanism to reduce turnover, or based on advanced education as an approach to human resources development.

Performance incentives

Financial incentives are commonly used for motivating employees. In fact, this approach is very popular. More than 90% of U.S. executives work under some incentive system, and approximately 25% of American companies offer incentives to their employees (Fox, 1980). A typical company incentive program may draw a 20% performance improvement after the first year of implementation (Fein, 1973) and may pay that percent as salary increases.

You should keep in mind that in order to properly realize the improvement potential of an incentive plan, it should be exposed to ongoing control and revision. If your organization does not intend to develop a maintenance program you should not start at all. Without monitoring, the system could actually cause performance deterioration. The importance of incentive maintenance should be looked at the same way as equipment maintenance; without a proper maintenance schedule, the equipment is bound to malfunction. Therefore, control of incentive systems should play a major role as a detector of deviations and indicator of future needs.

General principles

The principle behind an incentive system is that an employee, whether entry-level or executive, is paid a salary to attain certain standards of performance. As long as the employee's performance has not reached these standards, the employee 'has not justified' the payment of his base salary. Reward, or incentive, is paid only in those cases where performance exceeds the standard. The statistics on performance incentives for executives show that organizations believe in the effectiveness of this system. The reason that a significantly smaller percentage of shop-floor employees are covered by incentives probably stems from the complexity involved in developing a company-wide incentive plan, and from the fact that managers feel they are getting optimum performance without the cost of incentives, this despite impressive evidence to the contrary.

Requisites for success

An incentive system may fail because of poor design and installation, or due to unexpected circumstances which evolve. For example, a sudden drop in demand may force a company to reduce production outputs. Reduced production can be achieved through layoffs, or through production ceilings, which limit the potential incentive. It is critical that control be aware of several essential points which would improve the probability of an incentive plan's success.

The system should *permit earnings that are perceived to be of significant value*, usually considered to be an average of 25% of the base wage. A study by Globerson and Parsons (1985), indicated that the average incentive paid by American companies using incentive systems was 23% of the base salary. The minimum, satisfactory, and exceptional monthly incentives were 14%, 26%, and 41%, respectively. It is crucial that a plan, if it is to be successful, be based on incentives that the employees perceive as significant.

The system should be *easy to understand*, and calculations simple enough to be followed by all employees. In an ideal situation, an employee should be able to calculate his own wage incentive.

Performance *criteria included in the incentive plan should be within the control of the evaluated individual or group.* For example, telephone operators whose incentive is based on the number of calls taken, may have no control over slow days where they take only a few calls.

Sufficient *motivation for all the parties involved* is needed to properly maintain an incentive system. Relevant parties include the employees covered by the system, the immediate supervisor of the incented unit, the union, and the organization.

The *supervisor needs to be highly motivated to maintain the incentive plan*; he is in a position to cause a system to fail or to succeed. A supervisor may not cooperate if he is not included in the incentive system, or if the plan has reduced the income differential between him and his subordinates. The supervisor may also be insulted by the mere fact that improvements are attributed to the incentive system, rather than to his efforts. Involving the supervisor in the process of developing and maintaining an incentive plan is essential for a cooperative environment.

Local *unions are generally considered as partners* in the design and implementation of an incentive plan. If employees are not represented by a union, *it is in the organization's interest to involve the employees in the process.* Lack of employee involvement may have a negative impact on their willingness to improve their performance, even for significant incentives. Companies commonly establish labor-management committees to accomplish specific tasks such as introducing incentive systems. This approach leads to better cooperation between management and labor.

An incentive *plan must be continuously maintained*, otherwise the organization might find itself paying incentives for mediocre performance. Maintenance of an incentive system means periodic reevaluation of decisions such as the criteria and standards. Ongoing maintenance and control are an integral part of a sound incentive system.

Workers should be able to *clearly identify the connection between achievements and rewards* received; individual incentives for performance requiring individual contributions, group incentives for jobs requiring team work.

Cost-benefit analysis

A major objective in introducing an incentive system is to improve organizational performance. Therefore, it is important to compare costs with resulting benefits, and to evaluate the overall impact on the organization. The benefits of an incentive system are derived from savings generated as a result of introducing the plan; such a system may increase productivity by 20% or even more (Fein, 1973; Marshal, 1982). The general approach includes evaluating two major activities and cost components: set-up and maintenance.

a. Set-up consists of all activities required during the design stage of the incentive system. Typical activities are:

  - preliminary meetings with management;
  - meetings with labor;
  - becoming familiar with the organization's operations;
  - collecting and analyzing past performance data;
  - selecting the incentive system to be installed;
  - establishing the incentive equations;
  - presenting the system to management and labor;
  - establishing maintenance regulations; and,
  - training relevant personnel.

Resources required for set-up depend on the incentive system selected. An organizational incentive system requires fewer resources than a group or individual system, since it concentrates on macro measurements. Set-up costs consist mainly of remunerations to professionals, and in certain cases may also involve purchasing computers or computer software.

b. Maintenance of an incentive system includes:

  - monitoring performance;
  - calculating the incentive as a function of performance; and,
  - revising the incentive system as needed.

Whenever there is change in technology, product, or environment, there is a need to evaluate its impact and adjust the incentive plan accordingly. Maintenance cost is strongly influenced by the specific incentive system used. Organizational incentive systems are the least costly to maintain, and individual incentive plans are the most costly.

Level and intensity of coverage

The performance of an organization in many ways depends on the motivation of its employees. Individual motivation is greatly influenced by the relationship between the employee's perceived contribution to the organization and his reward. If an organizational unit consists of a number of employees evaluated as a team, then a high performing individual might not be motivated to maintain high performance if he is compensated according to the average team performance. It is usually claimed that the most motivated employee is one who works on an individual incentive, since he can clearly see the relationship between his contribution and his compensation. However, it is often impossible to develop an individual incentive plan for every member of the organization.

If an organization wants to install individual incentives rather than group or organizational ones, it most likely will not be able to cover all its employees. Intensity of coverage is measured by the percent of employees who are paid rewards based on performance. For example, a 20% coverage means that 20% of the employees are under some kind of incentive system. The organizational strategy may favor increasing the intensity as a way to improve overall performance. Therefore, evaluating present and potential coverage is of considerable significance, and may show that the current incentive system does not permit an easy shift to better coverage intensity. Possible recommendations may favor a change from individual to group incentives, so that more employees would be covered.

Obviously, an organizational incentive system covers all employees, but it may be less desired because of its weaker motivational impact. Evaluation of the improvement in motivation due to the incentive system is usually based on survey questionnaires and direct professional observation of performance. These aspects of incentive plan suitability and level of coverage are of particular interest to management control.

Incentive system and salary structure

As discussed above, in establishing a salary structure, an organization determines relative job values and the acceptable range within each job category. The flexibility permitted within each category helps to solve the problem of an employee who belongs to a lower category having a salary higher than an employee belonging to a higher category. Exhibit 14.1 describes a typical salary structure.

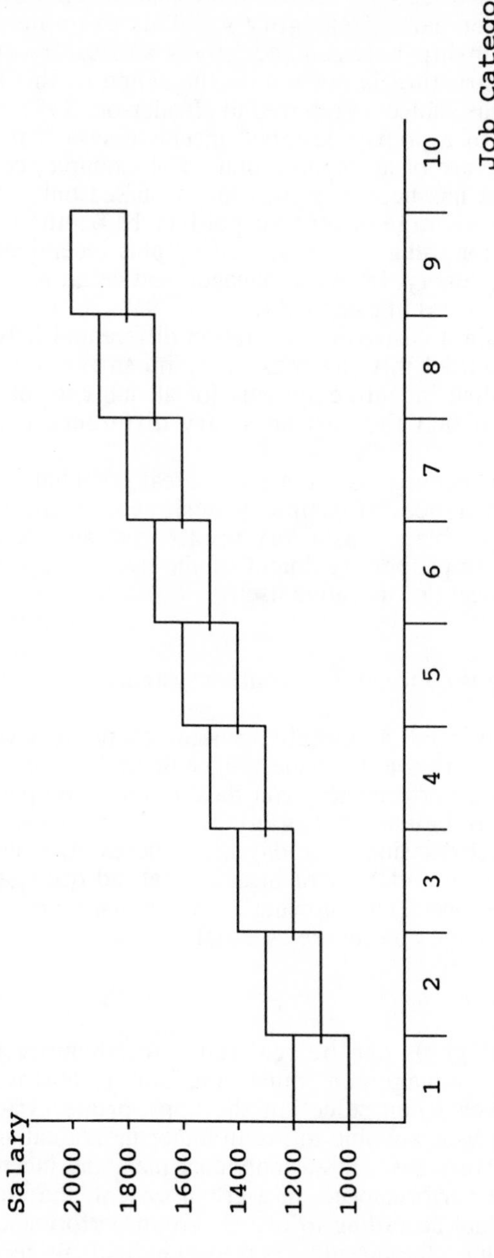

Exhibit 14.1 A typical salary structure

For example, the salary range for category 3 is $1200 to $1400 and for category 4 is $1300 to $1500. Therefore, an employee whose salary is in the upper part of category 3 is paid more than an employee whose salary is in the lower part of category 4. This example serves to illustrate the relationship between incentives and salary structure. Designing a salary structure is not within the scope of this book; the reader interested in this subject is referred to Handerson, 1982.

The introduction of a poorly designed incentive system may distort the entire salary structure of an organization. For example, consider an incentive system that has been designed and installed only for jobs in category 3. If the average incentive paid is 15%, then the total compensation range for category 3 (base salary plus incentive) exceeds the salary range of category 4. As a manager you could expect severe complaints from employees in category 4.

In order to maintain a desired remuneration differential between two categories, one should limit the maximum incentive. A feasible approach is to establish incentive systems for all job categories within the same facility, so that the desired salary difference can still be maintained.

In conclusion, an incentive system has a great potential to improve organization performance, if properly designed, introduced, and controlled. Failure to obtain satisfactory results from an incentive plan is generally due to improper treatment of the system rather than to weaknesses in the concept of incentive itself.

Management decisions concerning incentive systems

If you are planning to install an incentive system, there are several areas in which decisions will need to be made. Since these decisions will have a significant impact on performance, you must ensure a proper decision making process. Because an organization lives in a dynamic environment, a correct decision yesterday is not necessarily suitable for tomorrow. Therefore, the validity of incentive-related decisions should be continuously reviewed. The following are some major areas in which management decisions and control are essential.

Type of incentive system

Most organizations' goals can be realized through more than one incentive plan; thus management must consider its philosophy and operational objectives when selecting the appropriate system. For example, most enterprises are able to install either individual, group, or organizational incentive plans. In an individual plan, the incentive paid is related to personal performance. In a group system, the incentive is paid to every individual according to overall group performance. With an organizational system, the incentive is paid to individuals according to the overall performance of the entire organization. It is also possible to employ a combination of two or even three plans at the same time, as widely discussed in the literature (Globerson, 1985).

Exhibit 14.2 presents a comparison of the three major alternatives according to identical criteria.

Exhibit 14.2
Types of incentive systems

Criterion	Individual	Group	Organizational
Set-up cost	high	moderate	low
Maintenance cost	high	moderate	low
Individual motivation	high	moderate	low
Level of cooperation	low	moderate	high
Intensity of coverage	low	moderate	all employees
Frequency of feedback	daily	daily,weekly	monthly, yearly
Potential frustration	low	moderate	high

Relative importance of performance criteria

The relative importance of criteria may vary among organizations and among departments within the same organization. It may even change over time within the same unit. For example, profit is a very important criterion in commercial organizations, whereas it is irrelevant in nonprofit organizations operating under a set budget. Similarly, the number of items per man-hour is a relevant criterion for a production department, and not so for a research and development unit. The planning and organizational skills of a manager may be key in a start-up environment, but others may become more critical as the organization matures.

When selecting the criteria to include in an incentive system, you must make it clear that concepts and circumstances may call for a change in criteria or in their relative importance. Consider the example of an auto repair shop paying an incentive wage to the mechanics according to labor efficiency and spare parts used. This incentive plan motivates the mechanic to work faster and replace more parts.

Assuming an hourly salary of $10 and a commission of 5% on parts sold, the incentive paid to a mechanic who performs 46 standard hours of work in a 40-hour week, and installs $900 worth of parts in a week, is:

$$\text{Incentive} = (46\text{-}40)\,(10) + (900)\,(0.05) = \$105$$

His weekly salary is the sum of the base salary plus the incentive:

$$(10)\,(40) + 105 = \$505$$

Therefore, the mechanic's incentive, in percent of base pay, equals:

(105/40) (100), or 26.25%

In order to evaluate the relative impact of the two criteria, labor efficiency and commission on parts, we analyze two extreme circumstances, where each of the criterion is the only component of the incentive plan. If the mechanic's incentive were based on labor efficiency only, then he would not be motivated to replace parts, but would want to repair them, since he would earn more credit hours. If the parts were replaced rather than repaired, the mechanic might earn less, but the shop might make more money if the profit from replacing them were higher than from repairing them.

An analogous statement could be made if the mechanic's incentive were based on a commission on replaced parts. The mechanic is then motivated to replace as many parts as possible, even it if is more advantageous for the shop to repair a part than to replace it. It is important for the shop to determine the trade-off between spending labor hours on repairing parts compared to replacing them. A policy in this respect could be implemented using different weights for the two criteria in calculating the incentive.

In the same shop, it is possible to install another incentive plan, which might even be more effective. For example, consider a plan that is more strongly related to a major objective of the firm, such as increased profit. The shop can motivate the mechanic to increase the value added of his work by tying his incentive to this value. Value added, also referred to as gross profit, equals total sales expressed in dollars, minus the shop's cost of all materials, parts, labor, capital, and services.

Value of improvement

It is important for management control to estimate the contribution of each criterion included in the incentive system. For example, the value of improving efficiency by one percent in a given shop is $2000 due to reduced labor costs. Knowing the value of improvement per percent allows the company to establish a maximum justified level of investment in the production process and/or incentive. Through continuous control of the incentive plan, management should verify that its cost does not exceed the benefits achieved.

We will look at two examples where the impact of improvement can be evaluated in dollar terms, and a third example which requires a different approach, since it is not always simple to express improvement value in monetary terms.

Value of increasing labor efficiency. Imagine you manage a department and want to determine the value of improving its labor efficiency. The department's monthly base salary is $35,000, with benefits of $15,000, totalling $50,000 per month. Benefits include an individual pension fund and health insurance paid for by the company.

An increase of one percent in labor efficiency in your department, would mean a savings of $500 in labor costs. Without this change, it would cost you approximately $500 in additional staff or in overtime. The overall savings resulting from an increase in labor efficiency is higher than the labor cost of new staff, since there are additional costs related to hiring additional employees, such as those associated with additional equipment and space requirements. If you choose to use overtime, you would need to pay your employees 50 percent over the base wage. Therefore, it is justified to pay $500 for each percent increase in labor efficiency.

Let us assume that your company uses a conventional 'percent-for-percent' plan, that is, for every percent increase in efficiency, the company pays one percent incentive. In the above case, an increase of one percent efficiency would cost your company $350 (one percent of the base salary of $35,000), but saves at least $500, which would otherwise have to be spent on hiring new employees or paying overtime. Therefore, a net savings of $150 is created. Since management expects to obtain a certain return on incentive investments, control should continuously verify that the return satisfies expectations.

Value of improving quality. Let us assume you are working for an insurance firm and you want to estimate the value of improving the quality of work in the data entry department. The department is responsible for key punching documents into a computer system. Errors may or may not be detected by the system. A document with a detected error is recycled through the process until the error is corrected. A completed document with an undetected error generates a loss either to the company or the customer.

It is logical to assume that customers will catch, and want to correct, errors that have resulted in overcharges to them, but that undercharges will frequently go unchanged. In estimating the value of quality improvement, you realize that you should evaluate the potential savings resulting from both types of errors: those that can be detected by the computer software, and those that need human auditing.

You determine that the processing cost of a recycled document, which consists of clerical and computer costs, is $4.50 per document. The present average volume processed by the company is 5000 documents per day, with an average of 10%, or 500, recycled documents. A reduction in recycled documents of 1%, or 50 documents, will generate a savings of (5) (4.50) = $225.

You estimate, through sampling, that the company lost an average of $7.20 per document with undetected errors. You also estimate that 2.5 percent of the documents processed contained undetected errors. A one-percent reduction in these faulty documents would result in a savings of (50) (7.20) = $360 per day. This potential savings may serve as a guideline for establishing a corrective plan based on an incentive system designed to motivate employees to improve quality. This approach to improving quality through incentive wages is of particular interest to management, both as a policy and as a control tool.

Value of reduction in response time. As a manager in a mail order company, you decide to improve response time, defined as the average time which elapses from accepting an order to its final delivery. The current response time is 35 days. You feel that a response time over 30 days hurts the company's reputation and reduces the number of repeat customers. You do not have explicit information concerning the relationship between reduced response time and additional sales, but strongly believe it is important and are willing to pay more for a faster turnaround. You do not however, want the speedier service to be a result of higher inventory.

You decide to establish a quarterly incentive plan that ties a bonus to response time. Exhibit 14.3 presents the bonus which management is willing to pay as a function of response time.

Exhibit 14.3
Quarterly bonus as a function F average response time

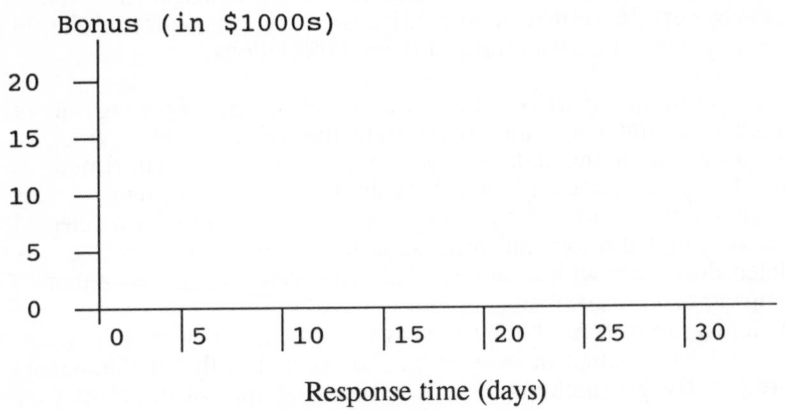

Response time (days)

The amount of $5,000 is established as the bonus for decreasing the response time to between 20 and 30 days. A greater bonus would be paid if the response time were further reduced, up to a maximum bonus of $20,000 for less than 20 days. Your implicit assumption in paying this bonus is that the improvement in customer satisfaction resulting from faster service will lead to a quarterly profit higher than the bonus paid.

When establishing an incentive plan of this nature it is important to monitor that improvements in the criterion on which the incentive is based were not achieved at the expense of other important criteria. In the case above, you would want to be certain that improved response time did not come at the cost of decreased accuracy or increased inventory.

Number of criteria to include

It may appear that the greater the number of criteria in the incentive system, the greater the expected improvement, because attention is paid to more operational factors. Although many criteria can be used for effective control in an organization, the same cannot be said with regard to the number of criteria in an incentive system.

If the incentive system includes too many criteria, the incentive equation becomes complicated, and the relations between performance and reward are difficult to comprehend. It has been found that the number of criteria used by companies in the USA and Canada ranges from 1 to 9, with an average of 2.4 (Globerson and Parsons, 1985). Fifty-six percent of these companies had 2 or more criteria included in their incentive systems. When asked, 79% of the companies recommend that 2 or more criteria be used, with an average of 3.2. It was also found that 70% using an incentive system with more than 5 criteria recommend using fewer criteria. It could be concluded that organizations find it beneficial to have a multi-criteria incentive system, with the number of criteria around 3 or 4.

The number of criteria is of relevance even if the company uses an integrated criterion to determine the overall organizational performance and incentive. A company can calculate the individual incentive by adjusting the organizational incentive with an individual criterion such as absenteeism or lateness. For example, calculation of an organizational incentive results in an average payment of 15% of base salary to its employees. This percentage is based on individual absenteeism: perfect attendance results in a bonus of 20%; a one-day absence reduces the bonus to 10%; while two days' absence disqualifies the employee from receiving any incentive.

Maximum level of incentive

An important decision made by management is the maximum incentive that can be earned by an employee. This decision has to be incorporated in the design of the incentive plan. A maximum incentive payment may be dictated by the need to maintain a certain salary structure within the organization. For example, an organization may decide that only production department personnel, including supervisors, will be included in the incentive plan. In this situation, the salary difference between the supervisors and the next managerial level is reduced, and there is a possibility that a supervisor might earn more than his superior. In such a case, management has two options:

a. Limit the maximum incentive paid to supervisors, with the limit incorporated into the incentive equation.

b. Design an incentive system that enables personnel of all levels in the organization to benefit from incentives.

The second option is preferred if relevant criteria are identified for all positions, and a sound incentive system can be established so that the wage structure is protected at the same time. This approach reduces the need for a ceiling on incentive payments, and therefore improves the potential effectiveness of the incentive system in promoting further improvements.

From a management control point of view, it is important to emphasize the following points:

1. More than one incentive plan can be designed for a given situation. Management should be involved in the selection of any incentive system, since its design is an expression of a management philosophy, having a direct impact on operational and human aspects.

2. The incentive paid should be correlated to, but lower than, the amount saved or advantages gained, as a result of improved performance.

3. Organizational strategy is implemented by assigning relative weights to the criteria included in the incentive plan.

4. Organizations should avoid using too many criteria in an incentive plan. The number should be held to a minimum and should concentrate only on the most relevant ones.

Auditing and revising the incentive system

An incentive plan should be audited continuously. The incentive audit should determine how effective the system has been in achieving congruity between employee behavior and management objectives. If the organization's objectives have changed since the incentive plan was installed, then the incentive system is likely to need revision.

Too long a delay in revising an incentive system can result in several pitfalls:

- Employee incentive is too low for perceived performance, leading to demotivation;
- Management pays incentives that are too high relative to profits, or performance;
- Improvement efforts made prior to the implementation of the plan become obsolete.

It is not uncommon for employees, management, or both to prefer a delay in the revision of the incentive system because of fear of the potential conflict which may arise as a result of any revision. For this very reason, it is essential to establish a periodic audit, and specify how, when, and by whom it will be performed.

There are some major issues that should be addressed when auditing an incentive system; group size, performance criteria, standards, and the performance/incentive equation. We conclude this section with a set of essential guidelines for maintaining an effective incentive audit.

Group size

An incentive program can be designed to cover each individual separately, a group of individuals, or the organization as a whole. There may be situations where circumstances change and call for a revision in the group size. For example, a small organization of 150 employees installed a profit-sharing system. Within five years, the company grew to 800 employees. Both employees and management felt that a group of 800 was too large to be used as an effective motivational unit, and preferred to establish departmental incentive schemes.

The opposite situation may occur as well; an organization decided that it was unaffordable to maintain an individual incentive system, and it switched to a group scheme, which although easier to maintain, resulted in similar achievements in output and incentive pay.

Performance criteria

The criteria included in an incentive plan are derived from the company's objectives. For example, a mail order house did not include 'response time' in its initial incentive plan, since it was not an issue at the time. It became important after the company grew, and there were a significant increase in customer complaints. It was important to draw attention to delivery time; this was achieved through the inclusion of 'response time' in the incentive scheme.

Standards

Standards have to be changed according to changes in product, process, technology, and environment. For example, the introduction of on-line computer technology to data processing has a significant impact on criteria such as cost per document and response time. However, an organization should avoid changing standards too frequently, since it takes time for everyone to adjust to them. A change in the standard should be significant enough to justify its revision. What is 'significant' depends on the potential impact of the change on organizational performance. Management control is extremely interested in adequate standards, which require their continuous review and maintenance.

The equation

The equation used to calculate the incentive defines the relationship between performance and incentive, assigning relative importance to criteria used. Examples of typical incentive equations where the criteria include:

EFF (efficiency),
DEF (percent of defects), and,
COMP (customer complaints) are as follows:

a. a model based on addition and subtraction:

$$\text{INCENTIVE} = (\text{EFF} - 1) + (5 - \text{DEF}) + (3 - \text{COMP})$$

b. a model based on multiplication:

$$\text{INCENTIVE} = (\text{EFF} - 1)\ (5 - \text{DEF})\ (3 - \text{COMP})$$

or a combination of these models can be used.

As the incentive equation represents management's objectives and preferences, it should change as the company's objectives change. Failure to change the equation may create a discrepancy between organizational objectives and employees' performance, since their performance is affected by the incentive equation.

Guidelines for an incentive audit

The following are guidelines for an effective incentive audit:

a. An audit program that regularly monitors the incentive system must be established. An audit should take place at regular intervals, at least once a year if no changes occur. In addition, whenever a change has taken place, the audit should ascertain if a revision of the incentive plan is needed or requested by either management or labor.

b. It must be understood and accepted, that the incentive system is being continuously audited. Revisions should be fair and follow consistent guidelines agreed upon by the parties concerned. The same level of seriousness should be applied to changes in the system as to establishing a new one.

c. Audit staff need to be competent, qualified, with background in incentive programs and system analysis. This will enable them to gain the confidence and trust of both employees and management.

d. Once the principles of the incentive plan have been agreed upon, further bargaining between the parties with regard to either the plan or revisions should be avoided.

e. The unit to be audited needs to be defined; it could be either an individual, a group, or the whole organization, depending on the incentive schemes used.

f. The scope of the audit should be defined; it could be very broad in nature and include evaluation of criteria, standards, and the equation used for the incentive, or it could be limited to the evaluation of the appropriateness of data collection.

g. The audit activity should be carried out without advance notice. Since, in many cases, the audit is used to compare actual performance to standards, it is essential to observe operations as they are normally performed.

h. Information obtained by the audit needs to be examined against the information used for the design and implementation of the incentive system. Deviations or lack of conformity are good reasons for reevaluating the system.

i. Audit results should be discussed with employees and management. The need for change, if any, should also be discussed and when agreement is reached, changes should be implemented as soon as possible. If action is delayed, future audit activities could be compromised.

In conclusion, it should be emphasized than an incentive system is not a sound one unless it is audited and revised periodically. However, management should be aware that it is harmful to practice frequent revisions, dropping and adding performance criteria according to temporary needs. Introducing changes in an incentive system too often hurts credibility and has a negative impact on the organizational culture.

15 Institutionalization of the control function

By now, you recognize the fact that the control process functions most effectively when it is a regular routine, and an integral part of the operations of an organization. Despite this, as we have pointed out before, the control function is frequently regarded as something extra. As a manager aware of its importance, you are in a good position to assist your organization in establishing the institutionalization of the control function. The term 'institutionalization' is used here to describe the formal structure and operation of the control function, and the place control has in a firm. We will examine this issue by focusing on three dimensions; the major areas in which institutionalization is required; the factors that influence the degree of institutionalization; and the relationship between institutionalization and employee attitudes.

Areas where institutionalization is required

Although almost all facets of control may be institutionalized, selectivity is required, because overdoing it is liable to create a system which is too rigid. It is most important to concentrate on three areas where formal structures are particularly appropriate. These are: the status of the control function; the control process; and relations between internal and external control.

Status of the control function

One way that organizations make a commitment to a function is to make that function *part of its structure*. The existence of a finance department gives authority to and requires accountability from those responsible for cash flow, investment, capital budgeting, accounting, etc. In the same way, a formal structure for the control function, enables this area to maintain a level of importance and responsibility equal to other departments. Even though the structure itself may be formalized, there are options concerning how strict or binding its authority will be.

Control my be either internal, external, or both. Most public, as well as large private organizations, are obligated to have some sort of internal control, to present periodic reports, and to project future plans and budgets. The most common forms of internal control structures are as follows:

1. Each employee evaluates his own performance;

2. Each team member evaluates and is evaluated by other members of the same team;

3. The superior evaluates his unit and his subordinates;

4. The superior evaluates his unit and his subordinates through a controller who is subordinate to him.

While forms 3 and 4 are most familiar to us in the United States, the team approach to control has been very effective in other countries, most notably in Japan. You are most likely familiar with the use of quality circles in that country. These are small groups of workers, which may or may not include supervisors, whose objective is to identify problems and propose solutions for their companies. While some observers question the effectiveness of the team approach to control in the U.S., one study of 300 service and manufacturing companies indicated that this method more that paid for itself (*Production and Inventory Management Review*, 10/84).

In addition to internal control, external control mechanisms are often put in place to ensure objective reporting. These include:

5. Headquarters and top management control and evaluate organizational units through an internal control system which is perceived by the units as external;

6. The organization is monitored by a control system entirely external to the company.

A company with exceptionally high performance requirements will not hesitate to submit its standards for external control. However, a company that fears external control, is likely to conceal records even from internal parties. This is sometimes done by using an outside agency to perform those activities which the organization is eager to hide. In general, organizations tend not to institutionalize external control, because of the fear of exposing weak or unpopular aspects of their operations.

Almost every organization is exposed to some form of external control, through legislation, consumer groups, or boards of directors. When we talk about the 'institutionalization' of external control, we are referring to control that goes beyond these; a situation in which upper management shows its commitment to the concept.

Another decision involving the formal structure of the control function is its *degree of centralization* within the organization. Maximum decentralization is when each employee serves as his own controller; maximum centralization exists when a professional unit has responsibility for comprehensive control. Exhibit 15.1 summarizes the advantages and disadvantages of centralized and decentralized control.

Exhibit 15.1
Comparison of decentralized and centralized control systems

Characteristics	Decentralized System	Centralized System
Scope	a micro approach	a macro approach
Cost	expensive to run	less expensive
Reliability	less formulated, and thus less consistent	greater consistency, thus more reliable
Human Relations	less formal, less objectionable to employees	tension between controllers and controlled
Dynamics	slow response on major issues; rapid on minor ones	rapid change of goals and major issues

It is doubtful whether there is a theoretical reason for, much less a preference for, one of these approaches over the other; each has a number of advantages. Thus, a synthesis of pragmatic, technical, and value considerations determine the choice for the organization. The institutionalization of the centralization/decentralization aspect of control is particularly important because of the wide variety of alternatives. Without a clear choice, the alternatives are ambiguous, and may generate much confusion. Exhibits 15.2 through 15.6 show five possible organizational structures with varying degrees of centralization.

The most prominent advantage of top centralized control (Exhibit 15.2) is that the chief executive is subject to control and evaluation as well as the rest of the organization. Responsibility for control rests with

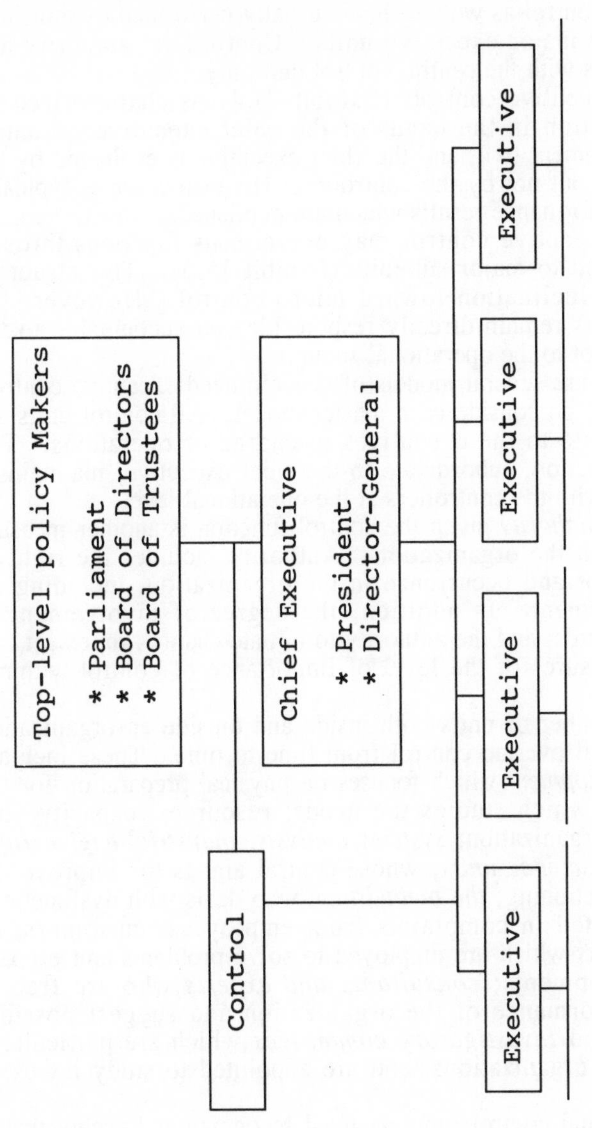

Exhibit 15.2 Top centralized control

the highest institution of the organization, be it the board of directors of a corporation, board of trustees, or government body. This structure puts major emphasis on macro control.

Top centralized control with extensions (Exhibit 15.3) includes aspects of micro control as well. This is usually performed by attaching controllers to the major executive units. Controllers' authority and accountability rests with the central control unit only.

Centralized executive control, (Exhibit 15.4), is characterized by placing this function in the hands of the chief executive. Control becomes a management tool, and the chief executive is evaluated by the board above him, but not by the controller. His evaluation is typically based on after-performance results which are published.

Centralized executive control may exercise its functions through extensions attached to major subunits (Exhibit 15.5). This structure demonstrates an inclination toward micro control. However, the attached controllers remain directly responsible and accountable to the central unit, and not to the operational subunits.

Although there are several models of decentralized executive control, Exhibit 15.6 could be considered a master-model. All control units are directly subordinate to the executives in charge of operations. The central control function, subordinate to the chief executive, maintains a staff relationship with the controllers at the operational level.

The *degree of authority* given the control function is another measure of its status within the organization. Authority includes the right to assess every factor and occurrence in the organization, including all levels of management. In addition, the degree of involvement in determining standards, and the authority to initiate change, represent two other critical measures of the level of importance of control within a company.

There are a number of units both inside and outside an organization whose function will overlap control from time to time. These include: *research and development* which focuses on physical preparation for the future; *planning* which studies the needs, resources, capacity, and standards of the organization; *systems analysis, industrial engineering, and management science units*, whose central aim is to improve the system and its functioning; *the ombudsman* who deals with dysfunctions which have resulted in complaints from employees, customers, or citizens; *think tanks* which are employed to solve problems and prepare for future developments; *consultants and experts* who are free to evaluate the performance of the organization and suggest possible improvements; and *investigatory committees* which are particularly popular in public organizations, and are appointed to study issues of public interest.

The organizational control function must recognize and accept that it has a dual relationship with these units. Although these functions are evaluated by control in the same way as is the rest of the organization, control serves them and is evaluated by them.

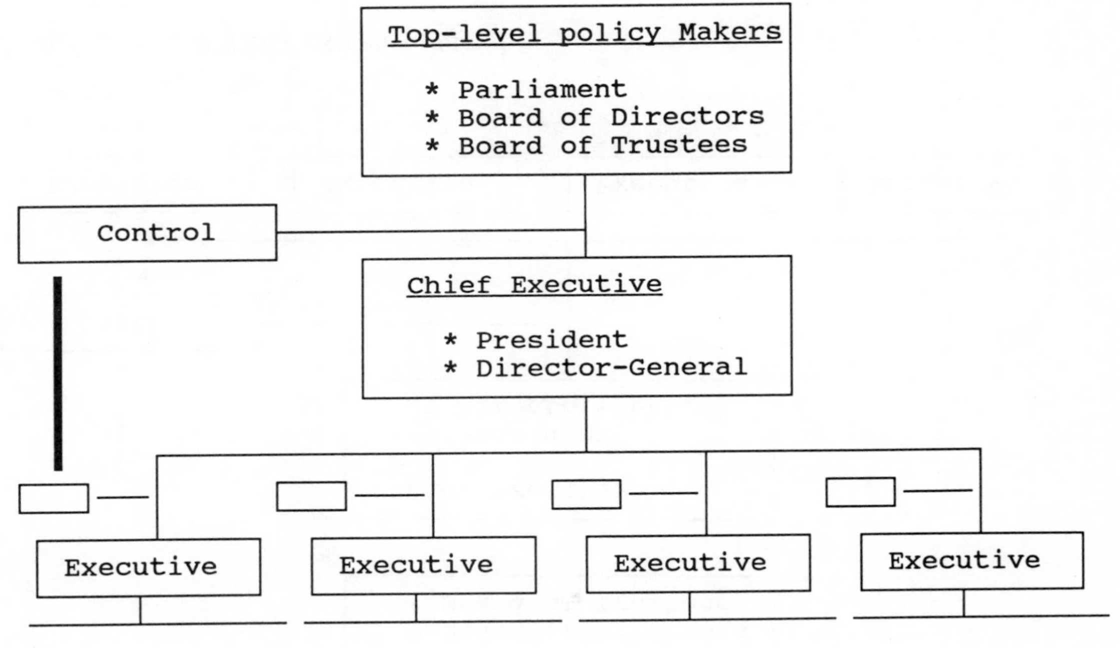

Exhibit 15.3 Top centralized control with extensions

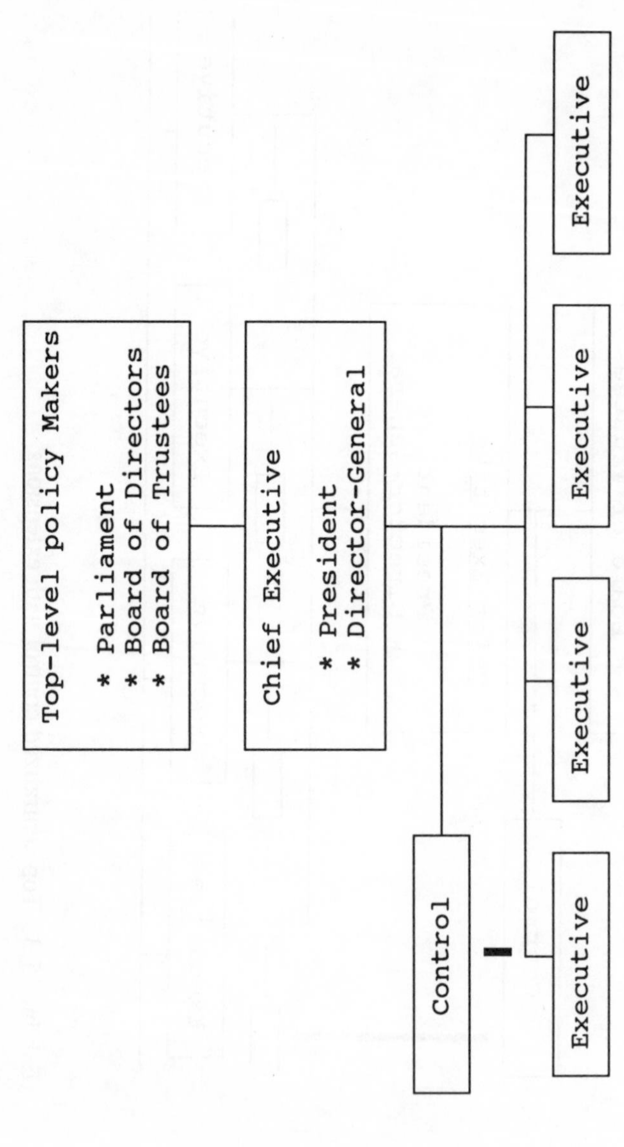

Exhibit 15.4 Centralized executive control

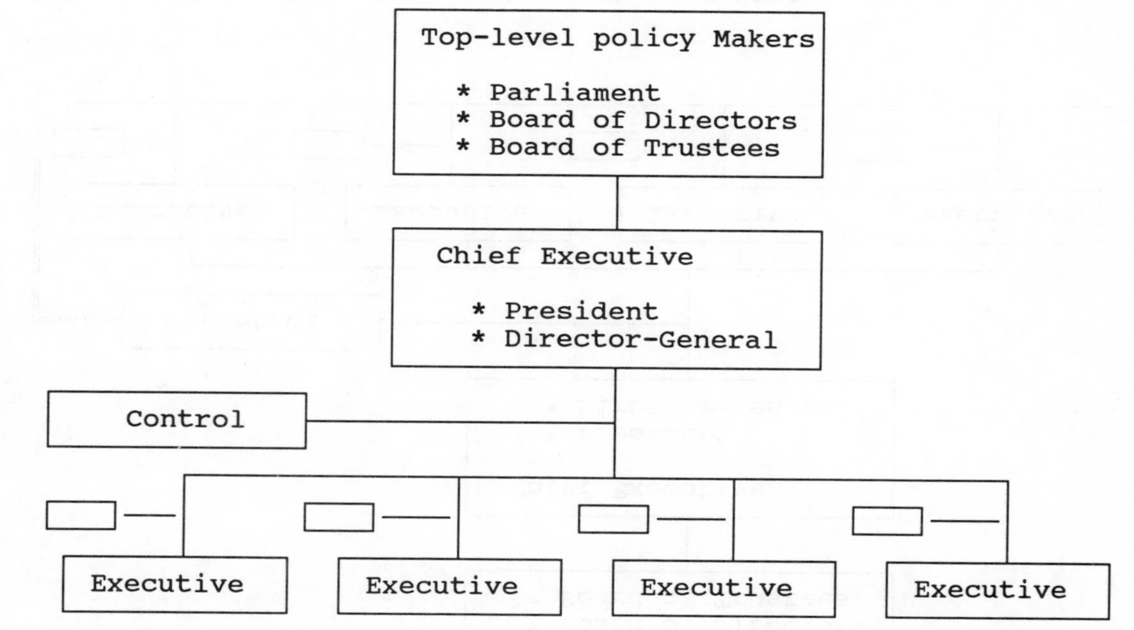

Exhibit 15.5 Centralized executive control with extension

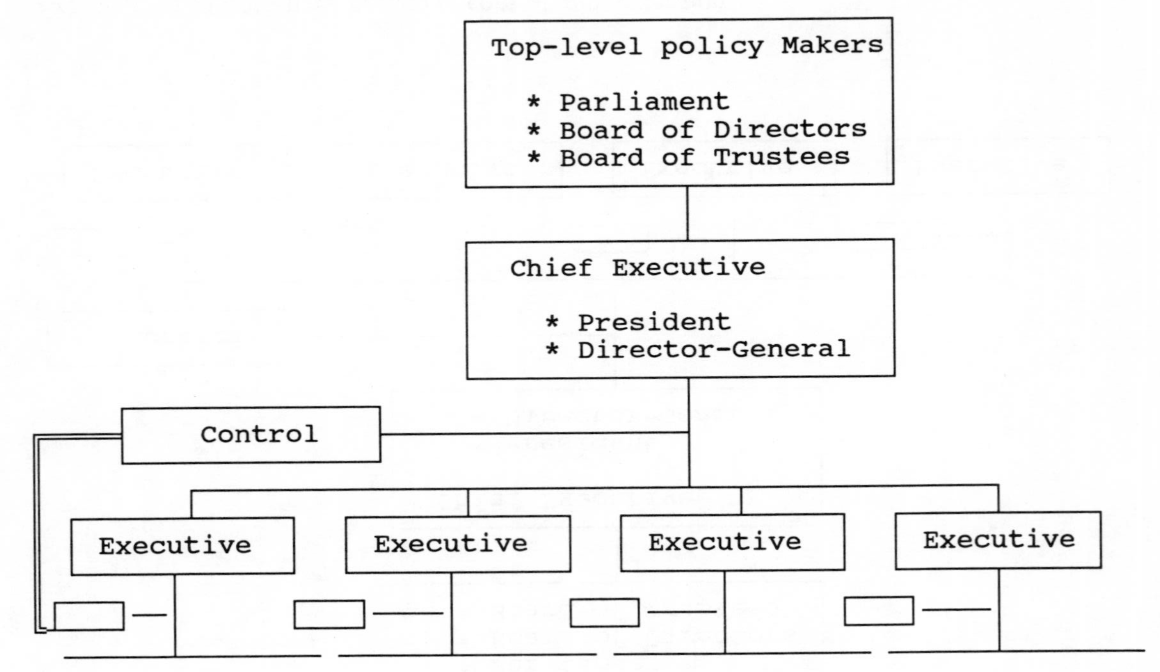

Exhibit 15.6 Decentralized executive control

Any discussion of the status of the control function within an organization must address the fact that control may be seen in one of several ways; as a staff function, an advisory body only, or it may have the authority to demand action. Either way, a formal statement regarding the status, structure, and authority of the control function, is an essential part of the institutionalization of control. The decision is part of the organization's strategy and management philosophy. But, whether control is granted wide or minimal authority, both controllers and controlled, must be aware of the nature and scope of these powers.

The control process

The process of implementing a control system must be institutionalized and not left to chance. While it is obvious that institutionalization does not guarantee the quality of control, it helps to ensure that the operations are carried out in a manner best fitted to organizational objectives. The need to institutionalize the control process is particularly important in three areas.

Planning of control involves the rational selection of what will be evaluated, how, by whom, and when. As already emphasized, it is impossible and unnecessary to subject 'everything' to control. The selection of the items to be controlled requires a detailed description of all organizational units and activities. By estimating the potential damage in case of a malfunction, you can identify those units and activities which should have tighter control. The matrix in Exhibit 3.1 serves as an aid in this selection process. Of course, management philosophy and external factors, such as legal requirements and competition, impact the choice of subjects and the depth of control.

In order to determine what methods to employ for control and evaluation, several questions must be answered. Who will carry out the control function? Will the information be solicited from the controlled units themselves or will an independent system be established? Will control initiate its own observations or will the information be given to it? Will interviews and questionnaires be employed? Is a sample population appropriate, or should data be collected from the whole population? The selection of methods depends on their relevance and validity for the respective control items.

Formal and institutionalized control requires decisions concerning the timing and frequency of control. An integrated and reliable control system usually includes the timing trichotomy, as already mentioned (pre-occurrence, current-occurrence, and post-occurrence control). Choices must be based on a cost-benefit analysis bearing in mind other requirements such as legal obligations.

The relative importance of timing varies. The most important time for control could be at the pre-occurrence stage, for example, in the development of a new product, or with the decision to establish an incentive system. Current-occurrence control might be more appropriate in the area of quality of conformance, and a focus on post-occurrence control would make sense in employee performance appraisal.

Accountability of control findings establishes the way in which the controller reports his finding and provides recommendations. The formalization of this process should include specifics as to the purpose of the report and what should be reported, how the findings should be presented and to whom the report should be submitted. Answers to these questions will depend on the nature and philosophy of the organization. Attention must be given to issues concerning confidential findings, recommendations for change, and whether the report is for internal use only. These deliberations, although they may seem technical, are essential to obtaining effective results from the control system.

Follow-up enables the organization to get the most out of the process. There is certainly a contribution made by the mere existence of the control function, however, its greatest value is in its ability to improve the system. All too often though, important recommendations are only partially implemented. Both the financial investment in control, and its potential to affect change, warrants a systematic follow-up of its conclusions.

Interaction between internal and external control

Every organization is subjected to some degree of external control. External control implies that the function is carried out by an outside body. This could be on the initiative of either the organization itself, or an another force, such as the law or the public. This issue becomes more complex in conglomerates and large, decentralized organizations, which maintain internal control at various organizational levels. Control of an organization by its conglomerate's headquarter is often considered to be external control. In other words, 'internal control' from the organizational perspective may be perceived as 'external control' by an organizational unit.

There is, in most organizations, an ambivalent attitude toward external control. Although the organizational culture may have come to terms with internal control, there is often a feeling that external control will expose deviations and faults. While controlled units seek the benefit of evaluation, and sometimes pay a high price for it, they also fear it. This can be true even when the organization itself initiates the external control.

Management must be aware of the advantages of external control. The extensive experience and knowledge that external control bodies accumulate in the evaluation of similar organizations, sharpens their ability to uncover problems and to recognize possibilities for improvement. Furthermore, it is widely accepted that periodic external control is essential because internal control can become accustomed to certain malfunctions of the system.

Assuming that the internal control system is aware of its limitations and of the relative advantages of external control, cooperative and complementary relations can be developed between the two. The quality of these relations depends largely on who initiates the external control. Such cooperation may be more difficult to achieve if external control is forced on the organization by suppliers, customers, or a legal authority.

We can easily identify several common types of external control; periodic control by accountants, consultants and experts hired by the organization, the organization's board of directors, or government bodies regulating areas such as licensing, health and safety, taxes, or employment. There are however many other, informal methods whereby external control is exercised. For example, the press, radio, and television have gained tremendous power in shaping public opinion. Control through the media, concerning a faulty product, an unreliable company, or a political scandal, is likely to have a significant impact on the organization under scrutiny.

In the political arena, demonstrations and boycotts by consumers, or strikes by dissatisfied employees, are forms of informal external control which point to dysfunctions in the organization. Elections are another form of external control. Whether electing members of a board of directors, or representatives in a political process, this is an accepted form of external control. In the United States, union organizing and the role of the political process once had more influence on business organizations than it does currently. However, consumer groups continue to exert pressure on organizations around environmental, health and safety, and disclosure issues in particular.

Major variables to consider

The content and form of control institutionalization depends on a number of factors, many of which are important to most organizations. We will discuss the six we consider most significant. These include: the size and structure of the organization; its management style; the nature of the organization; the nature of its operations; the level of employee performance; and the cost of control.

The relative importance of each of these varies with the situation, and they may even make contradictory demands. For example, the employees in an organization may be self-motivated professionals who require little supervision, yet the nature of the organization may be one in which strict government regulations apply, and tight control is required. This situation would exist in certain medical laboratories, where chemists, microbiologists and pathologists interpret test results. In any situation, the optimum level of institutionalization depends on the reciprocal relations among all the variables.

Size and structure

The larger and more departmentalized an organization, the greater the number of criteria required for controlling its performance. In addition, companies with many processes that cut across departments, require a higher level of institutionalization than small, concentrated organizations. Typically, there is a central control function in a large, departmentalized organization. It will concentrate on establishing the control set-ups, and then current control would be carried out by controllers assigned to each department.

Management style

A management whose philosophy tends toward centralism, and an autocratic approach, will generally tend toward a similar style in the institutionalization of control. This would mean a centralized control system, and a low level of employee involvement in the process. On the other hand, management with a commitment to a more democratic approach will aim for considerable involvement of employees in the control process. A good example is that of semi-autonomous work groups, in which group members participate in the design of standards and in carrying out control as well.

Nature of organization

Institutionalization of control is affected by the nature of the organization based on variables such as the type of ownership, the competitive environment, and existence of interest groups concerned with the product. For example, the more statutory the organizational nature, the more formal its obligation to maintain control and publish its findings.

A competitive environment is conducive to control as well. Organizations operating under such conditions are more likely to seek constant improvement. Monopolistic organizations, in contrast, are subject more to their own self-interest control or legal obligations; they often seek to avoid any external control. Thus, certain aspects of control are dependent on the existence of competitive conditions.

Organizations intended to fulfill essential needs and to respond to public interests have a greater obligation to report and publicize their control findings to the entire population. Institutionalization of control is of greater intensity in enterprises where outputs are related to the interests of the general public than are organizations which focus on relatively small sectors.

Nature of operations

The nature of the organization's activity also influences the characteristics of institutionalization of the control system. The more complex the production process, the higher the required level of institutionalization. A major consideration in determining the nature and frequency of control must be the possible consequences of deviations from standard, that is, mistakes. If a faulty product or service incurs minimal damage to the user, a low level of control will suffice. However, if poor performance entails critical, irreparable damage, a high level of control is required. This generalization refers to both the process and the outputs. For instance, control of food and drug production is highly institutionalized, both at the plant and the external level.

Employee performance

We have determined three major areas of employee performance which influence the nature of control institutionalization.

Employee skill. The less skilled an employee, the more supervision is needed. On the other hand, an unmotivated, yet skilled employee, requires intensive supervision. Therefore, skill must be treated in interaction with other variables such as motivation and incentives.

Motivation. The stronger the motivation to succeed and to achieve results at work, the less supervision and control is required. In contrast, the weaker the motivation, even if the work is not complex and/or the employees are skilled, the greater the need for institutionalized supervision and control.

Incentives. Incentives usually increase employees' motivation to produce output according to required standards. This factor is extremely important in the institutionalization of control, as it reduces the need for stringent control. However, it is important to note that poorly designed incentive systems may actually produce undesired results if employees narrowly concentrate only on the criteria specified in the incentive system. (This was discussed thoroughly in Chapter 14.)

Cost of control

Controls add to the cost of a product, and therefore should be adopted only if the potential benefits are proven, or control is required by law. The cost of control can be divided into two categories: set-up costs and operational costs. Set-up costs refer to all expenses related to the planning and installation of the system, including personnel, equipment, and materials.

Operational costs are those incurred in the ongoing activity of the control system. These increase as a function of the number of processes controlled, and with the frequency of control. Clearly, an organization's attitude toward the institutionalization of control is greatly influenced by the cost-benefit of the control process.

In summary, the impact of the above six factors in molding the institutionalization of control lies mainly in the interaction among them.

Ultimately, control effectiveness depends on the quality of integration of its various components.

Employees' attitudes toward control

Institutionalization of control requires careful consideration of the human factor, and especially employees' attitudes toward control. People tend to criticize more easily than to accept criticism. To perform the act of evaluation means to expose faults and deviations in performance and behavior. The idea of control often generates resistance among employees. Even if people 'get used' to criticism, it does not mean that they accept it, or become interested in it. Yet, all members of an organization, at all levels, are aware that some control is essential. Because of the importance of employee attitudes toward control, we will discuss the individuals involved as well as ways of handling conflicts among them. This is not a new problem, and is one which has been studied and discussed in management literature for a long time (Mann & Neff, 1959).

The individuals involved

The perspectives and interests of the people involved in control often differ, and their goals may be contradictory. Three main groups are active in the control process; those who set the standards and evaluate the control findings, those being evaluated, and the controllers.

Those who set the standards. Those who set the standards are usually the organizational leaders. They are frequently assisted by professional staff. Their interest is to establish standards that are competitive with similar organizations, but at the same time, to consider realistic performance levels.

Typical worries of management stem from fears that the standard is not realistic, or that it will work to the advantage of the competitors. Those who set the standards have a clear advantage over the other two groups, because they have authority over both the standards and the control findings.

The controlled employees. Despite the common wisdom that everybody in an organization is subject to control, institutionalization varies, often according to how easy it is to set standards for performance. The more quantifiable the criteria, the easier it is to control. When standards are easy to set, there is often better communication among the parties involved in the control process. As a result, evaluation is generally accepted at the operational level, where it is usually based on well defined and understood standards. Acceptance is also enhanced if employees' achievements are accompanied by rewards.

Managers are responsible for the output and achievements of others, and evaluating performance at these levels is more complex. Because of the difficulty in standard setting for senior levels, control is often based on subjective criteria, and these are often not even made clear to those being evaluated.

Often, those whose performance is evaluated, see control as a threat. They may feel that the standards are unfair, that organizational conditions have hindered their ability to function, that control is subjective and biased, or that the controllers are out of touch with what's happening in the field. The control process is apt to break down in these ways when the criteria are vague or not communicated clearly, when evaluators lack information or are not properly trained, or when the criteria are not based on a thorough job description or the measure is not valid or reliable. (These considerations were discussed fully in Chapters 4 and 6.)

Controllers. A controller is an employee whose job it is to examine an occurrence and to compare it to a standard. It is possible however, to examine an occurrence and to evaluate it without an unequivocal, quantitative standard. It is expected that the controller will operate in the spirit of those who set the standards.

Conceptually and psychologically, a controller is geared to trace deviations in performance, while the person being evaluated would prefer that no faults be found. This is the essential difference, and the basic source of conflict, between the controller and those subject to control.

Conflicts in control

Recognizing that there are differences in interests among the three groups involved in the control process, helps us understand the reasons for tension among them. In particular, three primary sources of conflict exist. *Standards themselves create pressure* for those being evaluated, they may decrease self-confidence or increase fears and uncertainty. A clear conflict of interest arises when those who set standards strive for high performance and those being evaluated want a lower standard, one which can be achieved with more certainty. This conflict can be lessened when workers are involved in, and feel part of, the control process.

Methods for measurement are usually determined on the basis of precision and cost. Tension can arise in a situation when the most precise and fair measurement is not selected because of its high cost. Other conflicts may arise when measurement techniques are too complex and difficult for untrained employees to understand.

The controller is expected to 'photograph' a situation, without touch-ups. This approach does not give rise to conflict if performance meets standards. However, the controller may be put under pressure, and tensions may rise, as *the gap between performance and standards* increases.

Minimizing conflict/maximizing participation

Control should be designed to avoid or reduce the conflicts that are inherent in the nature of this function. To this end, involvement of those being controlled in the design and functioning of the control system, and the depersonalization of control, are integral aspects of a successful system.

Involvement of those being evaluated. Employees' involvement in the process used for their own evaluation is likely to reduce conflict. This involvement is particularly important in determining standards and measurement techniques, analyzing findings, and making recommendation for correction and change. Trust in the fairness of standards and measurement requires that all employees know and understand the methods applied. This is an essential part of an evaluation process; its absence may have a devastating effect on the effectiveness of control.

Personnel involvement in the control process is likely to contribute on three levels: familiarization of employees with the process and techniques which will enhance the effectiveness of control; creation of a sense of fairness through just and objective treatment; and, creation of a sense of contribution and ownership in the system.

Depersonalization of control. Human interaction in the control process, constitutes a major source of conflict. Those being controlled tend to have differences with the other two parties. In their opinion, those who set the standards make excessive demands on them, and those who evaluate results fail to take extenuating circumstances into consideration, and are even biased. At the same time, those responsible for standards complain about employees who do not meet them, and controllers who fail to spot and prevent deviations from standards.

Tension and conflict may arise even without rational justification. It is therefore best to rely as much as possible on automated measurement processes and reporting. If measurement results and reporting are initially verified, there is a good chance that the control process will maintain a persistent high level of reliability. An automated measurement process replaces some of the operations fulfilled by the controller, thus reducing the risk of interpersonal conflicts.

While the variables presented in this chapter are not exhaustive, they do represent critical avenues to pursue when institutionalizing the control function. Organizations which do not structure the process, leave it open to chance. These organizations assume that things will go well, but there is much wisdom in the saying, "Make an assumption, make a mistake."

Even if a carefully considered structure for control exists, unless the structure, responsibilities, and evaluation techniques are clearly explained to all involved, you will probably have wasted your effort. Control can not exist without effective communication.

While it is evident that control must be institutionalized, so that the organization does not rely on incidental control, institutionalization does not assure the quality. However, in the absence of institutionalization, quality will almost certainly be low.

Bibliography

AICPA Professional Standards, Vol. 1, American Institute of Certified, Public Accountants, New York (1984).

Ahituv, N. and Neumann S. (1986), *Principles of Information Systems for Management*, 2nd edition, C. Brown.

Alewine, T. (1982), 'Performance Appraisals and Performance Standards', *Personnel Journal*, vol. 61, no. 3.

Allcorn, S. (1979), *Internal Auditing for Hospitals*, Maryland, London: An Open System Corporation.

Anderson, A. (1983), 'Budgeting for Data Processing', *National Association of, Accountants*, New York.

Anderson, D., Schmidt, L. and McCosh, A. (1973), 'Practical Controllership'.

Ansoff, H.I., Declerak, R.P. and Hayes, R.L. (1976), *From Strategic Planning to Strategic Management*, John Wiley and Sons, Inc., New York.

Anthony, R.N. (1965), *Planning and Control System: A Framework for Analysis*, Harvard Business School, Division of Research, Boston.

Anthony, R.N. and Herzlinger, R.E. (1980), *Management Control in Non-Profit Organizations*, Honewood.

Axelrod, R. (1976), *Structure of Decision*, Princeton, Princeton University Press, New Jersey.

Babbie, E.R. (1975), *The Practice of Social Research*, Wadsworth, California.

Bagozzi, R.P. (1986), *Principles of Marketing Management*, Science Research Associates, Inc., Chicago.

Bailey, A.D., Gagle, M. and Whinston, A.B. (1978), 'A Coordinated Approach to the Use of Computers in Auditing', *The EDP Auditor*, 7, no. 1, pp. 27-42.

Baird, L.S. and Thomas, H. (1985), 'Toward a Contingency Model of Strategic Risk', *Academy of Management Review*, vol. 10, 2.

Baird, L.S., Beatty, R.W. and Schnever, C.E. (1982), *Performance Appraisal Source Book*, Human Resources Development Press, Amherst.

Beach, L.R. and Mitchell, T.R. (1978), 'A Contingency Model for the Selection of Decision Strategies', *Academy of Management Review*, vol. 3.

Berczi, A. (1978), 'Improving Public Sector Management Performance', *Management International Review*, vol. 8, no. 2, pp. 63-76.

Berenson, M.L., and Levin, D.M. (1983), *Basic Business Statistics*, 2nd edition, Prentice-Hall, p. 764.

Bettenhausen, K., and Mimighan, J.K. (1985), 'The Emergence of Norms in Competitive Decision Making Groups', *Administrative Science Quarterly*, vol. 30.

Brown, W.B. and Moberg, D.J. (1980), *Organization Theory and Management--A Macro Approach*, John Wiley and Sons, Inc., New York.

Buffa, E.S. (1984), *Modern Production/Operations Management*, New York: Wiley.

Burrack, K. (1975), *Organization Analysis: Theory and Applications*, The Dryden Press.

'Businesses Are Signed Up for Ethics 101', *Business Week*, February 15, 1988.

Carroll, S.J. and Tosi, H.L. (1973), 'Improving Management by Objectives: A Diagnostic Change Program', *California Management Review*, Fall.

Carroll, S.J. and Tosi, M. (1973), *Management by Objectives: Applications and Research*, Macmillan.

Cash, J.I., Bailey, A.D. and Whinston, A.B. (1977), 'A Survey of Techniques for Auditing EDP-Based Accounting Information Systems', *The Accounting Review*, 32, no. 4, pp. 813-32.

Cerullo, M.J. (1973), 'Determining Post-Implementation Audit Success', *Journal of Systems Management*, 30, no. 3, pp. 27-31.

Chaffee, E.E. (1985), 'Three Models of Strategy', *Academy of Management Review*, vol. 10, no. 1.

Chase, R. and Acquilano, N. (1989), *Production and Operations Management*, 4th edition, Wiley, New York.

Cherlinitsky, D. (1984), 'Economic and Commercial Considerations in Implementation of Innovative Technologies', *The Factory*, pp. 38-46 (in Hebrew).

Comptroller General of the United States (1979), *Auditing Computer-Based Systems*, General Accounting Office, Washington, DC.

Comptroller General of the United States (1980), *Report to the Congress: Wider Use of Better Computer Software Technology Can Improve Management Control and Reduce Costs*, General Accounting Office, Washington, D.C.

Cook, T.M. and Russell, R.A. (1980), *Contemporary Operations Management*, Prentice-Hall, Englewood Cliffs.

Cooke, J.E. and Drury, D.H. (1972), *Managing and Accounting for Information Systems*, The Society of Industrial Accountants of Canada, Hamilton, Ontario.

Copeland, R. and Globerson, S. (1986), 'Improving Operational Performance in Service Industries, *Industrial Management*, July-August.

Cray, D. (1984), 'Control and Coordination in Multinational Cooperations', *Journal of International Business Studies*.

Cronbach, L.J., and Meehl, P.E. (1981), 'Construct Validity in Psychological Tests', in Mason, K.O. and Swanson, E.B. (eds.), *Measurement of Management Decisions*, Edison-Wesley.

Dachler, H.P. and Wilpert, B. (1978), 'Dimension and Boundaries of Participation in Organizations: A Critical Evaluation', *Administrative Science Quarterly*, vol. 23.

Dermer, J. (1977), *Management Planning and Control Systems*, Richard D. Kirwin.

Devenna, M.A., Fombrum, C. and Tichy, N. (1981), 'Human Resources Management: A Strategic Perception', *Organizational Dynamics*, Winter.

Dror (1985), 'Future Estimations: National Plan for Uncertainty', *Monthly Review*, no. 2 and 3.

Eilon, S. (1984), *The Art of Reckoning: Analysis of Performance Criteria*, Academic Press.

Elbing, A.O. (1978), *Behavioral Decisions in Organizations*, Scott Foresman, Dallas.

Farrell, P. and Aljian, G. (1982), *Aljian's Purchasing Handbook*, 4th edition, McGraw Hill.

Festinger, L.A. (1954), 'Theory of Social Comparison Processes', *Human Relations*, vol. 7, pp. 117-140.

French, W.L. and Hollman, R.W. (1975), 'Management by Objectives: The Team Approach', *California Management Review*, vol. 17, no. 3.

Gaither, N. (1984), *Production and Operations Management*, Dryden Press, Hinsdale.

Gerloff, A.E. (1985), *Organizational Theory and Design: A Strategic Approach for Management*, McGraw Hill Company, New York.

Gilb, T. (1971), *Reliable Data Systems*, Universitetsforlaget, Oslo, Norway.

Globerson, S. (1985), *Performance Criteria and Incentive Systems*, Elsevier.

Globerson, S. and Parsons, R. (1985), 'Multi-Factor Incentive System: Current Practices', *Operations Management Review*, vol. 3, no. 2.

Green, C.N. (1973), 'Causal Connections Among Managers' Merit Pay, Job Satisfaction and Performance', *Journal of Applied Psychology*, 58, pp. 95-100.

Griffin, R. (1982), *Task Design*, Scott Foreman.

Guiness, E.L. and Mann, L. (1980), *Decision Making Process*, Tel Aviv: Defense Office.

Hackman, R. and Oldham, G.R. (1975), 'Development of the Job Diagnostic Survey', *Journal of Applied Psychology*, vol. 60, no. 2, pp. 159-170.

Hampton, D.R., Summer, C.E. and Weber, R.A. (1982), *Organizational Behavior and the Practice of Management*, 4th edition, Scott, Foresman and Company, Glenview, Illinois.

Harrison, T.M. (1985), 'Communication and Participative Decision Making: An Exploratory Study', *Personnel Psychology*, vol. 38.

Hax, A.C. (1985), *Production Planning and Inventory Control*, Allyn and Bacon, Boston.

Heinritz, S., Farrell, P. and Smith, C. (1986), *Purchasing: Principles and Applications*, 7th edition, Prentice Hall.

Hendrick, T.E. and Moore, F.G. (1985), *Production/Operations Management*, Richard D. Irwin, Homewood.

Herzberg, F. (1959), *The Motivation to Work*, 2nd edition, New York.

Hofstede, G. (1978), 'The Poverty of Management Control Philosophy', *Academy of Management Review 3*, pp. 450-461.

Horngren, C. (1982), *Cost Accounting--A Managerial Emphasis*, Prentice Hall International, New Jersey.

(1970), *IBM.HIPO - A Design Aid and Documentation Technique*, 2nd edition, no. GC20-1851-1, IBM Corporation, White Plains, New York.

Ijiri, Y. and Jaedicke, R.K. (1981), 'Reliability and Objectivity of Accounting Measures', in Mason, R.D., Swanson, E.B. (eds.), *Measurement for Management Decision*, Edison-Wesley.

Jaeger, A.M. and Balighn, B.R. (1985), 'Control Systems and Strategic Adaptation: Lessons from the Japanese Experience', *Strategic Management Journal*, vol. 6, pp. 115-134.

Judson, A.A. (1982), 'The Awkward Truth About Productivity', *Harvard Business Review*, Sept.-Oct., pp. 93-97.

Juran, J. and Gryna, F. (1980), *Quality Planning and Analysis*, McGraw-Hill.

Juran, J.M. (1974), *Quality Control Handbook*, 3rd edition, McGraw-Hill.

Kaplan R. (1982), *Advancement Accounting*, Prentice-Hall.

Kaplan R. (1983), 'Measuring Manufacturing Performance: A New Challenge for Managerial Accounting Research', *The Accounting Review,* October, pp. 686-705.

Keeney, R.L. and Raiffa, H. (1976), *Decisions with Multiple Objectives*, John Wiley, New York.

Kerr, J.R. and Littlefield, J.E. (1974), *Marketing - An Environmental Approach*, Prentice Hall, Inc., New Jersey.

Kirk, D.E. (1970), *Optimal Control Theory*, Prentice Hall, Inc., New Jersey.

Kotler (1984), *Marketing Management, - Analysis, Planning and Control*, Prentice Hall, Englewood Cliffs.

Lander, G., Holmes, J., Tipgos, M. and Wallace, M. (1983), 'Profile of the Management Accountant', *National Association of Accountants*, New York.

Larsch, J.W., Baughman, J.P., Reece, J. and Mintzberg, H. (1978), *Understanding Management*, Harper and Row.

Lawler, E.E. and Rhode, J.C. (1976), *Information and Control in Organization*, Goodyear, California.

Lindbloom, C.E. (1959), 'The Science of Muddling Through', *Public Administration Review*, no. 19.

Locher, A.H. and Teel, K.S. (1977), 'Performance Appraisal -- A survey of Current Practices', *Personnel General*, vol. 56, pp. 215-254.

Lorsch, J.W., Boughman, J.P., Reece, J. and Mintzberg, H. (1978), *Understanding Management*, Harper and Row.

Lozer, R.I. and Wikstrom, W.S. (1977), 'Appraising Managerial Performance: Current Practices and Future Directions', *The Conference Board*, report no. 723, New York.

MacKenzie, K.D. (1985), 'The Organizational Audit and Analysis Technology for Organizational Design', *Human Systems Management*, 5, pp. 46-55.

Mazzolini, R. (1981), 'How Strategic Decisions are Made', *Long Range Planning*, 14 (3).

McGregor, D. (1966), *Leadership and Motivation Essays of Douglas McGregor*, Bennis, W.G. and Schein, E.H. (eds.), MIT Press, Cambridge.

Merchant, K., (1987), Fraudulent and Questionable Reporting, Financial Executives Research Foundation, Morristown, New Jersey.

Mills, A.E. (1967), *The Dynamics of Management Control Systems*, Business Publishers Limited, London.

Mintzberg, H.R.D. and Theoret, A. (1976), 'The Structure of Unstructured Decision Processes', *Administrative Science Quarterly*, vol. 21.

Monks, J.G. (1987), *Operations Management*, McGraw-Hill International Editions.

Murray, E.A. (1978), 'Strategic Change as a Negotiated Outcome', *Management Science*, vol. 24.

National Association of Accountants, Definition of Management Accounting, National Association of Accountants, Statement Number 1A, March 19, New York, 1981.

National Association of Accountants, Objectives of Management Accounting, National Association of Accountants, Statement Number 1B, June 17, New York, 1982.

National Association of Accountants, Standards of Ethical Conduct for, Management Accountants, National Association of Accountants, New York, 1983.

Newman, W.H. (1975), *Constructive Control: Design and Use of Control Systems*, Prentice Hall, New Jersey.

Newman, W.H., Summer, C.E. and Warner, E.K. (1977), *The Process of Management*, 3rd edition, Prentice Hall, New Jersey.

Ouchi, W.G. (1975), 'Relationship Between Organizational Structure and Organizational Control: Two Functions', *Administrative Science Quarterly*, 20, pp. 559-569.

Ouchi, W.G. (1977), 'The Relationship Between Organizational Structure and Organizational Control', *Administrative Science Quarterly*, vol. 22.

Ouchi, W.G. (1979), 'A Conceptual Framework for the Design of Organizational Control Mechanisms', *Management Science*, 25, pp. 833-848.

Ouchi, W.G. (1980), 'Markets, Bureaucracies and Clans', *Administrative Science Quarterly*, 25, pp. 129-141.

Parker, D.B. (1981), *Computer Security Management*, Reston, Virginia.

Pfeffer, J. and Salancik, G. (1978), *The External Control of Organization: A Resource Dependence Perspective*, Harper and Row, New York.

Porter, W.T. and Perry, W.E. (1977), *EDP Controls and Auditing*, 2nd edition, Wadsworth, California.

Prince, T.R. (1975), *Information Systems for Management Planning and Control*, 3rd edition, Richards D., Inc., Illinois.

Reeves, T.K., and Woodward, J. (1970), 'The Study of Managerial Control', in Woodward, J. (ed.), *Industrial Organization: Behavior and Control*, Oxford University Press, London.

Rice, R. (1977), 'Survey of Work Measurement and Wage Incentives', *Industrial Engineering*, vol. 9, no. 7.

Rockart, J.F. (1979), 'Chief Executives Define Their Own Data Needs', *Harvard Business Review*, March-Apr., pp. 81-93.

Rudwick, B.H. (1979), *Solving Management Problems--A System Approach to Planning and Control*, New York.

Schreyögg, G. and Steinmann, H. (1978), 'Strategic Control: A New Perspective', *Academy of Management Review*, vol. 12, pp. 91-103.

Shelly, G.B., and Cashman, J.T. (1975), *Business Systems Analysis and Design*, Anaheim, California.

Sheridan, T.B. and Ferrel, W.R. (1974), *Man-Machine Systems*, The MIT Press, p. 452.

Shetty, Y.K. and Verman, M. (1985), *Productivity and Quality through People: Practices of Well-managed Companies*, Quorum Books, West Port.

Simon, H.A. (1960), *The New Science of Management Decision,* University Press, New York.

Simon, H.A. (1976), *Administrative Behavior*, New York.

Sloma, R. (1980), 'How to Measure Managerial Performance', Macmillan Publishing Company, New York.

Stevens, S. (1951), 'Mathematics, Measurement and Psychophysics', in Stevens, S., Wiley, John (eds.), *Handbook of Experimental Psychology*.

Storey, J. (1985), 'Management Control as a Bridging Concept', *Journal of Management Studies*, vol. 33, no. 3.

Tabatoni, P. and Jarniou, P. (1976), 'The Dynamics of Norms in Strategic Management' in Ansoff, H.I.; Declerck, R.P.; and Hayes, R.L. (eds.), *From Strategic Planning to Strategic Management*, Wiley, London.

Tannenbaum, A.S. (1968), *Control in Organizations*, McGraw Hill, New York.

Tersine, R.S. (1982), *Principles of Inventory and Materials Management*, 2nd edition, North-Holland, New York.

Todd, Y. (1977), 'Management Control Systems: A Key Link Between Strategy, Structure and Employee Performance, *Organizational Dynamics*, vol. 5.

Tosi, H.L. and Carroll, S.J. (1976), *Management: Contingencies, Structure, and Process*, St. Clair Press, Illinois, p. 118-152.

Turner, A.N. and Lawrence, P.R. (1965), *Industrial Jobs and the Worker*, Harvard University Press, Boston.

Vlek, C., and Stallen, P.J. (1980), 'Rational and Personal Aspects of Risk', *Acta Psychologica*, vol. 45.

Vollmann, T., Berry, W., and Whybark, C. (1984), *Manufacturing Planning and Control Systems*, Richard D. Irwin.

Vroom, V.H. and Vetten, P.N. (1973), *Leadership and Decision Making*, University of Pittsburgh Press.

Weber, R. (1977), 'Implications of Database Management Systems for Auditing Research', in Cusing, B.E. and Krogstad, J.L. (eds.), *Frontiers of Auditing Research*, Bureau of Business Research, University of Texas, Austin.

Wendell, P. (1985), Corporate Controller's Manual, Warren, Gorham, and Lamont.

Will, H.J. (1978), 'Discernible Trends and Overlooked Opportunities in Audit Software', *The EDP Auditor*, 6, no. 2, pp. 21-45.

Willingham, J.J. (1971), 'Internal Control Evaluation - A Behavioral Approach', in Carmichael, D.R. and Willingham, J.J. (eds.), *Perspectives in Auditing*, McGraw-Hill.

Yelle, L.E. (1979), 'The Learning Curve: Historical Review and Comprehensive Survey', *Decision Sciences*, vol. 10, no. 2.

Zif, J. and Eyal, Y. (1976), 'A Basic Information System for the Marketing Management of New Products', *The Business Economics Quarterly*, volume 3-4/A January, pp. 43-58.

Index